THE FRAGMENTARY CITY

THE FRAGMENTARY CITY

Migration, Modernity, and Difference
in the Urban Landscape of Doha, Qatar

Andrew M. Gardner

CORNELL UNIVERSITY PRESS   ITHACA AND LONDON

First published 2024 by Cornell University Press

Library of Congress Cataloging-in-Publication Data

Librarians: A CIP catalog record for this book is available from the Library of Congress.

ISBN 9781501774980 (hardcover)
ISBN 9781501775017 (paperback)
ISBN 9781501774997 (pdf)
ISBN 9781501775000 (epub)

To all the many people who have built and inhabited Doha,
and to all the anthropologists who came before me

Among them, but not of them . . .

—William Gifford Palgrave, 1866

Contents

Preface

In this book, I speak from an ethnographic and empirical foundation to the experiences of the millions of transnational labor migrants, mostly from South Asia, who journey to the wealthy states of the Arabian Peninsula for some portion of their lives. I seek to convey an anatomy of the transnational migration system that shuttles those migrants to and from the wealthy states in which they are employed. Along the way, I articulate and analyze some of the fascinatingly unique and noteworthily interesting social, cultural, and urban arrangements that result from the unprecedented demographic concoctions of people gravitationally attracted by the region's hydrocarbon wealth. Nestled at the heart of those objectives is an enduring fascination with the cities of Arabia, and therein one will find the book's central thesis: Doha, exemplary of cities throughout the region, is a complicated tool by which state and citizenry manage their relationship with the rest of the world and by which they seek to govern those forces present in the urban landscape they have constructed. In that sense, this book is about the city of Doha.

Like most books grounded in the craft of ethnography, what follows is primarily a collation and discussion of other people's experiences intermixed with my own experiences as a participant-observer. Over multiple projects spanning more than two decades, thousands of transnational labor migrants and a constellation of other people have shared aspects of their lives, experiences, and perspectives with me and occasionally with my colleagues and my research assistants. This book aspires to remain true to those men and women and to the information they gifted me. The core of my analysis is built on that foundation. Although it is seemingly customary to thank many of our interlocutors by name in the preface of an ethnography, I will name none of those individuals here. I refrain because I find the custom of naming interlocutors that readers will not know to be oddly performative.[1] Nonetheless, I am grateful to all of them and comfortable with the fact that most of them—if they remember me at all—know that. A few of them remain close friends of mine to this day. I am equally grateful to the handful of institutions that played a key role in the production of this book—to Qatar University, the University of Puget Sound, the Whiteley Center, and a global coterie of scholars, colleagues, and friends who have helped me and this book along its way. I have learned a great deal from those people, and while I also list none of them by name here, most are aware of my deep gratitude.

Additionally, my students at those various institutions were particularly influential in shaping my understandings, and I am grateful for the opportunities I have had to teach and interact with young adults on several different continents. Jim Lance at Cornell University Press and the two anonymous readers he arranged had perhaps the most significant impact on this manuscript, and I am grateful to all of them. Finally, I am happy to name my family and express my gratitude to them: my daughter Astrid, and my parents, Gordon and Janice. Thank you for everything. You are the greatest blessing of my life.

Although my aspirations with this book are primarily anthropological, intellectual, and ethnographic, I hope this book will be at least vaguely recognizable as a creative work. In a previous chapter of my life I was a songwriter and musician of sorts, and I briefly attempted existence as an aspiring poet just prior to that. Photography is a useful and wonderful new hobby for me. Moreover, for many years I was married to a working artist. With all of that water under the bridge, it seems that creativity has been a lifelong passenger on my journey, and I continue to place a high value on the creativity that we might bring to the various disciplines and to the conversations that academics have stewarded through the difficulties of the previous century. In this book, that creativity has been mostly straitjacketed into the chapters and analyses that comprise an ethnographically moored book in the academic vernacular the present moment demands. Nonetheless, I hope that readers are able to glimpse that penchant for creativity in the photographs included here and perhaps in the stylistic and analytic latitude that anthropology has long allowed.

Although I will elaborate on the ideas by which this book is framed in the chapters to come and pontificate even further in the postscript, let me briefly turn to the destinations that I envision for the journey ahead. I certainly hope to convey how the city of Doha serves as a tool by which the Qatari people govern and regulate their relations with the world. I also hope to illuminate the transnational migratory conduits that bring tens of millions of foreigners to the Arabian Peninsula. I want to think about the kinds of social forms that blossom and proliferate in these unusual demographic circumstances. I also want to think about the fundamental nature of the astonishing cities that have arisen from the mostly empty deserts on the Arabian Peninsula. I will explore a variety of different angles on the tens of millions of people who arrive to work in Arabia, and I also want to think about all the other things that travel along those same migratory conduits—the money, the ideas, the various technologies, the germs and viruses, the natural resources, the liquified energy, the fashions and styles, and so much more. Throughout this journey, my emphasis will remain trained on the material circumstances, social relations, and cultural phenomena that coalesce in the city of Doha.

This emphasis may seem counterintuitive to some readers. A swath of eth-nographic scholarship exists, including contributions from a growing list of scholars concerned with the societies and peoples of the Arabian Peninsula, that is actively oriented toward a set of conversations that readers will find are largely omitted from this book. Though those works often march under the banner of anthropology, they are primarily engaged in a set of conversations concerning the emotional terrain of human life—succinctly, they are concerned with how people feel. This concern is often framed in terms of belonging, inclusion, and exclusion, but it also pervades a variety of other ongoing scholarly conversations. I see those conversations as a testament to what sociologist Frank Furedi (2003, 44) noted more than two decades ago—that "individual emotions and experi-ence have acquired an unprecedented significance in public life." His assertion might be usefully modified only by noting that this tendency seems most para-mount in America, or perhaps the West; in my estimation, the reorientation of anthropology around a concern with the emotional well-being of our subjects employs a therapeutic metric that is both undeniably and ethnocentrically en-twined with the American experience. In this book, I seek to remain focused, instead, on the complicated terrain and the varied circumstances in which the emotional states of my subjects are conjured—those material circumstances are the object of my objectivity (D'Andrade 1995). As this suggests, in the final ac-counting I view the emotional states of the diverse individuals who fall in the ambit of this ethnography as epiphenomena. They are an unpredictable variable which is only partially dependent on the material relations I seek to describe here.

In exploring this analytic pathway, my foremost commitment is to the disci-pline of anthropology, and to its exploration and long-standing veneration of the social and cultural terrain of human difference. In taking on the very same ob-jective that guided generations of anthropologists before me, my aim is always for impartiality and fairness in the analyses I present.[2] I hope that this book lives up to those aspirations. These aims are emblematic of the social scientific tradi-tion that was central to anthropology in its first century of existence. As the French anthropologist Claude Lévi-Strauss described it, anthropology's burden in the social sciences was always particularly cumbersome: "The objectivity aimed at by anthropology is on a higher level [than the other social sciences]: The observer must not only place himself above the values accepted by his own soci-ety or group, but must adopt certain definite *methods of thought*; he must reason on the basis of concepts which are valid not merely for an honest and objective observer, but for all possible observers" (Lévi-Strauss 1963, 364). Through the positivist and social scientific frame of the vantage point I have summarized here, I also seek the transcendent vernacular that Lévi-Strauss capably described so many decades ago.

This explication of the city and the social relations contained therein is offered as an example that might inform our conversations and plans for a human future that seems almost certain to be urban. From that vantage point, I have a variety of audiences in mind for this book. There are numerous stakeholders attuned to Doha and cities like it, and even more who compose the overlapping realms of academia concerned with cities, in general, with this city, in particular, and with the migrations and movement of all the various people who inhabit it. With that diverse audience in mind—Qatari citizens, legions of foreign workers, a diasporic middle class, other visitors and tourists, scholars and academics, policymakers, journalists, urban planners, and an array of miscellaneous others—we can conclude this: undoubtedly, the first two decades of the twenty-first century have been one of the most interesting, eventful, and historic epochs for the many residents of the Qatari Peninsula, and for the Qatari people. There is so much for us to learn from their experiences and from the city they have constructed in the desert. Follow me for a bit.

THE FRAGMENTARY CITY

CITY, SOCIETY, AND MOBILITY

In early 2008, a young Nepali man named Divendra made the arduous journey from his home village in the Terai—Nepal's low southern plain—to Kathmandu.[1] Upon arriving in the mountainous country's capital city, he spent several weeks navigating the complicated bureaucracy faced by all migrants destined for work outside Nepal. Eventually, after passports were stamped and boxes on various documents were checked, after that paperwork was filed and processed, and after various additional fees were paid, he boarded a plane bound for the Arabian Peninsula. This was Divendra's first time on an airplane, and he brimmed with anticipation for what he would encounter in Doha, his destination. The image of a new life in the cosmopolitan city had captivated him. In the years prior to his departure, a penchant for Hollywood movies had stoked his imagination of the possibilities—already he had envisioned himself on some high floor of a towering modernist skyscraper, frantically running documents to an important meeting, working in cadence with the busy energy of the office he pictured in his mind.[2] The glistening skyline he could now glimpse from the plane only spurred his imagination. In which of those skyscrapers would the next chapter of his life begin?

Readers will spend more time with Divendra throughout this book and will meet other people as well. The outcome of Divendra's aspirations will become more clear in subsequent chapters, but here I want to note that I, too, arrived in Doha that same summer, and the same skyline captured my attention as we approached Qatar's busy airport by air (see figure 1). That skyline also served as a backdrop for my imagination, and I puzzled over where the fates would fit me

FIGURE 1. Nepalese transnational migrants on break, with the skyline of Doha's West Bay in the background. Photograph by the author, 2018.

in this gleaming, mostly new city on the Arabian Peninsula. With additional flights in and out of Qatar in the subsequent year, I came to realize that Divendra and I were not alone in our musings. In fact, Qatar Airways' business class section, into which my new employer placed me on my increasingly regular transcontinental flights to and from Doha, was peppered with a variety of cosmopolitan professionals like myself, most of whom were in some way or another compensated for helping Qatar manifest its vision. Some were even involved in the process of helping Qatar articulate that vision. But among this class of professionals and assorted others peering out the windows of the plane at Doha's skyline were the architects, urban planners, and a coterie of others for whom the city was not just the backdrop of their imagined future nor the context for a new chapter in their life, but rather the direct focus of their attention and their

energies. Some of these individuals were helping to plan and design the astonishing urban trophy case that had so quickly sprouted from the barren desert
terrain; others, budding academic urbanists like myself, would inhabit this city,
and attentively go about their business as best possible in an urban landscape
that seemed to be under perpetual construction. Still other arrivals, like Divendra, both inhabited the city and helped to construct it, whether by driving ce-
ment trucks through the dusty urban landscape or manually carrying cinder
blocks from one place to another on a construction site. In some manner or another, so many of our lives revolved around the city itself.

In brief, this book concerns that city—the city of Doha, Qatar—and the various
people who inhabit that worlding urban junction. My concern is with the city itself
but also with the society that both produced that city and now inhabits it. The
methodological foundations of the book are ethnographic in nature—drawing
foremost from what ethnographers call data. Here, those data include interviews
with a diverse constellation of migrants, residents, citizens, visitors, and assorted
officials. These interviews are the result of a sustained sequence of research projects that stretch back more than two decades. But like any modern ethnographer,
my own stories and experiences also illuminate this book and comprise another
form of what anthropological ethnographers call data. As a result, the reader will
find the book peppered with a variety of details and tidbits—details about citizens
and their perspectives on the changes they have witnessed, stories of transnational migrants and their experiences crossing the Arabian Sea to toil on the hot
peninsula, fragments drawn from my experiences in the city and amid various
institutions therein, narratives about navigating the urban landscape of Doha by
foot and by car, and quite a bit more. These research methods and the projects
underpinning them are described in more detail in the next chapter, which coalesces in the point that I can succinctly convey here: the subject of this ethnographic work is both the city itself and the society that inhabits it.

Assessments of Doha and the other astonishing (post)modern cities of the
Arabian littoral are beginning to accumulate in the scholarly literature. Most of
them mention foreigners' presence to some degree, but this foreign presence
mostly skirts the margins in their conceptualizations and analyses. Doha is a city
in which nine of every ten urban residents are foreign temporary workers. One
finds similar demographic proportions in a few other cities in the neighboring
Gulf states. Most of the foreigners present in these cities can be described as
transnational labor migrants, an appellation that connotes both their place in the
working class and the temporary nature of their presence in Arabia. In light of
the unparalleled proportions of foreigners to citizens found in Doha and those
neighboring cities, this book is premised on the idea that these foreigners have
not figured centrally enough in our estimation of these cities.[3] There are valuable

historical contributions to our understanding of urban Arabia, and there are numerous new contributions focused almost entirely on the intricacies of urban planning and design (Fuccaro 2009; Al-Nakib 2016; Elsheshtawy 2008; Salama and Wiedmann 2016; Rizzo and Mandal 2021). To take one particularly excellent book as an example, in Ahmed Kanna's brilliant ethnography of Dubai (a city some 250 miles to the east of Doha), migrants are a feature of his analysis, but do not quite find their way to the central limelight of how he understands the city. Conversely, in much other ethnographic work, the city and the urban spaces therein are eclipsed by the migrant experience itself (Gardner 2010b; Vora 2013; Norbakk 2020; Wright 2021). In those contributions, the city serves more as a backdrop to the experiences of these communities of migrants, and therefore emerges as the sometimes-pertinent setting of an ethnographer's explication of those experiences.

In a few scholarly works, both the city and its inhabitants are analytically balanced in judicious ways. I take inspiration on this front from my mentor, Sharon Nagy, and the sequence of articles that explored Qatari society and urban space in novel ways (Nagy 1997, 1998, 2000, 2004, 2006). Yasser Elsheshtawy's work on the cities of Arabia is also exemplary and inspiring (Elsheshtawy 2008, 2010, 2019b, 2022). In his work the experiences of the migrant majority of Dubai's inhabitants figure centrally in the analytic portrait he paints of the city. One might make the same claim about Robina Mohammed's and James Sidaway's occasional contributions to the same scholarly conversations, about Laavanya Kathiravelu's impressive monograph, and about portions of Dalal Alsayer's scholarly work (Mohammed and Sidaway 2016; Kathiravelu 2016; Alsayer 2019b). Farah Al-Nakib is directly concerned with many of the same issues that preoccupy me here (Al-Nakib 2016). And Natasha Iskander's book homes in on the city of Doha and the migrant workers who construct it, and does so with unprecedented focus (Iskander 2021).

In this scholarship, the city itself, as well as the experiences of the humans who inhabit it, are considered in dialectic. In my rendition—an analysis of Doha, Qatar, and the work you have before you—I explore the migration system that feeds millions of transnational migrants into the city, I assess the experiences of the migrant majority in the city, and I seek to gauge how both city and society have taken shape around those mobilities. My goal is to provide readers with a vista point on the emergent and unusual permutations of city, state, and society produced by these transnational flows of people, capital, and ideas. Simultaneously, I seek to illuminate how the city serves as a complicated tool by which state and society seek to govern those flows. In summary, this book's goal is to shift the foreign presence in urban Arabia into the limelight, and to connect the active scholarly conversations concerning urbanism in Arabia with the burgeoning conversations concerning migration, mobility, and the transnational flow of humans in our contemporary era.

One key perspective underpinning this analytic journey is my commitment to an anthropologically moored epistemological diversity, and therefore to a deep and empowering engagement with non-Western otherness. Six decades ago, and coincident with the veritable crescendo of the modernist era, Bernard Rudofsky assembled his influential exhibit *Architecture without Architects* at New York City's Museum of Modern Art. Peering past the notable legion of luminary Modernist experts who, at that time, dominated global thinking about architecture, planning, and the urban form, Rudofsky's exhibit portrayed the magnificent creativity that humans, in an array of different cultural settings and different historical times, have displayed in constructing the built environment. Rudofsky's exploration of these diverse architectural vernaculars was a spark that, in retrospect, yielded a legacy that remains more vibrant and pertinent than ever.[4] For many decades, the dominant urbanist paradigm suggested that cities outside the ambit of the West—cities like Doha—were best understood as weak attempts to mimic the urban modernity exemplified by Western prototypes. Although contemporary analysis has largely abandoned this reading of the global urban form, one proliferate strain of scholarship concerned with cities and their planning today maintains the conceptual centrality of the West, only now, instead of those disparate cities being portrayed as poor mimicries of the Western urban ideal, modern critics trace complicity and guilt for the urban problems those cities endure to their purported Western source. This is the same essentialism under a different pretense, for in both calculuses the Western urban form remains the central and defining point of reference.

To exit this conceptual imbroglio, I follow Rem Koolhaas who, speaking to these Western critics in his 1995 essay about Singapore, declared that "The 'Western' is no longer our exclusive domain . . . it now represents a condition of universal aspiration. It is no longer something that 'we' have unleashed, no longer something whose consequences we therefore have a right to deplore; it is a self-administered process that we do not have the right to deny—in the name of various sentimentalities—to 'others' who have long since made it their own" (Koolhaas 1995, 1013). Whether our concern is with the Western, with neoliberal capitalism, with migration and mobility, or with the patterns taking shape in cities around the globe, the grand structural forces at work in these urban microcosms no longer have a clear geography. In this book, I seek to emphasize the agency that others display as they navigate the same structures of meaning and history that we, in a place like America, also face. I am, after all, an American anthropologist with a lifelong interest in cultural difference and the cities others have constructed.

In the remainder of this introduction, I frame the contents of this book with a discussion of several interrelated themes central to the journey ahead. The first thematic discussion concerns the city itself, here condensed into a brief jaunt through the expansive scholarly realms of urban studies, urban anthropology, and urban history. The second concerns society and culture, the twin concepts that carry readers to the heart of the anthropological discipline and its long-standing interest in the diversity of others' collective experiences in this world. The third of these thematic foundations concerns migration and, more broadly, mobility. Migration, in particular, is central to my expertise, assembled via several decades of active research in the region. But migration and human mobility are also empirical and demographic social facts—core features in the lives of the legion of foreign men and women who inhabit the city of Doha and many other cities like it. In each of these brief sojourns, the reader will take note of the scope of my interests. My framing discussions reach for what the French historian Fernand Braudel (1972) once called the longue durée—an approach to history that emphasizes the long term. With this book's ethnographic foundations, and with ethnography's penchant for the present and the particular, framing these essays in the longue durée is intended as an antidote, or at least a counterweight, to the ethnographic specificity to come.

On the City

If one can envision the whole of our species' existence for a moment, then the emergence of cities is clearly a recent development. Cities began to emerge some six thousand years ago on the heels of the Neolithic agricultural revolution and the tectonic effects it had on the organization of human life. Those effects were notable and varied, and their impact reverberated through time: the slow sedentarization of our previously mobile species commenced in this era; the predictable existence of surpluses became a common feature of the human landscape; and the need for organized, collective action—for increasingly large irrigation projects, for example, or for the erection of defensive structures to protect cities from marauders of various sorts—became a necessity. Changes to the infrastructural level of human existence, including to the way that some humans extracted sustenance from the environment, and to the technologies by which that extraction might occur, produced new sorts of relations and new social forms. Both resulted in an increasing social complexity. Cities can be seen as material manifestations of the increasing differentiation and social stratification that resulted from the tectonic changes of the Neolithic era. New sorts of hierarchies concretized the increasingly varied social and economic roles characteristic of the expanding landscape of inequality, itself the result of the surpluses generated by the agricultural revolution of the Neolithic era (Buras 2019, 66–70; Mumford 1961; Kotkin 2005). In Lewis Mumford's resonant analysis of humankind's historical trajectory, he further suggests that these changes pivoted on a singular key factor: "the most important agent in effecting the change from a decentralized village economy to a highly organized urban economy, was the king, or rather, the institution of Kingship" (Mumford 1961, 35). Queens, kings, emperors, pharaohs, tyrants, and other sorts of despots functioned as the governing hub of the "central nervous system" by which the increasingly complex urban societies and economies were individually coordinated.[5]

Inequality was a central and catalyzing factor in the formation of the city in human history.[6] The foundational and deeply historical connection between inequality and the urban form is also evident in the present era, for that inequality is visible at every turn in a city like Doha. But scholars' long-standing attention to the inequalities visible in the city only deepens the irony that it was amid the emergent urban landscape of inequality that, several millennia ago, democracy was born. Neither Doha, nor any of the neighboring cities on the Arabian Peninsula, are the product of democracies, but there is more to the association between cities and democracy than first meets the eye. It was in ancient Athens that the idea of the polis first emerged. The meaning of that word bends our English, for it refers to the city itself, certainly, but it also connotes the community bound by the obligation of collective management and governance of the city. In that second portion of the definition, we can see how the Hellenic concept of the polis conflated the material city with the ideas of citizenship, community, and belonging. All of this was pinned to the Athenian veneration of the polis, and most vitally, it was in the city that humans first disassembled the institution of kingship. It was via the governance of the polis that men first distributed and shared with other men the power and responsibility of Mumford's "institution of kingship." It is also at that same juncture where the idea of equality was born, and therefore, where the conceptualization of the rights that premise so much of our thinking today was ushered into human consciousness. In summary, the irony I am pointing to here is that the idea of human equality sprang directly from the manifestation of inequality that is the city.[7]

Although the city first emerged as an instantiation of the inequalities generated by the Neolithic agricultural revolution, our contemporary fixation on inequality in the urban landscape traces its roots back to the Industrial Revolution and the capitalist forces that reshaped the urban milieu in the nineteenth century. It was Friedrich Engels's analysis that first deployed inequality as the key lens by which we might assess the urban landscape. Indeed, the distribution of inequality in the urban landscape that so concerned Engels remains a central issue for contemporary urban theorists.[8] But underpinning the theses presented in this book, I suggest that we should be wary of consigning our analysis of the city to inequality alone.[9] Although readily encountered in any city, and so strikingly obvious in a city like Doha, that inequality is merely one facet of the broader differences and manifold diversities long integral to the urban ethos. Differences of all sorts coalesce in the city, and the estimation of that difference reaches into the depths of social theory: Adam Smith (1937) was concerned with the energies released by the same division of labor that fueled urbanization, for example. Emile Durkheim (2014) took stock of the organic solidarity that bonded such difference together in interdependence. Jane Jacobs (1961) contended that Manhattan's sidewalk ballet and the safety it conferred resulted from diversity in the urban social fabric. Ongoing scholarly conversations about the cosmopolitan ethos continue to speak to the value of the diversities and the differences that interact in the city: Douglas Saunders (2010) envisions cities as transitional spaces, as locations where so many of us—from different places and all part of the great human migration from village to the city—have clambered out of poverty; Elijah Anderson (2011) speaks of cosmopolitan canopies, those urban spaces that bring difference together and encourage deeply humanizing interactions. All of this, and much more like it, points to the thinness of inequality when considered alone. In the analysis presented in this book, I seek a more holistic assessment of difference—one that includes, but is not limited to, the economic renditions of inequality that first concerned Engels.[10]

With this grand history of the city as our backdrop, one meaningful thread woven through this history and the reservoir of scholarship behind it concerns the relationship between society and the city. For many generations, urban theorists have been attuned to how urban spaces shape our social and psychic life. The Athenian agora, a marketplace and, simultaneously, the urban space where citizens might meet, interact, and discuss any matters of urban governance at hand, is a classic example, and as an urban space, the agora is theorized to be integral in the emergence of the democratic form (Kitto 1951). The influence of space on social life permeates Elijah Anderson's extrapolation (2011) of cosmopolitan canopies as well, and in his recent book, Eric Klinenberg (2018) frames the value of these spaces by terming them a form of social infrastructure. These very same convictions were central to Frederick Law Olmsted's vision of how nature might better fit into the cities of the late nineteenth century, a conviction distilled in Olmsted's aspiration to find and articulate a sense of place in the urban landscape (Buras 2019). Even the key principles articulated by the Congress of New Urbanism, whose directives and ideals are perhaps the most influential paradigmatic force in recent urban planning history, are premised on the notion that good spaces yield good communities (Murrain 1996). Finally, echoing the portrayal of the Athenian agora as a public space vital to the birth of democracy, even a brief inspection of Jurgen Habermas's description of the public sphere conveys the integral role that, in his estimation, spaces played in the emergence of European democracies: British coffee houses, Parisian salons, and German reading clubs were the "institutional criteria" by which citizens established and maintained the public sphere that, in his calculus, provided a vital democratic counterweight to the powers instilled in the state (Habermas 1991; Mah 2000, 158–161). In summary, all these works—and a plethora of more work not mentioned here—theorize, explore, and assess the influential role that urban spaces play in shaping our social life.

In the most often-quoted tract from *The Eighteenth Brumaire*, Karl Marx (1996, 32) suggests that "[men] make their own history, but they do not make it just as they please in circumstances they choose for themselves; rather they make it in present circumstances, given and inherited." These sentiments not only reinforce the first and aforementioned thread that I discuss above—that spaces have the capacity to shape our social existence—but also point to an altogether different thread woven through these works in urban theory: that cities are material palimpsests of the human past. A *palimpsest*, of course, is a term for an ancient manuscript that's been partially erased for reuse, on which the evidence of the former text remains discernible.[11] It is an ideal metaphor for the built environment, and for the city itself: in a Beaux Arts structure from 1910, prominently located at the center of a small American city, we might see the collective investment in the civilizing discourse of a bygone American era, and the acquiescence of Americans of that era to the value of governance that such a building once signified. Conversely, deep in the folds of Le Corbusier's modernism and its repetitive uniformity we might glimpse the socialist egalitarianism that underpinned that twentieth-century movement (Le Corbusier 1967). Similarly, in the urban remnants of an aging Arabian *fareej*, with its narrow streets yielding spaces cloistered from the public hum of the city and its markets, we can glimpse the centrality of family and clan in the Arabian social tradition.[12] The acres of sacrificial space at the center of the pre-Columbian city of Cahokia invite speculation about the violent nature of North American hierarchy and social relations some 900 years ago (Kolson 2001). As these examples suggest, cities are complicated, multi-authored texts in which we might discern the enduring accumulation of relics and remnants of our past. In that sense, cities are a rich encyclopedia of past human relations. Like any city, therefore, Doha is a historical text.

On Society and Culture

The concepts of *society* and *culture* carry us into the heartland of the anthropological discipline. With the first sentence of his 1871 book *Primitive Culture*, Edward Burnett Tylor inaugurated the discipline of anthropology with his definition of culture. In his initial estimation, culture consisted of "that complex whole which includes knowledge, belief, art, morals, law, custom, and other capacities and habits acquired by man as a member of society" (Tylor 1958, 1). Eight decades later, the anthropologists Alfred L. Kroeber and Clyde Kluckhohn (1952) took stock of the definitional landscape in a book entitled *Culture: A Critical Review of Concepts and Definitions*. They looked for the common threads woven through some 164 different definitions of culture and eventually settled upon this distilled and often-quoted synthesis: "Culture consists of patterned ways of thinking, feeling and reacting, acquired and transmitted mainly by symbols, constituting the distinctive achievement of human groups, including their embodiment in artifacts; the essential core of culture consists of traditional (i.e., historically derived and selected) ideas and especially their attached values" (Kluckhohn 1951, 86). Hundreds of other definitions were in circulation as well, obviously, but in this definition one can recognize the common threads woven through most of the others—that culture is shared, learned, and multifaceted. Arguments about the precise components of these definitions continue to fuel anthropological debate, and as I often convey to students, asking a cultural anthropologist to define the concept at the core of her discipline is often the quickest route to a vista on scholarly befuddlement. In addition to its other attributes, the definition of culture has been unwieldy and unruly for more than a century.

Scattered throughout this book, readers will occasionally encounter the concept of a *social prism*. This is a conceptual tool I have developed, and as an aspect of culture, it merits a brief explanation here (see also Gardner 2019, 2021c). Along with all the other features of culture that we inherit from those before us, we might also discern the framework by which we classify and organize the continuum of human difference so readily encountered in this world. This framework is what I refer to as a social prism. Like any other aspect of a given culture, social prisms vary from one culture to the next. Even within the same culture, a social prism has the tendency to morph over time. And as a facet of culture itself, one's social prism is acquired by each of us as a member of our society. In the ethnographic canon, anthropologists have described castes, tribes, clans, moieties, genders, classes, ethnicities, phratries, sects, age sets, races, and countless other social ingenuities that are the substance of this framework. To remain open to cultural and epistemological diversities, I not only remain actively interested in other categorizations of human difference, but reflexively, I also endeavor not to reify the dominant American social prism in my analysis. Put another way, in this ethnography I make a conscious attempt not to privilege American social categories as primordial or obvious. Instead, periodically in the analyses presented here I seek to recognize those analytic categories as arbitrary and contingent social constructions, and to thereby subtly acknowledge that the categories of the hegemonic American social prism are oftentimes in service to the tattered remnants and vestiges of American imperialism.

Although I see this American social prism as a facet of the complex American culture, the concept of culture itself is also embattled today. A pressing set of long-standing (and ongoing) debates concern the boundaries of culture and thresholds of difference. In the waning decades of the twentieth century, a cadre of anthropologists contended that the model of culture bequeathed to anthropology by its American progenitor, Franz Boas, problematically overemphasized the static, cohesive, and place-bound essence of culture.[13] Perhaps it was no coincidence that these critiques arrived during the concentrated spate of global interconnection that characterized the last decades of the twentieth century—the precise period that commenced what I refer to as the era of mobility, and what we might also term the neoliberal era.[14] While I recognize the destabilizing effects that these expansive new mobilities and interconnections ushered into the terrain of culture, I nonetheless see mortal flaws in these popular (and widely accepted) critiques of the culture concept. Foremost, these critics' case is more an indictment of a caricature than any real and enduring anthropological legacy: as Ira Bashkow (2004, 444) convincingly argued nearly two decades ago, "most ethnographic studies today address the translocal connections that are entailed by neocolonial economic structures, regional exchange systems, diasporic communities, immigration, borderlands, mass media, evangelism, tourism, environmental activism, cyberspace, and so on." He further asserts that these same processes and forces were familiar issues to Boas and his students a century ago: their deployment of hybridization, diffusion, integration, and other such conceptual ingenuities were the mechanisms by which they emphasized cultural distinction and difference without implying that cultures were discrete and static. As Bashkow contends, arguments aimed at the Boasian legacy typically disregard the entirety of the conceptual toolbox that he bequeathed the discipline.

These conceptual frictions have an interesting parallel with my own fieldwork. On my first trip to the Arabian Peninsula in 1999, and far afield in the remote hinterlands of the Kingdom of Saudi Arabia's northeastern deserts, I found myself conducting a long ethnographic interview with an elderly Saudi man of bedouin heritage. A previous interview with another person had alerted me to the historical significance of the *dirah*, or the bedouin homeland, to the tribes and their enduring existence on the arid Arabian Peninsula. In the interview at hand, I pushed my bedouin interlocutor to delineate the historic boundaries of his tribe's homeland. He spoke with clarity and cohesion about the propriety of the wells at the center of that homeland, but my attempts to cull any precision from him about the boundaries of the *dirah* were oddly futile. His tribe's *dirah* ended "somewhere over there," he indicated, and then vaguely pointed to a distant mountainous ridge or some other feature of the landscape. I eventually surrendered my objective and moved on to another topic, and it was only after successive interviews and more introspection that I came to better see my missteps: I had been imposing my own (American) understanding of land and property on a different tenure tradition.[15] For all the pastoralists who once relied on the Arabian deserts for sustenance, the tribal propriety of the wells mattered greatly, as that water sustained all life in the desert. But the boundaries between one homeland and the next were blurry and indistinct, as further precision served no purpose.

I have come to think of this experience as a metaphor for the resolution of the dilemma concerning culture, boundaries, and place. Like those wells that once anchored the bedouin *dirah*, we might recognize the core and central elements of a given culture, and we might do so without the impossible requirement of delineating the precise boundaries between one culture and the next. Indeed, this view aligns with anthropologist Robert Lowie's memorable "antiprimordialist" take on culture, a view that emphasized the syncretic nature of all cultural assemblages.[16] But this looser definition of culture, and the imprecision that it allows, finds further support in our on-the-ground analyses of Doha and the other Gulf states. Migrants themselves recognize the core and central elements of the different cultures they encounter in the city. They think about each other with the stereotypical shorthand on which we humans often depend, and they deploy those reductive assessments and essentializations in their quotidian interactions with others in the city. At the same time, real and observable cultural differences are forged and maintained in diaspora by language, food, ethnicity, custom, religion, nationality, and the many other variables of difference that cohere to the concept of culture. For the legions of migrants from so many different places and traditions, those distinctions are produced and reinforced in everyday discourse and social interactions in Doha.

While culture has been discussed here at some length, we can dispatch with the concept of society more readily. Unlike culture, which is thought of as primarily a human attribute, society is the term we use for any group of interacting organisms. While culture is what those humans collectively build and share, the term society denotes the group of people who build and share it. In this sense, the concept of society conveys something both material and inherently communal. Yet the concept of society resembles culture in one integral way: both concepts, while central to anthropology, have the perplexing feature of being applicable across a variety of scales. This is particularly evident with culture. At one end of the continuum, for example, we might coherently discuss aspects of the culture of global capitalism. Additionally, one can talk coherently about the cultural ethos of much smaller accumulations of humans—the culture of the institution that employs me, for example, or the culture that diasporic groups carry with them as they move out into this world. While not prone to the same malleability, society also manifests these scalar flexibilities. One can speak of Qatar and the conglomeration of diasporic and transnational communities who inhabit the peninsula as a singular and pluralistic society. At the same time, we can also extract those individual components, and thereby speak coherently of Indian society in Qatar, or the norms of the Qatari society that hosts those communities, and in doing so, mean something particular and less comprehensive than the singular whole of pluralistic society found on the peninsula. The flexibilities with both culture and society, while puzzling, are also of great utility.

On Mobility and Migration

For those of us who do not reside on the African continent, it is worth recollecting that our distant ancestors began their walk out of Africa some fifty thousand years ago. Physical anthropology, further energized in recent years by successive revolutions in our capacity to analyze the human genome, has elaborated this story in great detail, but one aspect of that story only grows more clear with the accumulation of better evidence: migration, movement, and mobility have been integral and recurring features of human existence for time immemorial. Indeed, one might even argue that mobility is one of our species' defining characteristics. With a history seemingly composed of incessant movement, our eternal mobility undermines many of the claims, assertions, and assumptions that operate under the banner of indigeneity.[17] Regardless, migration and movement have always been central features of the anthropological lens. And as one would discover in the inspection of any place's deep history, migration and mobility certainly have a significant footprint in the history of the Arabian Peninsula's peoples. Scholars concerned with the Arabian Peninsula often bifurcate the social history of the people there into two groups characterized by their respective and interrelated modes of production: the bedouin (or *bedu*) people maintained a pastoral nomadic livelihood, and in occupying the interior regions of the Arabian Peninsula, they lived in a state of nearly constant mobility; the seafaring *hadhar* peoples of the coastal region, although foremost a merchant class based in the city or village, built livelihoods tethered to the sea and the mobility it allowed (Altorki and Cole 1989: 17–18; Crystal 1990; Longva 1997, 2006; Al-Nakib 2014).[18] In summary, our species' sedentarization some ten thousand years ago, and the more recent enclosure of humanity in the national containers that today shape our comprehension of the world, together suggest the exceptionalism of our present moment: the borders, boundaries, tenure, and stasis we've imposed on the landscape are notable exceptions to the human norms perceptible in the longue durée of our existence.

Setting these philosophical concerns aside, contemporary migration has undoubtedly had a significant and direct impact on Qatari society over the last century. The nation's first census was conducted in 1970, just a year before independence. Of the 111,113 individuals resident on the peninsula that year, some 45,039 were Qatari citizens. Composing just over 40 percent of the total population, citizens were already a minority in their own land in the years just before the OPEC embargo. In Qatar (and in the neighboring Gulf states) the proportion of foreigners would continue to balloon in the coming decades: in 1986, foreigners made up 73.3 percent of the resident population; by 2010, foreigners made up 85.7 percent of the resident population on the Qatari Peninsula. At the time of writing, nearly nine of every ten residents are foreign-born migrants, like Divendra—temporary workers with little possibility (and little expressed interest) in naturalization. Most of these workers are directly supporting a household at home (De Bel-Air 2017; Snoj 2019). Altogether, sustained migration to Qatar and the neighboring Gulf Cooperation Council (GCC) states comprises what is tabulated to be (after Europe and North America) the third largest transnational flow of labor migrants in the contemporary world (ECSWA 2007; Naufal 2011). On average, some eighty-seven migrants arrive each day in Qatar, and while these transnational workers hail from nearly ninety different sending countries, the most significant labor-sending nations are India (700,000), Bangladesh (400,000), Nepal (400,000), Egypt (300,000), and the Philippines (236,000) (Snoj 2019). To state the obvious: in history, and in the present, migration has been a central social fact in Qatar's experience.

Although the six GCC states contain just a tiny sliver of our global population, more than a tenth of the total number of transnational migrants in the world today were present there in 2016. The GCC states' proportion of global remittance flows is correspondingly substantial: in 2014, nearly a quarter (23 percent) of all migrant remittances (totaling some $98 billion) flowed outward from the Arabian Peninsula (De Bel-Air 2018). Other calculations reveal that, in 2021, the total outflow of remittances from Qatar, specifically, totaled some $11 billion, a number that was down slightly from previous years (Migration Policy Institute 2022). For comparison, the total remittance outflow for the United States in 2020 was $68 billion. With a total population of citizens that would place it among American cities like Anchorage, Buffalo, Lincoln, or Pittsburgh, it is clear that Qatar plays an outsized role in the flow of remittances in the contemporary world. Moreover, those remittances are directed at some of the most marginal and underdeveloped regions of the world. In summary, and to again state the obvious: migration, and the broader mobilities tethered to the Qatari Peninsula, are economically significant to millions of migrant households and the villages, towns, cities, and regions they inhabit.

The relationship between these migrations and the city itself is the central puzzle of this book. But Qatar, like its neighbors, is one of the most urbanized places in the world. For a nation-state so suffused with migrants and foreigners, one would certainly expect the city to be deeply shaped by migration. But migration does not cover sufficient analytic ground to entirely frame these chapters. Consider that nearly two decades ago, the anthropologist Paul Dresch (2006, 214) declared that "regional and local order has been threatened in the Gulf more than most places since the mid-twentieth-century by flows of trade, imagery, and foreign persons." The key point I take from his assertion is the breadth of his concern, and the causation that he envisions behind those flows of what he calls "foreign matter." In this book, and like any anthropologist, my interests are directed at people—both those on the move and those at home in the city of Doha. But I am also interested in all the other things that are on the move—the structures that Dresch hints at and the other sorts of foreign matter that sometimes travels via the same conduits and circuits as transnational migrants themselves. The concept of mobility aligns with this broader spectrum of matter-on-the-move, and although the book is more than two decades old, I often think about the matter of that mobility in the fields that Appadurai (1996) provided us; he spoke of contemporary human mobility and globalizing interconnection in terms of the ethnoscapes, technoscapes, financescapes, mediascapes, and the ideoscapes that comprise it. These terms, and the concept they together convey, reach for the breadth of the matter on the move in the world today.

As they already have, readers will also encounter additional dalliances with my notion that our contemporary era might be appropriately recognized as the "era of mobility." Human mobilities today, while varied, depend nearly wholesale on the ongoing exploitation of our planet's hydrocarbon resources and the readily accessible, nonrenewable caloric energy available there. That energy is also the reason for this book, for the migrations with an endpoint or a waypoint in Doha, and for the city itself—the urban construction in the limelight of this book. In labeling our time as the "era of mobility," I am articulating my suspicion that we will look back at these decades with a lens that's hard for us to envision from the vantage point of the present—that from our postoil future, we will regard the contemporary era, and places like Doha, as urban palimpsests of humanity's waning moments in the petroleum-fueled hyperactivity of the present. The readily accessible and nonrenewable caloric energy underground in Qatar is also deeply entwined with the city and society described here, and with the entirety of the world as we know it.

In summary, the era of mobility I posit as characteristic of our contemporary historical juncture is an attempt to grandiosely characterize the domain of the mobilities, the people, and the processes that I seek to ethnographically apprehend in this book. These concerns with mobility and migration inevitably lead back to a discussion of culture. Two decades ago, anthropologists confidently arrived at the conclusion that while globalization was changing lots of things, it was not simply snuffing out the cultural distinction and the many sorts of differences it engrossed. Rather, cultures (and the societies undergirding them) adjusted, evolved, changed, or, to use a verb that arose in the interim, "morphed" into something different. Yet via the identitarian nature of the contemporary moment—an American paradigm deeply in cadence with neoliberal capitalism, I might again add—culture is often now portrayed as a feature of one's identity that might be brandished or, alternatively, rejected. I find the American portrayal of culture to be steeply misguided, and in the countervailing thread woven into this book's analysis, I not only suggest the ongoing vitality of culture but also hold that culture is inevitably and always a collective project. To peer even further ahead in this book, I also assert that the production of culture remains a process that requires space, a point that will not be fully attended to until we reach the book's concluding chapters. But for clarification, one of the central theses of this book is that cities like Doha have evolved and grown the spatial infrastructure needed to maintain diverse cultures and difference amid the blizzard of human interaction fueled by this era of mobility. Hang on to that assertion.

FRIDAY ETHNOGRAPHY AND THE CITY

Many of the mainline disciplines at the heart of the liberal arts belong to the humanities—history, philosophy, the literary arts, religion, and the study of various languages are all emblematic examples. Other disciplines nestled in the heartland of the liberal arts, including sociology, psychology, and economics, trace their genealogical lineage to the social sciences and, therefore, to the scientific tradition. For a variety of reasons that need no elaboration here, the discipline of anthropology pledges fealty to both traditions, albeit in varying proportions according to the particular anthropologist; in short, anthropology is classifiable as both a humanity and a social science.

The portions of anthropology aligned with the humanistic tradition include the work that succeeded Clifford Geertz (1973) and the interpretive turn he forged in the 1970s. While the rendition of anthropology purveyed in this text owes some debt to the interpretive and humanistic traditions that constitute enduring and important realms of the disciplinary topography, my firmest commitments are to the social sciences and that tradition's legacy in anthropology. In summary, that legacy compels anthropologists to divulge their methods with clarity and precision; it asks us to present the evidence driving our interpretations and our analyses; and thinking more epistemologically, the social scientific legacy has long organized the anthropological mission around an orientation to the lodestar of objectivity. For clarification, and following Roy D'Andrade (1995), this objectivity is not a puritanical assertion of impartiality, as some postmodernist critics would suggest, but instead connotes something quite basic: a shared commitment to the description of the object in question.

FIGURE 2. The author (center-right) and a group of South Asian labor migrants, several of whom are also close friends. Photograph by Kristin Giordano, 2009.

Methods for Humans

Ethnography, as a method, is perhaps best defined as a toolkit containing many different research tools. What binds them together under the moniker of ethnography is not the component tools, but instead the overarching aspirations of ethnography's practitioners—to holistically understand, as best possible, the experiences, perspectives, and understandings shared by a group of people culturally unfamiliar to the ethnographer. Veteran ethnographers would likely add that this understanding is achieved only through sustained immersion in the foreign cultural world in question. There are caveats, exceptions, and matters of concern buried in the folds of this definition. Moreover, it is a definition ensconced in the anthropological tradition, where the method was born and elaborated over nearly two centuries. But the definition I have provided here is neither attentive to all of ethnography's adherents and numerous practitioners in many other disciplines, nor is it attentive to the permutations that we encounter in anthropology, in the form of anthropologists who seek to analyze their own cultural home, or those who, via auto-ethnography, suggest that with an internal dialogue they might treat themselves as a subject—as the quintessential key informant—in their research project. Despite these new permutations, the definition to which I adhere remains true to the ethnographic tradition and to the toolkit of methods pioneered over a century ago by a cadre of European and American men who sought to understand, from the inside out, the social and cultural differences readily encountered at the fringes of expanding European empires, as well as in the troubled spaces of westward expansion on the North American continent. Through that endeavor, anthropologists reached a leveling sort of relativism, thereby configuring an intellectual lens through which different ways of being in this world might be gauged and considered without judgment. This sustained academic endeavor produced the ethnographic canon—humankind's best (and only) comprehensive encyclopedia of the diversity of cultures our species has constructed in the past several centuries. Need I reiterate that this canon is an extraordinary and unsurpassed human treasure?

Before discussing some of the tools in the ethnographic toolkit that rests behind these chapters, it merits note that there is no particular research project underpinning this book. Rather, this book is the summation of a swath of different research projects reaching back two decades to my time in graduate school at the University of Arizona and to the first time I set foot on the Arabian Peninsula. The laborious indexing of those projects would overwhelm this chapter and would shift the reader's focus away from the path ahead. I recognize, that like other ethnographers, I sometimes take an authoritative tone in reporting my findings and interpretations, and that some assertions in this book may seem too disconnected from any evidentiary foundation to pass without notice. I also recognize that anthropologists' penchant for cultural immersion—for simply "being there," and the certitude it can yield—is oftentimes the principal vehicle for our analytic authority. For those reasons, a brief methodological overview of the portions of my research trajectory that directly pertain to the topics at hand seems apropos.

The craft of ethnography that anthropologists ushered through the twentieth century has accommodated various adjustments, permutations, and creative new directions with changing times and circumstances. Indeed, it is surprising that the practice of ethnography in the twenty-first century still closely resembles the practice of a hundred years ago. The anthropologist Caroline Osella coined the term "Friday ethnography" to describe one of those permutations characteristic of the ethnographic work with labor migrants in contemporary Arabia—our shared endeavor.[1] In short, most labor migrants on the Arabian Peninsula are busy with work six days a week. Many of the migrants I have worked with over the years would oftentimes depart their labor camps early in the morning, wade through stifling traffic for hours in a company bus that shuttled them to their worksite, then work a long day, and finally return to camp late in the evening, leaving only enough time for a quick meal and a bit of socializing before sleep beckoned. There is little space in that schedule for the curious—and sometimes inane—questions that accompany an anthropologist's presence. Fridays were a different matter, however. During my years in Qatar, most of my Fridays were spent with friends, acquaintances, and interlocutors in the labor camps (see figure 2). Sometimes we would stay there and visit; other times, we would go places together and do things—visit friends, shop for groceries, or seek out some new nook of the urban spectacle that surrounded us. In light of these ethnographic realities, "Friday ethnography" aptly describes those anthropological attempts at cultural immersion that by necessity are largely consigned to a single day each week.

During those times in the labor camps, and with countless other interlocutors on a dozen different projects, much of the data I collected took the form of interviews. More specifically, I commonly utilize the format that H. Russell Bernard (2011) refers to as the semi-structured interview. In this format, one embarks on an interview with a brief topical outline that lays out the basic waypoints to which the interviewer seeks to guide the conversation. Utilizing the same topical outline with numerous different interviewees yields a set of conversations with a similar (and analytically comparable) architecture. In the final accounting, the semi-structured interview is more of a structured conversation, and like any conversation, it is coconstructed. In addition to the topics predetermined by the ethnographer to be of interest, the semi-structured format encourages the interviewee to guide the conversation to topics and issues that she or he sees as pertinent or important. Using this format, I have interviewed bedouin pastoralists, members of the wealthy diasporic elites present in Arabia, the transnational laborers in the lowest echelons of the foreign workforce, Bahraini and Qatari citizens about the foreign presence in their homelands, about feelings of nationalism, about how those citizens go about constructing their own identities, and much more. Although numerous projects and communities of subjects have slipped out of this rough accounting, it is undeniable that the semi-structured interview is a key and recurring feature of the ethnographic toolkit I deploy.

Participant-observation is oftentimes referred to as the foundational method in anthropology, and in addition to the interview, it is another vital component of my ethnographic toolkit. The methodological impulse behind participant observation resembles the contemporary penchant for "experiential learning," which shares the underlying conviction that we come to understand things more concretely and comprehensively by doing them. For anthropological ethnographers, this takes the form of immersing ourselves in the quotidian activities of the culturally foreign worlds we seek to understand. The portions of my fieldwork with transnational labor migrants that utilized this tool would include those many Fridays cooking together, eating together, and meandering about the labor camps in the Industrial Area of Doha or, less frequently, elsewhere in Qatar. Broadly speaking, pedestrian activities such as going places and doing things together—be it shopping, sightseeing, exploring the city, or running errands—also fall in the ambit of contemporary participant observation. But the limitations of my participant observation should also be apparent: for a researcher concerned with the transnational migrant proletariat, as I have long been, an ideal form of participant observation would include signing a two-year contract, embarking on the journey to Arabia from some South Asian departure point, and enduring the various hardships and challenges these transnational migrant argonauts commonly encountered in the Gulf states. Indeed, some intrepid anthropologists have pursued this sort of participant observation in their research endeavors, but in this case, my skin, my passport, my fatherhood, and my eroding capacity to endure such hardships put any such attempt out of reach.[2]

Yet there are other realms where participant observation might also be recognized in the research projects underpinning this book. As a professional migrant employed in Qatar between 2008 and 2010, I was also subjected to the sponsorship system, and while my passport and the job that awaited my return to America insulated me from some of the pressures that many other migrants endure, class, position, and privilege do not simply inoculate one from the vulnerabilities and risks that are structurally embedded in the sponsorship system—a point brightly illuminated by Natasha Iskander (2021) in her work. In terms of participant observation, then, there was some experience I shared with other migrants as a result of being another foreigner employed in Arabia.[3] Similarly, considering the fact that the city itself is, in part, the subject of this ethnography, simply inhabiting (and thereby experiencing) the city also resembles a form of participant observation. The anthropologist Sulayman Khalaf (2006, 244) termed this aspect of the ethnographic method "participant living," and I hope that his methodological insight resonates with the work I present here. In summary, via participant observation, much of the understanding that I accumulated was the result of lived experience, as it remains in the present.[4]

Another methodological aspect of the research undergirding this book is the multi-sited nature of my ethnographic work. In the 1990s, anthropologists began to recognize that the social worlds we sought to understand increasingly seemed to require our presence in multiple geographical locations. The discipline conceptualized this permutation as an adjustment to globalization, or perhaps to the deterritorialization of culture and society in the contemporary era of mobility. In concrete terms, many of the labor migrants I have studied in Arabia live a quintessentially transnational existence. They are corporeally present in Qatar, for example, and toil there for two years, four years, or more. But their mental and spiritual lives are only partially moored in Arabia. Their gaze frequently remains trained on their faraway homes, on the family they left behind, and on their plans and intentions for whatever savings they have been able to accumulate during their time abroad. Multi-sited ethnography was configured to apprehend the complicated geography of these social fields. The multi-sited approach implies that any holistic, anthropological understanding of the transnational migrant's experience requires one to visit the places from which these migrants come, and to which almost all of them will eventually return if they have not already. Numerous projects have provided me with opportunities to ethnographically engage with the communities, households, and other institutions found in a variety of places in these migrant-sending states, including substantial fieldwork sojourns in Nepal, Sri Lanka, India, and Pakistan.

Importantly, a notable set of methodological shortcomings also undergird this book. Over a century ago, the anthropologist Bronislaw Malinowski (1922) essentially codified the ethnographic toolkit via his work with the inhabitants of the Trobriand Islands just off the coast of Papua New Guinea. Many of the proclamations he configured during his time on the islands remain integral to ethnographic practice: anthropologists should endeavor to stay for a year or more, immerse themselves in the social and cultural imponderabilia of everyday life, endeavor to live among their subjects when possible, and anthropologist should speak to those subjects in their own language. The last of those criteria merits discussion here. In 1999, I arrived in Saudi Arabia with a middling, intermediate capacity in Arabic, but the intervening years have not been kind to my abilities. Moreover, Arabic proved largely useless as my focus shifted to the culturally and linguistically diverse population of foreigners resident on the Arabian Peninsula. As a population, these resident foreigners, and particularly the vast component of that population that I refer to as the *transnational proletariat*, speak dozens of different languages. I speak none of those languages. Arabic, Hindi, and Urdu have some currency as the lingua francas amid the superdiversity one encounters in Arabia, but no language has the same footprint as English.[5] In my fieldwork, I have operated almost entirely with English and have utilized a cadre of translator-researchers whom I have hired, befriended, and trained since 2002. I have learned a great deal from the long and sustained relationships I have established with these translator-researchers, many of whom also have life experiences as the labor migrants I have long studied. Nonetheless, readers should recognize that without facility in any of the languages indigenous to the working class of migrants, the research and findings underpinning the entire arc of my ethnographic work are inattentive to the nuance and detail that fluent conversations would allow.

Of the sustained string of projects underpinning this book, I will briefly describe three in more detail here to give readers a vantage point on the evidence presented in the remainder of this book. First, in 2002 and 2003, my time in graduate school culminated with a year of ethnographic research in the Kingdom of Bahrain. That research was funded by the Fulbright Program and by the Wenner-Gren Association, and my presence in the Kingdom was sponsored by the Bahrain Training Institute. Although my project was originally conceptualized around an ethnographic assessment of the relationship between citizens and foreigners on the islands, within weeks of my arrival I tightened the focus of the project to an assessment of the diasporic and historic Indian community's experience there. Over the course of my time in Bahrain, I conducted formal interviews with sixty-six individuals, most of whom were migrants. In the legacy of participant observation, I also joined several Indian-dominated fraternal organizations and spent quite a bit of time at the many Indian social clubs in the city. Through one of those social clubs and its outreach efforts, I was able to begin frequent visits to some of the labor camps where the lowest echelon of transnational migrants dwelled. The portion of the migrant world I encountered there captured my attention and remains central to my concerns (Gardner 2005, 2010a, 2010b).

The second project was funded by the Center for International and Regional Studies (CIRS) at Georgetown University in Qatar under the guidance of Mehran Kamrava. Between 2008 and 2010, my small family and I lived in Doha, where I taught at Qatar University. For three preceding years of teaching at the University of Puget Sound, I had been reading Philippe Bourgois's ethnography *In Search of Respect* with my students, and through our class discussions I had developed an appreciation for the depth of insight that Bourgois had been able to assemble by focusing on such a small cadre of ethnographic subjects. Via a project supported by a CIRS grant, I sought to follow a set of ten newly arrived labor migrants from several different sending states through two years of their life in Qatar. Periodic interviews—sometimes monthly, sometimes biweekly—allowed me to better envision the arc of the experiences that migrants encounter upon arrival in Qatar. Repeated interviews also allowed me to grow close to some of these transnational migrants on a personal level. Moreover, the grant provided funds for me to visit many of these migrants' families in Sri Lanka,

Nepal, and India, and thereby better understand the places and contexts from which they came. Several of the young men I befriended as a younger man at work on this project remain close family friends to this day (Babar and Gardner 2016; Gardner 2012a, 2012b, 2017).

The last project was funded by the Qatar National Research Fund (QNRF) as part of its National Priorities Research Program. In seeking this funding from the state in 2010, we contended that, to that date, scholarship concerning labor migration to Qatar (and, indeed, all of Arabia) relied on small-scale, qualitative, and sometimes ethnographic findings, and more occasionally, on quantitative analyses utilizing nonrepresentative samples of a slightly larger scope. With funding and support from the QNRF, and in collaboration with Qatar University's Social and Economic Survey Research Institute, between 2010 and 2013 we conducted the first large survey of low-income labor migrants built upon a random sampling frame, thereby yielding a representative set of quantitative data. That sample allowed us to extrapolate our findings for all low-income migrants in Qatar. Our team surveyed 1,189 labor migrants, and the project included additional components built around qualitative interviews and a series of focus groups. Interestingly, our quantitative findings generally corroborated many of the findings reached by previous, small-scale ethnographic projects but also led to significant revisions in the research community's understandings of some aspects of the migrant experience in Qatar (Gardner et al. 2013).

These three projects are merely notable examples from a longer array of ethnographic work conducted over more than two decades. Before turning to a description of the methods I used to apprehend the city itself, I want to conclude this section with an ethnographic vista point that I reached only at the tail end of those two decades. In the earlier years of my work among the population of transnational labor migrants on the Arabian Peninsula, the problems and experiences those migrants conveyed to me had a pressing immediacy that permeated my writing and analysis. But many of those same migrants remain my friends to this day, and the problems that loomed so large in their (and my) consciousness in our first encounters are now distant features in the rearview mirror of their lives. What I was unable to see as a neophyte ethnographer was how the issues, problems, challenges, and frustrations they described to me fit into the larger arc of their lives—into the longue durée of a modern human life. This awareness roughly corresponds with a shift from a synchronic perspective on our ethnographic subjects—as a portrayal of their world as a snapshot in time— to a diachronic vantage point that seeks to convey our subjects' experiences across time. This book, and much of my work nowadays, leans more toward this diachronic perspective.

Methods for Cities

The ethnographic toolkit I have described here was configured for the study of humans in their natural social environments. For most of Qatar's residents, and for the residents of the highly urbanized neighboring states, those environments mostly consist of the city itself. Although the city can be "read" in the archaeological sense—as a palimpsest, yielding evidence of the social relations and the ideals fixed in the material vestiges of eras now past—the city obviously cannot be interviewed. And although Khalaf's notion of participant living helps connect the ethnographic tool of participant observation to an assessment of the urban form, ethnography itself does not provide a sufficient toolkit for a comprehensive analysis of the city. Or, at least, modifications are needed if an ethnographer wishes to, as the anthropologist James Holston (1989, 314) once put it, take "an entire city as a unit of study." As a result, I pursued a different methodological approach for this objective, and in the remainder of this chapter, I will briefly convey the methods I used to apprehend Doha's varied urban landscape. This approach to the city itself complemented a constellation of interviews with various subjects about their life in the city.

Following others, the term I will use to describe this methodological approach to the city is *urban drifting*. The taproot of this approach to the urban form is oftentimes traced to Baudelaire's descriptions of the Parisian *flâneur*—the archetypal urbanite and nineteenth-century European man, the leisurely Parisian stroller, the *boulevardier*, the adroit observer of contemporary urban life "who everywhere rejoices in his incognito"(Benjamin 1999, 443).[6] Lurking in Baudelaire's description of the *flâneur* are connotations of detachment, and perhaps a subtle condescension to otherness that I wish to extricate from my iteration of this method. To accomplish this, I would turn to Baudelaire's contemporary, Friedrich Engels, and thereby complement Baudelaire's aloof *flâneur* with Engels's forensic attention to the forces of inequality contouring the city, his grip on the sensorial register of the British slums rendered by the Industrial Revolution, and his gradual recognition of the organismic character of the cities he encountered. The thread that connects Engels to Baudelaire's *flâneur* most clearly is the experiential nature of their engagements with the urban milieu. Like ethnography as a whole, and like the impetus distilled in the practice of participant-observation, the value of "being there" was a central tenet in both of these early renditions of what I term urban drifting.

While we might trace the taproot of this urban method to the nineteenth-century works of Engels and Baudelaire, the methodological approach of urban drifting was more clearly articulated and codified a century later by the Paris-based Situationists in the 1950s.[7] Their methodological explication of the *dérive* (often translated as urban drifting) outlined a method of engagement that yielded what they termed the *psychogeography* of the city. For the doyen of the Situationists, Guy Debord, this technique of urban exploration compelled one to seek "swift passage through varied environments" (McDonough 2009, 78). The Situationists' aspirations were to encounter the hidden, to see the overlooked, to experience and engage those places and those neighborhoods beyond the quotidian circulations of bourgeois urban life. The Situationists gravitated to the unexpected and consciously sought the happenstance encounters that urbanity allows and perhaps encourages. From one angle, their methodological explication sought to ensure an encounter with the sorts of urban spaces that Engels had so compellingly described a century before.

In Debord's estimation, urban drifting was inevitably a flexible endeavor: a *dérive* "unfolds in a few deliberately fixed hours, or even fortuitously during fairly brief moments, or on the contrary over several days without interruption" (McDonough 2009, 82). The experiential engagement with the city codified and articulated by the Situationists is a recurring feature in scholarship concerning the city. Lewis Mumford (1961, xi), an American contemporary of the Situationists, conveyed the essence of those sentiments in the preface to his magisterial *The City in History* when he declared that his "method demands personal experience and observation, something unreplaceable by books." More recently, Douglas Saunders (2010, 2) echoed the same in describing his habit of introducing himself "to new cities by riding subway and tram routes to the end of the line, or into the hidden interstices and inaccessible corners of the urban core." In between Mumford and Saunders, and even more so in the present moment, a constellation of others—too many to list here—corroborate or otherwise affirm this experiential approach to the city.[8]

There is a substantial and storied legacy to the experiential engagement with the city. And this method, termed urban drifting, shares an enormous amount of ground with ethnography itself. Like ethnography, the method of urban drifting is experiential by design; it is exploratory in nature, as practitioners seek out the unexpected, the hidden, and the unforeseen in the urban landscape; and like ethnography, in this methodological approach the practitioner herself serves as the research instrument. Those are three key elements that can be traced back to the nineteenth century and to some of the first writings concerned with the social topography of the city. The same key elements connect the methodological approach of urban drifting to the storied ethnographic tradition. Yet unlike practitioners of the past, in the contemporary era we have a key addition to this methodological toolkit, for many of us now have cameras in our pockets, often at all times. As a result of the camera's ubiquity, we can add photography (and the images that result) to the list of key items found in the toolkit utilized in apprehending the city via urban drifting.

Photography and anthropology have a long and tangled history. This is partially a product of their coincident arrival in the mid-nineteenth century. Photography played a prominent role in archaeology because of the subdiscipline's central concern with space, and photography was utilized in a variety of other manners throughout the first century of anthropology's extrapolation and development. But Jacknis observed that while photography proliferated in the discipline—sometimes serving as a form of research data for anthropologists, perennially central and useful in presentations to the professional community of other scholars, and always a notably important feature in the public's waxing and waning attention to the discipline and its practitioners—photography's methodological stature in anthropology was never secure. Even into the 1980s, photography was portrayed and deployed as a component of research that was decidedly supplementary to the ethnographic mission (Banta et al. 2017). Only with the advent of the digital age and the concomitant proliferation of the image in ways that even Benjamin (1999) had not foreseen did photography ascend to a more central place in the ethnographic toolkit. This shift was accompanied by a spate of scholarship and by the extrapolation of new vantage points on the role of the image in contemporary society.

Although photography played an ancillary role in anthropology's methodological toolkit for much of the twentieth century, in architecture and in the related fields concerned with urbanism and the urban form, photography and the image have been much more important for a much longer period of time.[9] Le Corbusier's 1933 *The Radiant City*, for example, provided a captivating amalgamation of photographs, sketches, and architectural renderings heralding the arrival of high modernism. Similarly, Benjamin's unfinished *Arcades Project*—assembled from the notebooks he carried to the Spanish border in his attempt to flee the Gestapo's grasp—contained numerous sketches, drawings, and images intended to complement his writings. Rich with images, these early works established the template for the study of architecture and the urban form for the remainder of the century. As one of the countless examples, each of the 253 "patterns" elaborated by Christopher Alexander (1977) and his team in *A Pattern Language* commences with a photograph intended to convey the archetype they seek to describe. Just a few years earlier, Denise Scott Brown and Robert Venturi's famous sojourn to Las Vegas also relied heavily on photography. As Brown later recalled, "photography was our primary tool," and in *Learning from Las Vegas* (the book resulting from that sojourn), textual elements seem to yield the spotlight to the image itself. This balance seems strikingly apropos for a book often heralded as helping to usher postmodernism and its bottomless concern with representation into existence and scholarly circulation.

In this book, my capacity to include images is limited by the associated costs, but in an ode to Christopher Alexander's book, each chapter contains an image, or several images, that might conjure some additional fragment of insight for readers.

Concluding Thoughts

For numerous scholars and researchers concerned with the juncture between urban spaces and the human experience therein, photography has served as a key tool—as a form of empirical evidence that is particularly adept at portraying both spatial and symbolic features of the city, and as a mode for conveying those findings to others. In this book, the evidentiary foundation is ethnographic in nature. But as I have sought to articulate here, significant parallels exist between the ethnographic tradition and the methods described here for apprehending the city. Foremost among those parallels is the experiential foundation of these modes of understanding and the embodied nature of both participant observation and the experience of "being there" in the city. Moreover, both photography and ethnographic data are empirically curated by the provisioner, which inevitably confounds any puritanical notions of impartiality.

To recapitulate, the methodological underpinnings of this book convey a commitment to the social sciences—to a description of the methods I used and the implication of the replicability and also to the presentation of empirical evidence to support my analyses. These are only the first steps toward the higher level of objectivity that Lévi-Strauss envisioned, as articulated in the preface to this book. Building on that tradition, the proliferation of the camera phone and the ubiquity of the image itself also suggest that the anthropological definition of evidence should be expanded to include the photograph. But that seems of minor importance here. More vitally, the inclusion of occasional photographs will hopefully allow readers to better gauge my analysis and, more precisely, gauge the relationship between my evidence and the analytic conclusions I reach.

INVISIBLE GAS

In his analysis of the petroleum industry's footprint in the villages of the Niger Delta in Africa, Michael Watts (2004, 251) discerns a "miserable, undisciplined, decrepit, and corrupt form of 'petro-capitalism,'" a concept he compellingly delineates in his critical assessment. The form of capitalism he observes is harnessed by the petroleum complex he also identifies. That complex consists of an intricate conglomeration of arrangements, laws, institutions, corporations, and security forces conjured in those states found atop our planet's remaining subterranean reservoirs of hydrocarbon energy. One can see evidence of this petroleum complex in Qatar and the other Gulf states, although in its Arabian manifestation that complex is largely indiscernible from the state itself. Moreover, most of the various components of the petroleum complex portrayed by Watts have been trimmed, organized, managed, or otherwise assuaged by the Gulf states so that they appear as nothing more than another example on the continuum of contemporary bureaucratic and institutional normalcy in the neoliberal era.

This elision of the forces at work in the Gulf states is only enhanced by the nature and geography of Qatari extraction. Qatar sits atop one of the world's most productive fields of natural gas (see figure 3). Most of that gas is located offshore, beneath the peninsular nation's territorial waters. The gas itself is invisible to the human eye. Yet while the Nigerian villagers Watts observed lived amid the pollution and the nocturnal glow of an industry engaged in extracting the delta's precious resource, to the residents of Qatar—that is, to citizens, migrant workers, accompanying families, and assorted others—the industry itself

FIGURE 3. An oilfield pipeline gate valve, similar to those that Qatar's invisible gas must pass through. This image is of an exhibit at the National Museum of Qatar. Photograph by the author, 2020.

is largely invisible, like the gas it extracts. Offshore and beyond view from the city, gas is pulled from the ground and brought to the surface of the sea. It is then relocated, processed, and liquified, thereby allowing large quantities to be transported in a single ship. The gas is then loaded into tankers, and once those ships exit the Straits of Hormuz and scurry past those portions of our planet's seas within reach of Somali pirates, that gas has truly reached the global marketplace. Fascinatingly, few junctures of the productive process in Qatar require land, and almost all of the requisite production process occurs at some distance from the city. In terms of Watts's notion of petro-capitalism and the petroleum complex that it conjures, Doha—the city itself—is the primary manifestation and the sole edifice of an invisible commodity whose production and departure to the global marketplace occurs offstage.

Qatar's contemporary wealth is a stunning historical turnabout for the desert state. For millennia, including much of the last century, Qatar was a mere
footnote in the world's concerns with Arabia and with the broader Middle East.
The peoples of Arabia endured colonialism in the long Ottoman period, and then
a sort of quasi-colonialism in the British era in which the region and the nation-
states carved from it were principally cogoverned as "protectorates"—as bureaucratic addenda to British India. The Arab Gulf states achieved independence in
the latter portion of the twentieth century, although several expressed misgivings
about independence and the impending British departure. But independence and
the financial boon resulting from the OPEC embargo quickly resulted in a fertile
soil in which nationalist ambitions blossomed anew. In the 1970s, Kuwait shined
and Bahrain seemed ascendant; beginning in the 1980s, Dubai emerged as a
place people around the world recognized and knew. Qatar's emergence into the
global theater of attention commenced in the late 1990s as its vast reservoirs of
gas finally began to reach the global marketplace. Gauging Qatar's level of wealth
on a per-capita basis, the peninsular nation most closely resembles the United
Arab Emirates to the south; Kuwait's wealth and relatively small citizenry also
place it in this ambit. But these small states are dwarfed by the demographic
titans in the neighborhood: the Kingdom of Saudi Arabia, adjacent to Qatar,
and mighty Iran, just across the waters of the Persian Gulf.

In many of the scholarly conversations focused on the peoples and societies
of the Arabian Peninsula, substantial effort is devoted to understanding the
unique historical experiences of the respective Gulf states. These conversations
have been rich and informative, and remain so, but that sustained discussion
concerning each nation's historical peculiarities often obscures the parallel journeys these states followed into the contemporary era, as well as the cadences
observable in those states' respective histories. The similarities run deep. Despite
notable differences and historical particularities, these states' histories are woven together by geography, culture, environment setting, ethnicity, the presence
of lucrative hydrocarbon resources, a similar experiences with the Ottoman and
British empires, and by quite a bit more beyond that. Numerous families, clans,
and tribes maintain social relations across national borders, and several of the
ruling families trace their ancestry to related tribes.

The Gulf states also share a history—again, from the vantage point of the
longue durée—enmeshed and interconnected with the Indian Ocean world. This
historical experience contrasts sharply with the insularity by which the various
peoples of the Arabian Peninsula are typically characterized. The conclusions I
draw at the end of this book suggest the vestiges of that insularity are dialectically entwined with the peninsula's sustained interconnectedness to this Indian
Ocean world. That interconnectivity is tied to the historical mobilities of the

peoples of the peninsula. In the interior of the Arabian Peninsula, bedouin tribes amazingly sustained themselves for millennia in perhaps the most trying environment on the planet, and their mobility was an essential feature of their endurance. The port-dwelling, sea-focused *hadhar* Arabs built and occupied the busy ports on the seashore, and for much of history shuttled pearls into a regional trade network of great significance in the Indian Ocean world and beyond. These preexisting mobilities and interconnections grew and changed in the colonial era, but they confirm the fact that for millennia the Arabian Peninsula has been a busy juncture at a cosmopolitan crossroads (Onley and Khalaf 2006; Bishara 2017; Roberts 2021).

The GCC states are most recognized for their hydrocarbon wealth, and for the global prominence the afterglow of that wealth has allowed them to forge. Qatar, the focus of my research for more than a decade, is an excellent example. The peninsular state has an extraordinarily high per capita GDP, and by some measures the small state also contains the densest accumulation of millionaires in the contemporary world (Davis 2013). The situation is similar in the United Arab Emirates and Kuwait. A century ago, however, the foundations of the pre-oil regional economy were annihilated when the Japanese entrepreneur Mikimoto Kokichi first pioneered the commercial production of cultured pearls. This resulted in the rapid devaluation of the region's pearls, and amid a broader global depression and the enduring presence of the British colonial apparatus, these were difficult and penurious decades. The Arab Gulf states became independent in the second half of the twentieth century, and their hydrocarbon reserves, conceived by many as a gift from Allah, began to elevate these desert societies to unprecedented heights. Although scholars often emphasize differences, numerous factors—small indigenous populations, the task of crafting new nationalisms, the presence of that hydrocarbon wealth, monarchical leadership cast in the tribal form, and the rapid infrastructural and social development characteristic of the past five decades—comprise the foundational and obvious parity observable in the historical experiences these states share.

To outsiders, the citizens of the Gulf states appear extraordinarily homogeneous, even uniform. This perception is exacerbated by the steady convergence of *khaleeji* fashion and style around a singular and gender-bifurcated mode. Despite appearances and fashion, these populations are somewhat heterogeneous. As previously noted, the peoples of the Arabian Peninsula include the *bedu*, or those who trace their lineage to the nomadic pastoral peoples of the subcontinental interior, and the *hadhar*, or those who trace their lineage to the merchant and seafaring peoples of the port towns and minor cities. But that is only one of many sociohistorical fissures and differences that comprise the citizenry. There are both Sunni and Shi'a components of the indigenous population. Of the Persian immigrants, both old and new, some claim an Arab ethnicity, and others do not. The *abd* component of the population trace their ancestry to the slaves brought to the Arabian Peninsula from Africa and are mostly assimilated into the indigenous structures of social organization.[1] Another former slave population was drawn from Baluchistan, an ethnic region now split between Iran, Pakistan, and Afghanistan. These vectors of difference, and more like them, interlace with the revitalized conception of the tribe and tribal belonging on the Qatari Peninsula. This tribalism provides a social form more specific than ethnicity but more encompassing than the notion of an extended family predominant in the West (or even in South Asia). For citizens, these aspects of identity construction are cast against the backdrop of a proportionally vast population of foreign residents, workers, and visitors.

Amid this diversity, one of the central features of society and state in Arabia is the ongoing construction, development, and maintenance of a coherent sense of national belonging. In most regional cases, the impulse for a relatively new nation to determine and elucidate a shared history has simultaneously affirmed the legitimacy of the ruling families and the tribal hierarchies that the British established to lead the protectorates and proto-states carved from the Arabian Peninsula. Significant portions of these states' contemporary activities can be tied to the articulation of the narratives to which these nationalisms are pinned. Hosting global mega-events invigorates this sense of nationalism. Constructing spectacular cities asserts singular, coherent nationalisms to a global audience. National museums articulate these narratives in great detail and specificity. But thinking of both Clifford Geertz and Benedict Anderson, the nationalist narrative at the heart of these processes is also a story Qataris are telling themselves about themselves.[2] The energetic "heritage industry" so active in the region— an industry coalescing in the form of the aforementioned museums, in particular—facilitates the distillation and codification of these singular national narratives.[3] Foreigners are employed throughout the heritage industry that's arisen around the ongoing construction of these national identities, and increasingly seems to be evoking a collective nostalgia for the premodern past.[4] Simultaneously, and perhaps paradoxically, the activities of this heritage industry simultaneously project a refined, cosmopolitan, and thoroughly modern image to a global audience, an ongoing act that also quietly asserts the benevolent leadership of the ruling families, whose role at the apex of these relations is to guide progress, to choose tastefully, and to choose well.[5]

Migration and the Shape of the State

Migration has had a deep impact on the shape of Qatari society and has left an indelible impact on the whole of the Arabian Peninsula. Although the topic of migration was introduced in earlier chapters of this book, my mission here is to further illuminate this aspect of the peninsula's history, and to better articulate how migration shaped the relationship between state and society in Qatar. It is important to recollect that mobility and interconnection with regional and global trade networks were already key features in the social foundations and traditions of the peoples who inhabited these arid regions by the twentieth century. The *bedu* of the peninsula's interior relied on mobility as a pastoral adaptation to the arid environment, and via the camel, had built livelihoods around long distance trade with the interior portions of the Arabian Peninsula and beyond. The *hadhar*, or coastal urbanites, meanwhile, had cultivated livelihoods tethered to the sea and the mobilities that it allowed. In the intertwined history of these two livelihood systems, trade and exchange were always central features, but notably, neither livelihood system was particularly focused on the incorporation of migrants and the facilitation of migration to serve these modes of production.

One notable exception to this assertion is the trade in human slaves. As Hopper (2015) noted, the rags-to-riches narrative oftentimes used to describe the arrival of petroleum wealth in the twentieth century can be misleading, as it obscures the region's increasing interconnections with the global marketplace that predated the hydrocarbon era (see also Bishara 2017; Roberts 2021). In the preoil period of the early twentieth century, as Qatar navigated the imperial presence of the Ottoman and British empires, the production and export of pearls and dates increasingly connected the region to the vicissitudes of the global marketplace. Labor power was in great demand. Although Britain had made the abolition of slavery an increasingly central feature of its imperial presence in the nineteenth and early twentieth century, Qatar was a protectorate, not a colony, and the whole of the region remained largely out of focus to these distant empires. In that context, and with labor demands tied to the production of pearls and dates, the slave trade remained economically vital to the regional economy. In his estimation of economic life in the Western Indian Ocean of the nineteenth century, Bishara (2017, 47) concludes that the presence of slaves "infused every transaction, every promise to deliver, and every line in the ledger book."[6] Qatar was no exception: under Ottoman rule in 1905, "Africans" comprised an estimated 22 percent of the population of Qatar—a surprisingly large figure for an era in which the primary source of slaves had again switched back to Baluchistan and other Eurasian sources (Hopper 2015, 9). It would be nearly five more decades until slavery was finally abolished in Qatar in 1952.

It is analytically conceivable that the legacy of slavery in Arabia helped normalize the idea of looking outside the region for the proletarian elements of the labor force. But the gravitational core of contemporary labor migration did not come into view until the petroleum era commenced in full. Oil was discovered in Bahrain in 1932, but the industry's vast expansion would await the conclusion of World War II. In the decades following the war, the region's burgeoning hydrocarbon industry drew labor foremost from other Middle Eastern states. In the early 1970s, Qatar and several of its neighbors were newly independent of Britain, and in response to Israel's 1973 war with several of its Arab neighbors, the ensuing OPEC embargo elevated GCC states' profit levels to unprecedented heights. It was in this context—newly independent states flush with hydrocarbon profits—that the political-economic trajectory of Qatar and its neighbors was solidified, and the gravitational core for transnational migration was established. In Omar Alshehabi's analysis (2015, 10–12), this trajectory coalesced around the construction of the "petro-modernist state," configured foremost around the objective of deeper integration in the global capitalist system.[7] It was against this backdrop that Qatar and the other GCC states began to increasingly turn to South Asian labor sources. In the first two decades of the new millennium, South Asian labor predominates throughout the GCC, and this is particularly true at the bottom of the socioeconomic ladder. In our 2012 survey of low-income migrants in Qatar, some 89 percent of the migrants earning less than QR 2000 (US$549) hailed from South Asia, with another 5 percent arriving from the Philippines; at this income level, the largest remaining Arab component in our survey were Egyptians, comprising only 3 percent of our representative sample (Gardner et al. 2013).

One manifestation of this petro-modernist state and this history is the formation of the rentier state, a theorization descriptive of those states whose productive income is almost entirely derived from the external sale of a natural resource. Qatar sells almost all of the natural gas it produces to others in the global marketplace. Rentier regimes—prototypically arranged, like Qatar, so that the state itself is the primary recipient of externally derived wealth—maintain the economic and political satisfaction of their citizenries through the distribution of wealth to those citizen-subjects. In Qatar, the primary channel for that distribution is through public sector employment.[8] Rather than comprehensive engagement in economically productive activities for work, citizens' "primary economic role is confined instead to being consumers and beneficiaries of state-distributed or privately generated rent" (Alshehabi 2015). Nearly all Qatari citizens work in the public sector; however, the millions of noncitizen labor migrants present on the Qatari Peninsula predominate in the private sector, while foreign labor continues to stock countless positions in the public sector as well.

In a sense, the invisible gas that drives Qatari wealth and development is at the core of the state and the migration system that is grown and evolved around it. That invisible gas is also deeply implicated in the city itself, a topic which I turn to next.

A City in History

Although people were present on the Qatari Peninsula for time immemorial, the city of Doha first came into recognized existence in the early nineteenth century. Initially nothing more than a pair of villages on the shores of the Persian Gulf, the city was conjured around the lucrative pearl fishery of the adjacent shallow sea, as well as by the trade and interconnections that the sea enabled. The town grew steadily in the remainder of the nineteenth century, and various districts and neighborhoods evolved, shifted, and merged over the intervening era. Estimates concerning the middle and late nineteenth century indicate that 4,000 to 6,000 people resided in what we now think of as Doha, and that number would double with the pearling boom that commenced at the end of that century. Just decades later, however, the international market for pearls collapsed, and with the subsequent global economic depression that ensued thereafter, the city remained in a sort of stasis for decades into the twentieth century. The city's population would not begin to grow again until the 1950s, just after the first shipment of crude oil left the peninsula (Fletcher and Carter 2017). In the ensuing decade, Doha grew in leaps and bounds: people who had abandoned the city in the difficult decades of the early twentieth century began to return, Qatari tribes from elsewhere on the peninsula were drawn to Doha and all it promised, and wave after wave of migrants from outside Qatar began to settle in the city.

Describing the seaside village of Doha in 1949, the Qatari journalist and author Nasser Othman (1984, 1) noted that "The village had developed by a natural process without any thought for such modern ideas as town planning." But this "natural process" was not the unbridled chaos that the urban Orientalists of yesteryear once sought to portray.[9] The archaeologists Richard Fletcher and Robert Carter (2017) convincingly portray a set of twelve "structural principles" visible in Doha's historical urban growth—principles tied to the social, political, economic, and environmental context in which the port cities of the Arabian littoral emerged.[10] In addition to items like the importance of the sea, the general climate of the region, and the walls, forts, and towers of a defensive posture typically woven into the urban landscapes of the region, their evidence points to a constellation of social features characteristic of these cities. These include the separation of residential districts from zones of economic activity, the "compartmentalisation of residence along kinship and community lines," and the integral role of both central administration and patronage systems in the societies that built and inhabited these port cities (Fletcher and Carter 2017). Although the preoil town was perhaps not planned, Doha and neighboring port cities were coherently structured by these forces which, together, seem to suggest a distinctively *khaleeji* urban tradition connecting the urbanity of the present with the city's urban past.

Cities everywhere in the world are envisioned as spaces where diverse and different people come into contact with one another. This pluralism, and the demographic diversity that underlies it, is integral to the very definition of the urban milieu. Although Qatar and other Gulf societies have often been portrayed as insular and homogenous places (and sometimes these are even self-portrayals), a sustained line of scholarship has clarified that port cities of the Arabian littoral have been waypoints in the Indian Ocean world for the entirety of their existence (Gupta 2008; Fuccaro 2009; Bishara 2017; Roberts 2021).[11] In his frequently reproduced description of the port of Manama, just to the north of Qatar in Bahrain, for example, W. G. Palgrave (1866, 211–212) penned the following description in 1866:

> Mixed with the indigenous population are numerous strangers and settlers, some of whom have been established here for many generations back, attracted from other lands by the profits of either commerce or the pearl fishery, and still retaining more or less the physiognomy and garb of their native countries. Thus the gay-coloured dress of the southern Persian, the saffron-stained vest of "Oman, the white robe of Nejed, and the striped gown of Bagdad, are often to be seen mingling with the light garments of Bahreyn, its blue and red turban, its white silk-fringed cloth worn Banian fashion round the waist, and its frock-like overall; while a small but unmistakable colony of Indians, merchants by profession, and mainly from Guzerat, Cutch, and their vicinity, keep up here all their peculiarities of costume and manner, and live among the motley crowd, 'among them, but not of them."

This captivating quote illuminates the circumstances and context in which these cities and societies developed. While that context was a shared condition, Doha was a smaller mercantile entity than Manama, Kuwait, or Dubai, and through the machinations of its leaders, a century ago the city was less suffused with the South Asian demographic presence that British interests had helped cultivate elsewhere in the region (Fletcher and Carter 2017, 459).

Like those neighboring cities, Doha was indelibly shaped by the wealth generated from its oil and gas resources. Although many contemporary scholars seek to emphasize the continuities that connect the pre- and postoil eras in the GCC states, the resulting monies did have a clear, significant, and notable impact on the built environment.[12] As Fletcher and Carter convey, "the first direct oil revenues (beginning in 1950) had an immediate effect, and, within three years, Doha's town plan had begun to change, with the appearance of tarmacked roads and the construction of new planned districts" (Fletcher and Carter 2017, 449; Hay 1959, 110–111).[13] To that list, we might add an airstrip, court buildings, a variety of new administrative offices for the state, headquarters for the police, new schools, a power plant, and much more. One of those administrative offices was the Ministry of Public Works, which charged with guiding infrastructural development and new housing. The construction of social housing emerged as a key vocation of the Qatari state, and under the guidance and consultation of foreign planners, the city sprawled out into the open desert (Nagy 1997). Ring roads B and C—beltways that encircled the urban core of Doha at the time of their construction—are from this era and remain important features of the center city today. Additionally, in this era, the Qatari state began to "reclaim" land from the sea, thereby expanding or moving the available waterfront.

The central city grew into shape during the apex period of architectural modernism, and in the aging city center one can still encounter the architectural vestiges of this era tucked between the postmodern hotels, office buildings, trophy museums, and urban developments that now crowd the corniche (Gardner 2021a). In the closing decades of the twentieth century, however, the aging city center was residentially abandoned by Qatari citizens as they dispersed to the suburbs. For Qatari citizens, the aspirational ideal shifted from the semi-private *fareej*—those aging districts or neighborhoods populated along "kinship and community lines"—to the stand-alone late modernist villa surrounded by a high wall enclosing a verdant garden (Fletcher and Carter 2017, 449). The sociologist Khaldoon Al-Naqeeb (1990, 91) had once noted that the periphery of the cities of the region was occupied by "something resembling a decrepit lumpen proletariat in air-conditioned ghettoes on the fringes of the 'metropolitan petroleum cities'." But after citizens' suburban migration in the waning decades of the twentieth century, the aging and modestly modernist neighborhoods at the urban core of the city were abandoned to the burgeoning transnational proletariat at work on the peninsula.[14] As a result, they became ghettoes, albeit vibrant and transnational. At the outset of the twenty-first century, however, the pendulum has swung back yet again: a variety of urban redevelopment projects have sought to revitalize the aging city center, and the legion of foreign workers now mostly resides at the periphery of the city. True to the nature of a palimpsest, nearly all these urban eras of the past are still visible in some form, discernible via an urban drift through the dense city center (Gardner 2021a).

Although Doha continues to sprawl into the surrounding desert, the ongoing revitalization of the city's dense urban core is heralded by an array of gargantuan projects remaking central districts. Souk Waqif, the labyrinthine central market both restored and improved to the threshold of simulacra, is located on the same grounds where it always stood and remains one of Qatar's most popular attractions for residents and visitors alike. Nearby is the Museum of Islamic Art, designed by the starchitect I. M. Pei on a parcel of "reclaimed" land just offshore from the city's waterfront corniche. Adjacent to the souk is Msheireb Downtown Doha, a thirty-one-hectare super-block consisting of more than one hundred buildings. The urban redevelopment is promoted as "the world's first sustainable downtown regeneration project" (Msheireb Properties 2021). For years, gargantuan machines tunneled the Metro's now-completed pathway under the city center. These projects, and countless others like them, point not just to a surplus of capital but to the increasingly prominent role of the city as a symbol. Certainly, Doha is a capital city, and thereby symbolically represents the Qatari people to a global audience. But the city is also an architectural trophy case, and thereby falls into a consumerist sort of calculus. Against the backdrop of that global audience, the trophies in the city resonate in a cosmopolitan index of architectural taste. All of this points to the key connections between state, city, and society: as Fuccaro (2009, 3) once noted with succinct clarity, "Gulf metropolises have become instruments of statecraft, tools to promote state formation."

Concluding Thoughts

In part, this brief overview of the political economy that results from extractive industries is intended to infuse the reader's understanding of the forthcoming points in this text. At the same time, it also speaks to the political economic foundation of my understanding of society and culture not just in Qatar but in all human societies. Much as Marvin Harris (1979) contended some decades ago, I also believe that we assemble, arrange, and adjust our intricate cultures and our hierarchical societies around the material bedrock of collective human existence. This seems clear in a city that is doubly yoked by Allah's grand gift of hydrocarbon wealth; the city is built with the profits of that extraction, and thereby yoked to its service as a repository for the surplus capital generated by the extraction of valuable hydrocarbons, as David Harvey (2008) would suggest. But in unfolding into its current shape, Doha is also yoked to the urban infrastructure that humans' dependence on hydrocarbon energy has produced. Automobiles have indelibly shaped the city, and airplanes facilitate the mobilities around which Doha is configured. In Qatar, the whole of the city is fueled by invisible gas.

THE JOURNEY TO ARABIA

The journey that transnational labor migrants take to Qatar and the neighboring states of the Arabian Peninsula is both complicated and variable, and as ethnographers often claim, no single example can stand for the diversity of experiences that migrants encounter. At the same time, these stories about migrants' journeys, their tribulations, and their reasonings—aspects of migration narratives—are the foundational form of evidence that we ethnographers often rely upon in crafting the portraits of the world that we seek to provide. In the next chapter, I will convey to readers a basic anatomy of the migration system that shuttles millions of migrants to the peninsula. That anatomy is culled from the experiences of hundreds of migrants with whom I (and, sometimes, various research teams under my supervision) have spoken. In providing that anatomy of a migration system, I will be pointing out some of the recurring patterns in those migrants' experiences and the common junctures that pepper their journeys.

But drawing on anthropology's social scientific legacy, I suspect readers might also benefit from digesting these ethnographic data in a more raw form. In this chapter, and in the preface to the anatomy of the Gulf migration system I present in the next chapter, I provide four examples of the sort of evidence with which I work and on which my understandings are based (see figures 4–7). The presentation of lengthy and detailed examples of ethnographic data is a strategy with a long and sustained history in anthropology. Important examples in my own intellectual development include Serena Nanda's *Neither Man nor Woman: The Hijras of India*, and the several chapters that she devotes to conveying specific hijras' experiences and stories. Additionally, one might mention

FIGURE 4.   A labor migrant in Qatar. This image (and the others in this chapter) were part of a photographic project titled *Skyscrapers and Shadows* that, in reaching for migrants' individuality, sought to portray them out of the uniforms, away from the labor camps, and outside the workplaces where they are typically encountered en masse. None of the men pictured in this chapter are those detailed in the text. Photograph by Kristin Giordano, 2008.

Bourgois and Schonberg's *Righteous Dopefiend*, Oscar Lewis's *Five Families*, Vincent Crapanzano's *Tuhami*, and Josiana and Jean-Luc Racine's collaboration with Viramma on the book named after her—*Viramma: Life of an Untouchable*. These are all examples of ethnographers' penchant for including singular interlocutors' histories and experiences in accompaniment to the summarizations they oftentimes convey. I have previously made frequent use of this writing strategy and have told portions of some of these migrants' stories in previously published work. In summary, then, before turning to an overarching anatomy of the Gulf migration system, in this chapter I present four Gulf migration synopses.

In all four cases, these synopses are distillations woven together from multiple interviews, sometimes conducted over a span of many years. Notably, the first migration synopsis presented here continues with Divendra, whose story briefly commenced this book.

Divendra from Nepal

Divendra knew that these late hours of the night would be his last moments with his infant daughter. When he saw her again she would be toddling, he figured, or perhaps even walking. He watched her as she slept, and he studied each line of her face in the hopes that he might preserve every detail in his memory. Tears welled in Divendra's eyes, and he was overcome with emotion. Shortly before dawn he would make his way to the bus station in the city center, and after an arduous day's journey to Kathmandu, and then weeks of preparation and paperwork, he would depart for distant Qatar. After months of anticipation, Divendra's journey out into the world beyond the low Terai plain of southern Nepal was about to begin. At times he felt anxious about this decision, and he knew he would miss his daughter so terribly, but more often than not he felt a vague sense of conviction: he had to go. He had to provide for his family. He had to earn.

The events preceding this decision were noteworthy. Several years earlier Divendra had borrowed a substantial sum from his father, or more accurately, from his family as a whole. With that loan he opened a computer training facility in the central district of a small city on the Terai plain. Sadly, the business failed, and his dreams were dashed. Although complicated political machinations and the troublesome Maoist insurgency had made operations extremely challenging for the fledgling business, it was electricity—or lack thereof—that had most directly torpedoed his plans. In those years, electricity was available only for a few hours of the day, or sometimes night, in Nepal. How could he run a computer training facility when the computers could only be operated for a few odd hours of the day? As he discovered, it proved impossible.

In his description, afterward Nepal felt like a land without opportunity for him. Around that same time, his childhood friend Sam, currently at work in faraway Qatar, contacted him, and Divendra listened intently. Sam told him about an opportunity—they would work side-by-side in an office in Qatar until Divendra was fully trained. Then Sam would depart for home. Divendra would receive a salary of QR1000 (US$275) every month. This was more than he could earn in Nepal, and unlike most of the other returned migrants he had spoken with, there was no labor broker standing between him and this opportunity. Thanks to Sam, Divendra's new employer would arrange everything, and in addition to this salary, the employer would provide both accommodation and a food allowance. Altogether this sounded like an excellent opportunity, and shortly thereafter, it was decided. With a last farewell, he bid his infant daughter goodbye and made his way into the night.

Divendra's journey to Qatar was eventful and memorable. His luggage, stowed atop the bus to Kathmandu, was thoroughly soaked by a monsoon rainstorm on the ten-hour journey. Much of the pocket money he had saved was handed to the laundryman in Kathmandu, who cleaned and dried his luggage's contents. He returned to the hotel for another few hours, and after calling his parents and family for one last goodbye, he found himself alone in his room, in tears. Perhaps he should call it all off? He pressed on. The airport was a new and confusing experience for Divendra. He was befuddled and out of sorts until a kindly, experienced traveler took him under her wing and guided him to his appropriate departure gate. The leg of his flight to a Dubai stopover was his first time aloft, and he marveled at the bird's-eye view of Nepal. Unaware of the customs surrounding wine, Divendra took offense when the flight attendant poured only a tiny sip into his glass. Why was he being disrespected like this? Harsh words came from his mouth. His temper rose again when security agents at the Dubai stopover airport groped his clothed body and prodded his luggage in their standard procedure.

After arriving in Doha, and after enduring all the required entry procedures, Divendra exited the airport to find Sam waiting in the seemingly ever-present throng that coagulates outside the airport's arrivals hall. His old friend was gladdened to see him, and Sam promised to take him to their accommodations straightaway. After a barrage of Divendra's questions went unanswered, Sam ominously responded with a brief request: "don't kill me, old friend—just wait until morning and everything will be cleared up."

From the airport they skirted the central city on one of the ring roads before turning away from the glistening skyscrapers that hugged the urban oceanfront. Together they proceeded out to the fringe of the city, passed through several kilometers of nondescript suburbs, and just beyond the edge of the city they turned to enter the Industrial Area. This neighborhood would be the geographic epicenter of Divendra's life in the years to come: the Industrial Area, as it is called, is an accumulation of light industry, warehouses, and dormitory style labor camps that house a legion of foreign workers. Sam and Divendra's vehicle continued into the night, weaving its way through the vast grid of streets before entering the hardscrabble dirt parking abutting Divendra's new accommodation—his "camp." Upon arrival he was shown to the small dormitory style room he would occupy with Sam and several others. He unloaded his luggage on one of the bunks inside. He was then introduced to his new roommates, and although Divendra was brimming with questions, he was drained by the long journey. Questions would wait for tomorrow. Soon all the men were asleep.

The next day he awoke, and after a short journey to work, he began his new job. The office itself was a small, low-slung building in the heart of the Industrial Area—a far cry from the gleaming skyscrapers of West Bay he had imagined in Nepal and then glimpsed from the plane. Divendra would take over for Sam and run the small office, as the four Palestinian brothers who oversaw the business had little patience for the official forms, emails, invoicing, and accounting required of contemporary businesses in Qatar. Although not construction workers per se, the company that Divendra learned to manage was in the construction industry: they leased cranes, trucks, and other construction equipment to various larger concerns and projects, all of whom were in the business of constructing some component, project, or feature of this astonishing modern city arising from the sandy hardpan desert.

The ensuing years were full of travail. The unfinished labor camp to which they were assigned was overcrowded. The South Asian migrants—his coworkers—complained about the food almost constantly. The generator that provided electricity to the camp periodically broke down, stranding them in the fringes of the Industrial Area without light, water, and air conditioning. The four brothers who ran the small enterprise that employed them were difficult to work for; they berated Divendra and the other South Asian workers daily. Wages were withheld, salaries went unpaid, and monies for unspecified fees and penalties were deducted from the wages they sometimes received. The Egyptian component of the small company's workforce clashed with the South Asian contingent, and those frictions—even fisticuffs—were an everyday reality for men at the camp. After training Divendra to run the office, Sam returned to Nepal on his contractually promised vacation, and in collusion with Divendra, planned to never return.[1] Divendra, now in the mastery of the office, struggled with his positionality: while he felt exploited and abused by the four brothers, as the accountant and office manager he was also the tool by which they exploited and abused the other transnational migrants, including his own countrymen. It was Divendra who had to prepare the forms, documents, and payroll ledgers that implemented these exploitations, and he grasped at the weapons of the weak to quell his comrades' frustrations and lessen their difficulties (Scott 1985).

Divendra and I met shortly after his arrival in Doha, and we fit together in multiple ways: although an unpleasantly cold term, he was an anthropological "subject" in one of my ethnographic projects; he was subsequently a research assistant integral to the broader scope of my ethnographic fieldwork on multiple projects; and he was a friend I came to know well and upon whom I depended at multiple junctures. For Divendra, the city that he imagined and then glimpsed

FIGURE 5.   Another labor migrant from the *Skyscrapers and Shadows* collection of images. Photograph by Kristin Giordano, 2008.

from the plane is a city that he would slowly explore over subsequent years, and one that we would sometimes explore together. Although his tribulations and challenges were far from over, those explorations of the city first helped me begin to see the city through others' eyes. Although he would struggle mightily with extracting himself from the imbroglio of his employment, and there is much more to Divendra's story in Qatar, we will depart his migration synopsis here.

Roshan from Sri Lanka

My first interview with Roshan was on his seventh day in Qatar. He was on his afternoon break, and we sat in a large, cool, and modern room in the institution where he worked as a custodian. As we talked, I noticed that his hands were covered with writing. I asked him about this, and he replied that these were simply the names of his family and loved ones—the people he missed so dearly, the people he had been thinking about every day in his first week in Qatar.

A quiet, kind, and graceful young man, Roshan's demeanor was perhaps a strange by-product of a life immersed in conflict and violence. His natal village, just a half-day's journey from Jaffna, lay deep in Sri Lanka's northern province— the regional epicenter of Sri Lanka's long civil war. His father was a farmer, and his mother was a homemaker. As his mother later described it to me, Roshan was born into war: the conflict first swept through the village when he was a young toddler, and like many of their neighbors, the family fled their home in search of safety. They lived as vagabonds, moving here and there, and were gone for nearly four years. When they returned, Roshan was finally able to start school. Although he was older than the other children, he flourished in the classroom, and by the conclusion of secondary school he was the strongest student in the class. Education beyond secondary school, however, would take him away from the small village, away from his family, into uncertainty, and perhaps into danger. His uncle's family had already been interned in one of the state's "welfare villages," and in 2008 the conflict seemed to be reaching another crescendo. Danger was everywhere.

On a late April day of that same year, Roshan left the village with his mother and one of his uncles to attend a wedding some distance away. His sister and her fiancée remained behind with Roshan's elderly father. Their journey to the wedding passed without incident, but shortly after their arrival a phone call from home sent them into a panic: the rebels had stormed through Roshan's village and conflict had erupted. Roshan and the others rushed home to discover his future brother-in-law had been shot and killed in the melee between the rebels and the state's forces. His family was devastated, and his sister was disconsolate. Months passed in a haze. Roshan gave up on the idea of school and eventually found work at a hospital. Slowly he grew comfortable with the job. At the end of that month, his supervisor asked him to accompany him and several other employees on a trip to a nearby town. The men were stopped at a military checkpoint, questioned at length, and then beaten by the soldiers. Their identification and money were confiscated, and Roshan and his supervisor were taken to jail. They were both accused of involvement with the Liberation Tigers of Tamil Eelam (LTTE)—the rebel forces in Sri Lanka's long civil war. He was held for many days. Roshan's brother arrived and tried to plead his case, but he, too, was beaten. Finally, his family raised 15,000 SR Rupees (US$75), which allowed him to be released.

Several other men from his village were working in Qatar, and his mother told him that he would go to Qatar as well. It was described to him as an amazing place—a great place to make a living. For Roshan, it would also provide an escape from the violence encompassing his life in Sri Lanka, his parents thought. It took many months for the plan to come together, and the arrangements were not straightforward. His mother sold the jewelry that she had accumulated in marriage, and the family borrowed lots of additional money to pay the fee for Roshan's work visa, which totaled about $1,000. After paying this money to a labor broker, Roshan was shown his work contract. It guaranteed him QR 1,200 (US$330) per month, and he would be working as a custodian, or "cleaner" in the parlance of the migrants who work in Qatar.

The flight to Qatar was a traumatic experience for Roshan. It was his first time on an airplane, and he was out of sorts. He developed a fever, and the heat of Qatar only seemed to make things worse. For reasons that remain unclear to him, his employer shuttled him between different camps for weeks after his arrival. He moved and moved, and moved yet again. The food at these various labor camps was unfamiliar and, in his estimation, was roundly awful. Finally, his employer relocated Roshan to what would be his permanent camp on Street 43 in the Industrial Area. Other than the bus ride to and from work, the Industrial Area is the only Doha that Roshan really knows after more than a year in Qatar.

Roshan works sixteen hours a day, six days a week. He and the other men leave the camp at four in the morning, and they return at 10 p.m. He and his roommates cook when they get home, then sleep. Roshan, like most of his roommates, spends about QR 250 (US$69) on food every month. The camp itself holds perhaps three hundred men, all of whom are from India, Nepal, Bangladesh, and Sri Lanka. When he arrived, his small room was home to six other men. Recently, however, the company has doubled up all the rooms: the men sleep two to a bed, four to a bunk. They suffer in the cold of the winter season as they lack sufficient blankets. The camp has other problems, as well: a massive trash pile just beyond the camp walls caught fire near the end of summer, immersing the camp in a hazy stench. This continued for weeks. The water supply was also insufficient, and he and the other men clandestinely collected water for drinking and cooking at the institution they clean at Education City. The men smuggle water home on the bus, and Roshan showers at a friend's camp on Friday, his only day off. In these conditions, it is difficult to do laundry, and the employees at the institution he cleans periodically complain about the workers' appearance, their hygiene, and their smell.

When Roshan arrived in Qatar, he discovered that the company would not pay him the 1,200 Qatari Riyals (US$330) a month he was promised in Sri Lanka. Instead, they would pay him 600, although there were vague promises of possible overtime. Moreover, upon arrival his employers held his first two months of salary—this money, he was told, would ensure that he would not illegally abscond to another position in Qatar. He had not been issued an ID card after more than a year in Qatar, and is not certain that he will be issued one, as many others who had been working there a long than him still did not have their cards. Without an ID card, Roshan was unable to buy food on credit at the local store, and he was petrified of any chance encounters with the police.

Roshan has never met his Qatari sponsor. His point of contact with the company is a Filipina woman at the manpower agency that employs him, but she was not able to help with most of the problems he faced. There was also a Sri Lankan supervisor who monitored the men as they would come and go from the camp. With all the challenges, Roshan had not divulged much about his difficulties to his family back home. But he had trouble explaining to them why he had been unable to send home the money they were expecting. His parents were clamoring for his financial help—after all, he was working in the Gulf, where the streets are paved with gold!

On Fridays, he and a friend have been slowly cooking up a plan to sneak away and travel back to Sri Lanka. His only wish, he noted at the end of one of our interviews, was to leave this place and return home. For the two years of our friendship, Roshan was burdened by homesickness that never let up.

Binod from Nepal

In early 2008, Binod made the decision to migrate to the Gulf. In the years leading up to his death, Binod's father had steadily whittled away at the family's small fortune with his habits of drinking and gambling; since then, his family had invested heavily in his sister's dowry via a combination of loans and mortgages. As a result, the family faced an economic crisis of spiraling debt. Binod had experience driving large trucks in the region of Nepal that he called home, and after contacting a labor broker in a nearby city, he secured a position as a heavy truck driver in Qatar. The debts incurred to this labor broker for the work visa were a substantial addition to the family's debt, but Binod figured that within a year he could pay off the loan with his earnings, and could then begin to save some money for the family and for the future.

Binod left Nepal almost immediately. Once he arrived in Qatar, he was taken directly to a labor camp at the far end of the Industrial Area. Conditions at the camp were difficult: crowded bunk rooms, bad plumbing, and an insecure water supply were at the top of his list of concerns. For six months Binod drove a water truck to and from various construction sites in and near the city. Then, the company's general manager told all the drivers that they were using too much diesel as they drove about the city for work. The manager refused to calculate for the fact that most of the drivers' time on the road was spent in traffic—and often at a standstill.

FIGURE 6. Another labor migrant from the *Skyscrapers and Shadows* collection of images. Photograph by Kristin Giordano, 2008.

Unconcerned with those reasons, the manager began to penalize the drivers with deductions from their salary. In protest, the men refused to drive under the circumstances newly imposed upon them. Things continued to escalate; once they stopped driving, the company retaliated by ceasing to pay the men their monthly salary.

The striking workers eventually found their way to the labor court and filed a case. The court case took an enormous amount of time and a substantial investment from each of them. At one point, Binod persuaded his roommates to sell their collectively purchased television so he could extract his share of its value for court fees. In the subsequent six months, the men sat in the camp in a long, slow standoff with their employers as their case percolated through the legal system. Finally, many months later, the case was resolved in their favor. Binod would be going home with all the salary due to him. Good riddance to Qatar, he thought.

Before he could depart, however, the general manager of the company—a savvy and vengeful man—filed a countersuit claiming Binod had "misused QR 10,000 (US$2,747) worth of diesel." The manager's intention was to punish Binod; with a new case in the court system, Binod would be prevented from returning home. For several additional months the spurious case against Binod bounced through the court system in Qatar. Meanwhile, his employers began to cut off the electricity at the labor camp during the day, so Binod and the remaining drivers on strike suffered in the stifling heat as they endured the slow resolution of their case.

After months of languishing in the long summer heat, the spurious case was dismissed. Binod was finally going home. He received several thousand Qatari Riyals in back pay, but most of the money went to the various friends and acquaintances who had loaned him money over the many months he went with-

FIGURE 7. Another labor migrant from the *Skyscrapers and Shadows* collection of images. Photograph by Kristin Giordano, 2008.

out pay. He boarded the plane home with less than QR 500 (US$137) in his pocket—his savings for more than two years in Qatar.

Vasu from India

Born to a Christian household in a small agricultural village in the Indian state of Andrah Pradesh, Vasu's mother and father both came from farming families. In the first decade of the twenty-first century, profits grew increasingly slim, and times grew tough for many in the village, including his extended family. Midway through the tenth grade, his parents informed him that they needed money for his sister's dowry, and as a result, they could no longer afford his school fees. Moreover, by leaving school behind to earn a salary, Vasu might start contributing to household finances, they noted. Although his younger brother would eventually make it to the eleventh grade before departing for work, early departure from school was typical for most of the young men in the village, Vasu clarified in one of our earliest interviews.

As he sought some sort of gainful employment, Vasu joined an uncle in the nearby city of Vizag (Visakhapatnam). There he learned to drive in the bustling city. Eventually, Vasu returned to the agricultural village of his birth and continued to work as a driver there. It was at this juncture of his life that his heart was captured: Vasu fell in love with the young girl next door. Although her family was only slightly better off than Vasu's family, her father was displeased with the prospects of this neighbor boy. But unlike a typical Indian marriage arranged by families, Vasu and Latha were in love. He began hastily planning their "love marriage" wedding. Latha's father remained displeased and hinted that Vasu might compensate for his shortcomings by planning a truly grand wedding for his daughter. Driven by the possibility of acceptance, Vasu planned a truly impressive wedding for the whole of the village. Although Latha's parents paid the customary dowry, Vasu borrowed even more from a moneylender and from another wealthy neighbor to pay for the lavish celebration. In retrospect, Vasu recognized that the legacy of his matrimony was debt, and in the months following the wedding, the moneylender's ruffians ensured that Vasu's financial obligations remained at the front of his consciousness.

Latha gave birth to a daughter the next year, and Vasu's new family squeezed into a small, government-constructed home with Vasu's parents and brother. Straining under the debts of his sister's dowry and the costs of the wedding, the extended family scrambled for a viable financial path forward. Friends from the village were already working in Qatar, and his mother would soon join this migration; she departed shortly thereafter for work as a domestic servant in the suburbs of Doha. Those same friends reported back that Vasu might triple his salary abroad, and after his uncle also departed the village for employment in Qatar, his father made preparations for Vasu to follow the others across the Arabian Sea. The household took out a loan approximately equivalent to US$1,415 to pay for Vasu's work visa and for the airline ticket that would carry him to a job that his uncle, already resident in Qatar, helped arrange.

Vasu worked as a tea boy for a service-focused manpower agency contracted to serve the offices of Qatar Petroleum. It was easy work, he recalled. Vasu worked from 6:30 a.m. to 2:30 p.m., five days a week, and that work required little more than preparing and serving tea in a large office. On the weekends, Vasu would always take one day to attend church. On the other day, and in the afternoons during the week, Vasu sought out part-time jobs washing cars or cleaning apartments to enhance his QR 900 (US$247) monthly paycheck. Settling into this routine, Vasu was able to limit his own spending to about QR 400 (US$110) a month for food, essentials, and credit for his mobile phone. The remainder he sent home to his father. After sixteen months of work, the debt incurred to send him to Qatar in the first place was paid off, and the monies that he and his mother remitted home now brought them ever closer to the dream of building a house large enough to accommodate the growing extended family.

Vasu sometimes cleaned a European man's car and tidied up his apartment for a bit of extra money, and although his uncle pursued the same sort of work on the weekend, his uncle had not seen inside a European's household. Vasu invited his uncle to accompany him, and on that fateful day they made their way through the streets of central Doha to the European man's apartment. The city of Doha is seemingly always under construction, and as they were navigating past one of many urban construction sites, a speeding Qatari driver—busy texting on his phone—smashed into both men. Their bodies were catapulted through the air and into the construction site emptied for the weekend. The driver attempted to flee the scene. Although his legs were mangled beyond use, Vasu was eventually able to crawl back up to the road and wave down a passing car. The two men were transported to the hospital; his uncle would awake from a coma after twenty days only to perish from his injuries. Vasu survived.

The surgeries that followed were difficult, and the hospital seemed to dispense no pain medication, Vasu noted. The pastor and some congregants from his church visited him in the hospital, and he relished human contact. He thought to keep his accident and his uncle's death a secret from his family at home, but word eventually made its way back to the village about the disaster. His aunt had convinced the entire village that Vasu was responsible for his uncle's death, but he had no time to worry about village politics. His employer promised him three months' salary for recovery, and his five roommates helped with caretaking during Vasu's long recovery. During this period, he moved in with his mother for a few weeks, as the kind Qatari family that employed her was deeply concerned about Vasu's well-being.

After a few months, he tried working again, but he could not keep up with the other tea boys. Supervisors at the company began to question his fitness for employment in Qatar. Maybe they were seeking bribes? Maybe he should just return to Andrah Pradesh? But returning home would be more difficult than he initially perceived: his employers retained his passport, and his Indian supervisors in the office would not process any of the paperwork without bribes. Moreover, after learning of the accident, the police visited him in the hospital, and he was prohibited from leaving the country until the courts cleared a case filed against the driver. Although he recognized it as a lie, the quickest path home was through a confession: by falsely admitting to the court that he and his uncle had been carelessly crossing the street when the driver hit them, he might be allowed to exit Qatar. As Vasu recalled, 'I couldn't say it out loud, so I wrote it on a piece of paper and signed it. I didn't want to have to say it out loud!"

In our last conversation, his plans to return home were tabled yet again. The company had found employment for him at a gas station, although his salary there was significantly lower than before. The change in his job meant a move to a new labor camp, and he had just befriended his new roommates at the camp—other men from Andrah Pradesh. His new work schedule prohibited Vasu from attending church on the weekends, but he clung to the idea that more work in Qatar might elevate his family's financial position. Perhaps the new house was still within reach.

In our closing conversation, I posed this question to Vasu: "If a young person in your village were to approach you and tell you that he's planning to go to Qatar, what would you say to him? What advice would you give him?" Vasu's response was sadly reflective of his travails: "I would advise him not to go to Qatar because you will have to pay a lot for the visa and the first two years you will only spend clearing these loans . . . I just think that it's a colossal waste of time and energy, a waste of your youth. You'll spend all of your young adult life here and for what? . . . Look at how much I lost by coming here: I lost my uncle, I almost lost my leg, I will not be able to ever drive again, and my family is tearing apart . . . He would be better off if he stayed in India, close to his family. A man needs to be with his wife and children."

Concluding Thoughts

These four migration narratives provide a window into the building blocks of the analysis provided in this book. As any ethnographer would point out, none of these migration narratives should be framed as typical, for human lives are varied, different, and diverse. But in these four narratives—from South Asian men in the lower echelons of the migrant workforce toiling in Qatar—one can glimpse some of the recurring threads that connect these experiences and inform the anatomy of the Gulf migration system, to which I turn in the next chapter.

THE GULF MIGRATION SYSTEM

This chapter conveys the primary waypoints, the principal components, the key relations, and the significant stakeholders that altogether comprise the Gulf migration system. I use the concept of a migration system to describe this complicated transnational conglomeration of actors and institutions. The concept allows us to remain cognizant of the fact that as a complicated, multifaceted, and historically variable whole, one migration system—such as the Gulf migration system—can (and does) differ significantly from other migration systems extant in the world. For example, the features, actors, institutions, and history of the Gulf migration system are recognizably different from the same conglomeration of components found in the American migration system, and both differ from the migration system that shuttles migrants to Europe today.

The Gulf migration system can be envisioned as encompassing six destination states in the transnational movement of a massive labor force. Since 1981, those six states have formed the GCC.[1] Proceeding north to south along the western shores of the Persian Gulf, the GCC includes Kuwait, Saudi Arabia, Bahrain, Qatar, the United Arab Emirates, and Oman. The features, qualities, and patterns described here as characteristic of the Gulf migration system generally apply to all six of these states. Together, this region has been described as the third most significant destination for transnational migrants in the contemporary world, after North America and Europe, and the most significant migratory conduit with both the sending and receiving states located in the Global South (ECSWA 2007; Naufal 2011; Rahman 2020). Although the six GCC states include less than 1 percent of our globe's total population, nearly a quarter (23 percent)

FIGURE 8.   Young Nepalese men in Kathmandu preparing to depart for work on the Arabian Peninsula. Photograph by the author, 2016.

of all outbound remittances are sourced from the Gulf states, for a total of US$98 billion in 2014 (De Bel-Air 2018, 7).

Beginning in about 2010, the figure of twenty-five million has been a convenient estimate for the total number of foreigners at work in these six states. Unlike the migrations to North American and European destination states, however, almost none of these twenty-five million foreigners hope to naturalize as citizens in the GCC, nor do most migrants aspire to remain on the Arabian Peninsula in old age. There are, of course, some exceptions to this generalization in the middle and upper classes of foreign workers who reside in the region, and there is a growing body of work concerned with migrant children raised in diaspora.[2] Nonetheless, few of the foreigners at work on the Arabian Peninsula desire either naturalization or, more broadly, social integration. Both possibilities are also actively prohibited by the policies put in place by the GCC host states. As a result, the tens of millions of migrants at work in Arabia are best conceived as temporary workers, for the most part. While they may spend the better part of their working lives in one or more of the GCC states, their gaze typically remains fixed on the home they left behind or, for more privileged migrants, on other migratory endpoints beyond Arabia.[3]

The estimate of twenty-five million migrants needs more explanation here. While that figure has been a useful and convenient approximation of the annual stock of migrants present in Arabia during the second decade of the twenty-first century, it is also a figure that can obscure more than it reveals. In our 2012 survey of low-income migrants in Qatar, for example, we were able to determine that the mean duration of stay for low-income migrant workers in the country was, at that time, five and a half years, and furthermore, that over half of the migrants we sampled had been present in Qatar for less than four years (Gardner et al. 2013, 5). As these data points suggest, the figure of twenty-five million might provide us with a synchronic glimpse of the migrant population at work on the Arabian Peninsula, but migrant turnover is high, and the mobilities orchestrated by this migration system are oftentimes cyclical in nature.[4] From a diachronic vantage point—across the last decade, for example—many more millions of migrants are coming and going from the Arabian Peninsula than is apparent in any single year. Put another way, the estimate of twenty-five million migrants who might be present in any particular year excludes all of this coming and going. Additionally, the great majority of those transnational migrants arrive alone, and as I will contend in more detail later in this chapter, these solitary arrivals are best conceived not as agentive individual migrants but rather as the emissaries of household systems (and for readers familiar with South Asia, oftentimes emissaries of large, complicated "joint" households consisting of three or more generations of individuals related by blood or marriage). For both reasons, the figure of twenty-five million feels much too small to encompass the total number of humans embroiled in the Gulf migration system.[5]

Speaking of the GCC as a whole obscures some other unusual and noteworthy aspects of the spatial distribution of migrants in the constituent states and cities of the region. For example, in all six GCC states, temporary foreign workers make up a majority of the total workforce. But in Qatar and in several of the Emirates, foreign workers make up nearly nine of every ten residents—proportions somewhat unprecedented in the history of the nation-state. These dramatic proportions resemble those found in Kuwait, and also those found in some other cities and geographical pockets throughout the region. With so many foreign workers, and drawing those foreign workers from so many different sources, Qatar and the neighboring GCC states seem like an unusual permutation of the demographic superdiversity increasingly characteristic of the era of mobility.[6] Additionally, in all of the GCC's constituent states, migrant workers almost entirely stock the private sector's workforce. Conversely, over many decades, employment in the public sector has emerged as the ideal form of employment for citizen-Arabs. As a result, in several of the Gulf states (including Qatar), nearly all employed citizens work in some capacity for the state itself, and although this bifurcation is beginning to erode in some places, it remains particularly characteristic of those states with the highest per capita levels of wealth.

Outmigration in the Gulf migration system is more geographically complicated. Speaking broadly, since the 1970s the bulk of the foreign workforce toiling on the Arabian Peninsula has been drawn from South Asia—from India but also from Pakistan, Bangladesh, Sri Lanka, and Nepal. The Philippines and a handful of other Southeast Asian countries also contribute migrants to the demographic stock of foreign workers in Arabia. Other Middle Eastern citizens, once numerically and culturally dominant among the migrant workforce in the region, continue to be important components of the transnational workforce present in the GCC, but this geographical contingent's numerical dominance waned in the 1970s (Babar 2017; Norbakk 2020). Scholars of a variety of disciplinary stripes have explained the shift away from Arab labor in different ways: was the growing predominance of South Asian workers a reverberation of transnational connections established under the dominion of the British empire? Perhaps Gulf employers felt more comfortable exploiting the labor power of non-Muslims? Or were political concerns and anxieties about the fractious foreign Arab workforce at the front of the policy decisions that reshaped the Gulf migration system decades ago? Although all these explanations seem plausible, they hint at a more obvious certainty: the stock of migrants feeding into the transnational conduits of this migration system has evolved over time.

Those evolutions and changes have been apparent to me over two decades of research. In my time in Bahrain, for example (2002–2003), Nepalese migrants were a relatively new component of the foreign population at work there. In my time residing in Qatar (2008–2010), Vietnamese labor migrants were a new feature in the labor camps of the Industrial Area. And in my frequent visits to Qatar and to other states on the Arabian Peninsula since 2010, I have observed the presence of new migrant populations, particularly from several West African sending states. Through in-depth ethnographic scrutiny levied at the portion of this migration system operating in Nepal, my own analysis of the shifting constituent populations of the Gulf migration system points to this: over time, intrepid first migrants return home and help establish durable transnational conduits, a process often referred to as "chain migration." In these regions of intensive, sustained, and circular migration, communities steadily accumulate a collective and informed understanding of the Gulf migration system.[7] As a result, members of those communities have more knowledgeable and more experienced veteran migrants to draw upon for information; thus, potential migrants in these communities are better able to assess opportunities abroad. As those potential migrants and their communities become more knowledgeable, they become less exploitable and thereby more costly to employers. In this logic, the Gulf migration system inherently searches out greener pastures—including new migrant-sending states but also including more peripheral and far-flung regions in the current array of migrant-sending states. In my analysis, these mechanics help explain the constantly shifting migrant demography that I have observed over more than two decades of research.

Ethnography has been a particularly insightful tool in assessing the circumstances behind migrants' decisions to enter the Gulf migration system, and to spend some portion of one's working life in a place like Qatar (e.g., Osella and Osella 2000a, 2000b; Gamburd 2000). Via the numerous stories I have heard and collected in ethnographic interviews over the years, crises are a recurring and central feature of those circumstances. Readers encountered some of these threads in the previous chapter: wells dry up in sustained droughts, leaving small-scale agricultural households with an impendingly bleak future; the erosion, collapse, or absence of basic infrastructure (like electricity) torpedoes competent business plans and drives human capital to look beyond the proximate horizon for opportunity; patriarchs carry their families to bankruptcy with bad decisions and various vices, and households subsequently spiral into economic crisis and desperation; civil war, violence, and conflict render homelands dangerous or unlivable, with protagonists like the LTTE in Sri Lanka or the Maoists in Nepal peppering many of the stories I have collected. These are only a few examples of the specific circumstances that one encounters in sustained conversations with migrants about the motivations behind their departures from home. But these specificities belie the recurring general conditions that most potential migrants face: widespread unemployment and the absence of opportunity are conditions plaguing numerous regions, some entire countries, and arguably even portions of entire continents. Those larger geopolitical inequalities and the absence of the sorts of opportunity suggested by modern global capitalism reside at the foundations of the departures that fuel the Gulf migration system.

As noted earlier in this chapter, another key feature to recognize in the circumstances driving outmigration to Arabia is the fact that, in many cases, the migrants present in the Gulf states are best conceptualized as emissaries of household livelihood systems. Inspection reveals that migrants oftentimes hail from notably complex households, like the South Asian joint households. In short, the decision to migrate is frequently a household-level decision—a decision interwoven with the household's attempt to navigate the sorts of crises described above, for example, or premised on the objective of paying for an older sibling's continued education, or perhaps undertaken to repay the loans taken by the household unit for a sister's dowry, or maybe just vaguely conceived as a pathway to help the household improve its general circumstances. In all these examples, the decision to migrate is pinned to the interests of others, and to the viability of the household as a coherent actor. Considering the fact that global policy environments remain dominated by the highly developed states of the global north, and moreover, that cosmopolitan scholarly conversations and critiques are epistemologically dominated by that same geography, there is a recurring tendency to treat Gulf migrants as rational individual agents, and to highlight the centrality of the nuclear family, rather than the complicated family structures that remain typical elsewhere in the world and in many of the sending states in the Gulf migration system. Both of these paradigmatic fragments—the conceptualization of migrants in the individualistic model of *homo economicus*, and the ongoing emphasis on the nuclear family in both the migrant's social field and the policy environments that govern it—speak to the epistemological ethnocentricities that seep into our understandings of global difference and, in this case, our understandings of the Gulf migration system.

Although there are good reasons to remain attentive to the complicated circumstances from which Gulf migrants depart, the ethnographic approach is also well-configured to grapple with the motivations that migrants convey about their journey. These topics have been explored at length elsewhere (Gardner 2010a, 2012b). In summary, the wages and salaries available to potential migrants seeking work on the Arabian Peninsula are higher than those available at home, and are certainly the first and principal reason motivating almost all young men and women entering the Gulf migration system. To emphasize that point: the possibility of higher remuneration often figures centrally in individual migrants' descriptions of the motivations behind their departure from home. Better remuneration is also a key feature in the calculus of migrant-sending households. But the importance and centrality of these financial concerns can also divert our attention from the constellation of other reasons and justifications that also drive outmigration. Some migrants frame their journey in terms of a search for opportunity—they are compelled simply by the possibilities of those Rumsfeldian "unknown unknowns." Others see the Gulf states as a proximate location where one might interface with the more developed and wealthier strata of our world. Their migrations are perhaps conceptualized as attempts to reach the circuits of global modernity, or to join portions of the world they have glimpsed in the global mediascape. For still others, the journey to Arabia is an escape from the strictures and limitations of home; migration to the Gulf might allow an Indian widow to escape the burdens of life in the shadow of a deceased husband, or allow a young Filipino to explore his homosexuality in the urban, cosmopolitanism context that the Gulf states foster.

Although my objective is to remain attentive to the specificity and diversity of migrants' intentions, another feature of this migration system where outmigration's social context and individual migrant motivations coalesce is in the emergence of Gulf migration as a veritable rite-of-passage in these sending states (see figure 8). Particularly in those regions with long-standing transnational connections to the Gulf states, the symbolic meaning and the social connotations of outmigration to Arabia have supplanted any specific motivational calculus. As a rite of passage, in some places migration to the Gulf states is what young men do—a quotidian and commonplace feature on the pathway to adulthood (Osella and Osella 2000a, 2000b; Bruslé 2009/2010, 154).[8] Here, the general tenor of adventure, intrepidity, and an exploration of the unknown eclipses specific reasoning or pressing financial needs. In lectures and conversations with my American students, for example, I often suggest that a young migrant's journey to Arabia sometimes seems to resemble my students' decisions to venture off to college. In pondering their own decisions that led to their presence in my classroom, many can recognize that those decisions were untethered from any specific calculus, and that for many, college is what comes next upon concluding their secondary education.

For various combinations of these reasons, a young adult, often in coordination with his or her household, may intend to seek work in Arabia. Next, they must enter the Gulf migration system. The process of entering this migration system illuminates the array of stakeholders that constitute it, as well as the transnational footprint of the whole of this system. The multiple and various pathways to entry, in Iskander's estimation, "straddle the line between legal and illicit activity" (2021, 235). But typically, labor brokerages in the migrant-sending states receive manpower requests from companies in the GCC states; in Nepal and other parts of South Asia, independent subagents oftentimes roam more rural areas, seeking to profit from connecting potential migrants to the employment opportunities listed by the labor brokerages. Some potential migrants can circumvent these brokers and subagents—particularly migrants, like Divendra, with personal networks that reach directly through other migrants to Gulf-based employers. Although expressly forbidden by various states in the Gulf migration system, the visas permitting migrants to work in the GCC states remain a commodity with high market value. In 2012, our survey of low-income workers in Qatar determined that migrants paid an average of US$1,031 for the right to work for two years in Qatar, and anecdotal evidence suggests these costs remain in place in most sending states.[9] For many migrant-sending households, accumulating these entry fees to the Gulf migration system can be financially challenging. Households might sell off valuable and productive assets, mortgage property and land, pull other children from school, otherwise borrow the funds from moneylenders or banks, or configure some combination of these strategies to accumulate the necessary monies.

The aforementioned subagents, labor brokers, and moneylenders are only one phalanx of stakeholders in this migration system. In the sending states, we might add to that list the agencies that train workers in basic workplace skills. We should certainly include the sprawling and expanding government bureaucracies that seek to regulate outmigration, and deliver stamps, approvals, and required documents in exchange for fees. We could also include the burgeoning NGO sector that seeks to scrutinize and regulate outmigration. Let us not forget the hotels and guesthouses where predeparture migrants reside as they navigate this increasingly cumbersome departure bureaucracy (see figure 8), nor should we omit the many components of the transportation infrastructure that have arisen to carry millions of aspiring migrants from the rural hinterlands to urban hubs in migrant-sending states. The airlines shuttle migrants to the Gulf states, and upon arrival, migrants encounter employers, sponsors, new bureaucracies, and a constellation of additional stakeholders cultivated by these migratory conduits. In sum, this abbreviated anatomy certainly reveals the transnational nature of the Gulf migration system, for the various components of that system are indubitably cast between sending and receiving states. Considering that each of these stakeholders extracts some sort of fee or tax from the migrant's journey, this anatomy also helps illuminate a point similar to the political scientist William Walters's contention concerning what he called the deportation industry. Thinking about this transnational constellation of stakeholders in the Gulf migration system, we might more clearly refer to this system as a migration industry configured to extract profit from the mobilities seemingly requisite for many in the global, late-capitalist system and the era of mobility that it has produced.

Early in my attempts to interview migrants and learn more about their journeys I stumbled upon what anthropologist and methodologist James Spradley (1979) once called a grand tour question—the sort of question that seems to elicit a rich array of detail, emotion, and imagery from our ethnographic subjects. This is the precise stratum of ethnographic material and detailed information that fascinates those of us who are, foremost, concerned with trying to viscerally understand the experiences of others in this world. In shorthand, the grand tour question I stumbled upon asked migrants to recollect the details of their first day upon arrival in the Gulf. The resulting stories, impressions, and recollections are, like the migration narratives as a whole, replete with common threads and recurring experiences. For many of the Gulf migrants I have spoken with, those stories began with descriptions of their first plane ride, and many recollected anxiously marveling at their first experience aloft. Those stories contained numerous examples of confusion about various procedures in transit—at security check, disembarking from the plane, and so forth—and I have been perennially stunned by how many migrants recall spending many hours, and sometimes days, waiting to be retrieved from the airport and transported to their accommodations. Migrants commonly recollect the long drives through the glistening cityscape to those accommodations, and those memorable journeys often conclude at dormitory-style labor camps located at the periphery of the city. Most poignantly, these migrant recollections frequently narrate the moment when the dreams and aspirations they have brought from home meet the grave and often-challenging realities now visible before them.

The Kafala

In her seminal 1997 monograph *Walls Built on Sand*, the anthropologist Anh Nga Longva identified the sponsorship system as the key feature structuring the relationships between citizens and foreign workers in Kuwait. That sponsorship system, widely referred to by the Arabic term *kafala*, distinguishes the Gulf migration system from many other extant migration systems.[10] Building on the vantage point that Longva (1997) first provided to us, in my analysis I suggest that the *kafala* orchestrates relations between foreign workers, citizens, and the state. Although there has been much discussion of the *kafala* and its role in shaping social relations on the Arabian Peninsula, Diop and his coauthors usefully reduce the *kafala* to three key features for the purposes of our analysis: via the *kafala*, migrants may enter the country only under the sponsorship of a local person or legal entity; in the relationship established by the *kafala*, the sponsor assumes responsibility for the migrant's living and working conditions; and finally, by the *kafala*'s strictures, a sponsor's permission is required to change employment or to depart the country (Diop, Johnston, and Trung Le 2016).

This is a useful distillation of the foundational elements of the contemporary *kafala*, and there are several important points to make here. First, while the policies and regulations vary between countries, scholars generally agree that the *kafala* exists somewhere between custom and law.[11] In my analyses, I often point to the customary norms and attitudes that have sedimented in sponsor-migrant relations in the region—sedimented around the highly unequal relations structured by the *kafala* (Gardner 2018; see also Alloul 2021). Second, we might recognize that the *kafala* takes responsibility for governing foreign workers from the state and, instead, distributes that responsibility and those obligations to citizen-sponsors and employers. As the scholar Noora Lori (2019, 140–141) describes it, "the mechanisms for enforcing temporary residency are widely dispersed while authority over residency decisions remains highly concentrated."[12] In essence, we might recognize that the *kafala* invests citizens with responsibilities and duties that many Western analysts and critics envision instead as the appropriate purview of the state. With that vista point in mind, Natasha Iskander (2021, 8) illuminatingly suggests that how citizens deploy the rights and powers afforded them by the *kafala* is of central interest in grappling with the impact of this migration system on the foreign workforce.

Third, and perhaps most crucially, in distributing those responsibilities to citizens and their proxies, and in the context of the unfree labor market that results, one can also perceive the underlying mechanics of the dramatic variability in migrant experiences resulting from these systemic arrangements. In the *kafala* system, migrants' fates are pinned directly on the behavior, goodwill, and capacities of their sponsor. Should a new migrant arrive in Qatar to find a sponsor who is concerned about his well-being, who pays him on time, who abides by the complexities of the law, and who perhaps helps the migrant overcome the unexpected calamities that can arise in human life, migrants may have an entirely positive experience. With remittances fueling new possibilities for a household back home, the migrant may opt to return for additional contract periods, which are typically two years in length. Other migrants arrive in Qatar to encounter sponsors who are unconcerned or exploitative. With the unconcerned sponsors, I am also seeking to clarify that sponsors and employers are, in Qatar, oftentimes not the same individual, and that as a result of these commonplace arrangements, many migrants have little or no direct contact with their official sponsors after arrival. Exploitation at the hands of the sponsor's proxies—the migrant's employer, typically—can happen without the sponsor's knowledge. While those sorts of arrangements are common, there are also exploitative or otherwise problematic sponsors of all sorts, as one would expect. Via the *kafala*, the migrant lacks the capacity to seek employment elsewhere or to depart the country altogether.

All of this is to say that as a result of the *kafala* and the social relations it orchestrates, migrants' experiences are highly variable. The structural arrangements of this system, built as they are around the individual sponsor, explain the extraordinary variability in the migrant experience observed in Arabia. This variability makes the whole of this migration theater prone to journalistic and analytic cherry-picking; in any Gulf state, it is easy to find ten migrants with horror stories about their experience, and easy enough to find ten others who are happy with their fate, if not journeying along a veritable rags-to-riches trajectory. In the context of such variability, it is perhaps noteworthy that many journalists, activists, the algorithms that drive social media platforms, and some researchers (including ethnographers) oftentimes present, highlight, or emphasize only stories at the negative extremes of the Gulf migration experience.[13]

No summarization of the *kafala* would be complete without a discussion of the changes now afoot on the Arabian Peninsula. For the two decades that I have pursued an ethnographic understanding of migration to the region, the constituent Gulf states have periodically (and publicly) announced the dismantling of the *kafala*.[14] Just a few years after I departed my fieldwork in Bahrain, for example, the island Kingdom announced the *kafala* would soon be abolished.[15] There are numerous similar examples announced by various GCC states in the interim, but in 2015, Qatar began to amend the law regulating entry, exit, and residence of foreigners on the Qatari Peninsula, and then subsequently announced its intention to dismantle key portions of legal framework underpinning the *kafala*. With decades of similar announcements from GCC members amounting to little or no significant change in migrants' actual circumstances, there is plenty of ridicule and sustained criticism being directed at Qatar, despite the changes implemented or otherwise underway.[16] For example, in her largely even-handed early assessment of these changes, Iskander (2021, 69–71) notes that these revisions to the *kafala*'s legal footprint have essentially taken powers and rights formerly distributed to the sponsor or employer and consolidated them in the state itself.

These sorts of insights and long-standing criticisms of the *kafala*, while invaluable, should not eclipse the more fundamental changes clearly visible here. In Qatar, migrant workers no longer need their employer's permission to change jobs, and the state has ceased requiring foreign workers to obtain permission from employers to exit the country. In addition, and beyond the ambit of the *kafala*, Qatar also implemented a new minimum wage of QAR 1,000, while also stipulating additional minimums for the costs of food and housing.[17] In addition to introducing the region's first nondiscriminatory minimum wage, Qatar also moved previously excluded domestic workers under additional protections parallel to the national Labor Law. Several neighboring nations have now announced similar intentions to deconstruct aspects of the *kafala*.[18] Again, with these substantial changes afoot, it remains too early to assess the impact of these changes in Qatar or in the neighboring states. While we await impartial and empirically grounded assessments of these tectonic changes to the foundations of the Gulf migration system, or at least to its Qatari manifestation, however, journalists and activists will continue to set the tenor of the global public's reception of the changes proposed to the *kafala*.

Assessing the Gulf Migration System

This anatomy of the Gulf migration system provides a generalized birds-eye view of the transnational system that functions as a central structural force in the lives of many millions of transnational migrants, their citizen-hosts, and the households from which those migrants come. Although the scope of this anatomy has allowed me to briefly visit numerous different junctures and actors in this migration system, there are also notable omissions here. For example, for the most part I have treated the population of migrants at work on the Arabian Peninsula as a whole, and devoted little attention to the hierarchies, stratifications, and differences that have coalesced in this transnational field. These stratifications, although materially anchored in class, often manifest on identitarian lines: migrants' nationality, ethnicity, gender, religion, caste, linguistic capacity, perceptions of that migrant's racial location, and numerous other features shape the overall migrant demography on the Arabian Peninsula, and any individual migrant's experience therein. The structure and nuances of those hierarchies are the central topics of the next chapter. But this overview also omits any discussion of the process by which migrants find their way to illegality in the system I have just described, nor have I addressed the role that misinformation and disinformation play in the calculus of potential migrants' decisions to venture to the Gulf (Gardner 2012; Pessoa, Harkness, and Gardner 2014). Moreover, in this sustained focus on the Gulf migration system, the city itself has slipped out of focus.

While others may see things in this anatomy that I fail to recognize or address, there are two threads woven through this material that I suggest merit attention. First, the sociologist and political economist Stephen Castles (1999, 10) took an estimation of the integral role that social networks played in enabling the migrations and movements that, from the vantage point of the present, now seem to be quotidian features of the contemporary era. In speaking to their power, he also noted that these social networks can "metamorphose into an alternative and competing form of institutional regulation: the "migration industry" with its plethora of informal and commercial recruiters, agents and other facilitators for international migration." This seems prescient for the time: in the Gulf migration system, these "informal and commercial" elements remain a durable presence in the migration narratives summarized in this anatomy. Writing just a few years after Castles, the political scientist William Walters turned his attention to the enduring prevalence of deportation in the world, and expanding upon the idea that Castles's had previously ventured, Walters (2002, 266) established a more expansive definition of what he terms a deportation industry: "a system which implicates all manner of agents—not just police and immigration officials, but airline executives, pilots, stewards, and other passengers. Most pointedly, we are reminded that private companies make money from this form of suffering. Deportation is a business."

Again, there is good and somewhat obvious evidence that connects the Gulf migration system to Castles's notion of a migration industry. Many rural Nepalese migrants' journey to Arabia commences via a *dalal*, a word used to describe the informal subagents who roam the rural hinterlands (and a word that can also be translated to English as a pimp). There are a variety of other informal and commercial junctures along the migrant's path, each another juncture at which some small profit might be extracted from the aspiring migrant for some service or another. Like Walters, in assessing the migration narratives at the root of this ethnography, I fail to see any clear distinctions between the subagents at the very front end of a Nepalese migrant's journey and the statal bureaucracies that extract fees for some necessary form or official stamp, nor between the *dalal* and the official bureaucrat who may move the migrant's paperwork along only after a bribe has been received. Like Watts's concept of a petroleum complex discussed in an earlier chapter, there is some coherent logic to a holistic apprehension of the migration system that's arisen around these transnational mobilities. Recognizing all these junctures and stakeholders—the institutions, businesses, agents, entrepreneurs, bureaucrats, hoteliers, employers, sponsors, and more—as components of a singular whole allows us to better perceive the profit-seeking nature of the Gulf migration system, and therefore, its footprint as a complicated, vast, transnational, and decentralized industry. As Natasha Iskander (2021, 225) notes in her careful and detailed analysis, some even contend that this migration industry, more than simply facilitating transnational mobility, now actively drives the outmigration process.

I also think there are good countervailing arguments to consider here. As an anthropologist, I am wary of the quasi-Marxist classification of these varied and diverse actors into the essentializing categories of either exploiters or the exploited. In that simplistic logic, how might we classify the families that send their son to the Gulf, or those men like Sam, the return migrant from the previous chapter who helps send other young men along the same route he once pioneered? What about Vasu's mother's employer and sponsor, who in the previous chapter provided a room for Vasu while he recovered from his injuries? And I am equally wary of the fact that, unlike the subjects in Walters's deportation industry, most migrants to Arabia enter this system voluntarily.[19] In summary, while I can see the logic of framing the Gulf migration system as a profit-extracting industry, the simplifications and reductions required therein fail to encompass the human complexities of the many different agents and stakeholders who comprise this whole.

It is this penchant for analytic simplification—for the reduction of the ambivalences and complexities we find everywhere in the human experience—that leads to a second concluding point by which we might draw together several other threads woven through this chapter. While countless others in contemporary academia are adroitly attuned to extant imperialisms, to the legacy of colonialism, and to the role that the production of knowledge seems to play in either establishing or preserving various aspects of the inequality characteristic of all human societies, few of those academicians are concerned with the sort of epistemological ethnocentricities that I perceive lurking in the anatomy of Gulf migration I've presented here. Those ethnocentricities, together, can fuel a sort of epistemological and interpretive imperialism that continues to dominate our global intellectual landscape.

As the philosopher Kwame Appiah recently noted, ethnographers have long devoted substantial energy to introspection, to assessing the veracity of their own frameworks of understanding as they navigate their analysis across thresholds of cultural and historical difference.[20] In presenting this anatomy of the Gulf migration system, my attention has been, in part, devoted to the framework of our understanding itself. For example, as discussed earlier, the idea of family promoted in much migration theorization and in many migration policies is typically a conceptualization of family cast in the Western image. Likewise, in theorizing about migrants and the calamities they may encounter in this migration system, scholars often promote a kind of rationality and individualism that also traces its roots to Western liberalism. Similarly, the social prism by which we oftentimes conceptually subdivide the stock of transnational migrants in Arabia (frequently to critique some aspect of that migration system) also reflects its American (if not European) pedigree. Even the lodestar of integration—not elaborated in this chapter, but the absence around which so many critical assessments of the Gulf migration system orbit—seems like another American value that has slipped into the deep mechanics of our scholarly calculations and the conversations that result. Although I have tried to sidestep these epistemological ethnocentricities as best I can, and thereby to live up to Claude Lévi-Strauss's (1963) notion of reasoning on a basis sensible to all possible observers, I am uncertain if the impartiality I advocate has been fully demonstrated here. Nonetheless, it's difficult to shed the conviction I first encountered upon concluding Iskander's critical assessment about the politics of skill in this migration system: that via our collective attempts to improve the conditions of the many and diverse migrants on the move in the contemporary world, are we perhaps facilitating the consolidation of those various migration systems, and, in the process, reconstructing them to be in tighter alignment with neoliberal norms and American values?

SEGREGATION AND SPACE IN THE MODERNIST CITY

The overarching objective of this chapter is to present and discuss the enclaving and segregation of transnational labor migrants in the urban landscape of the city. As I seek to demonstrate, transnational labor migrants' place in the city is shaped by a variety of different forces and processes, some of which are clearly the result of enduring structural features of the *kafala*, the sponsorship system that has long orchestrated transnational migration to the region. For most members of the legion of transnational labor migrants at work on the Qatari Peninsula, constraints on their mobility in the city are an everyday feature of their experiences abroad. But to understand foreign workers' placement in the urban landscape, we must first try to understand how difference works in this complex demographic context, a task that requires us to grapple with the overlapping hierarchies that characterize the diverse population of humans resident on the Qatari Peninsula. As we will see, foreign communities' variable positions in that hierarchy have much to do with their place in the city.

In reaching for both objectives—explaining the predominant features of the social hierarchy present in Qatar, and explaining how, as a result, those differences locate people in various parts of the city—I seek to simultaneously remain attuned to the social prism by which I organize my analysis of the city's diverse residents. As scholars from other parts of the world might recognize, discussions of inequality and difference are arenas of both great attention and militant friction in American academia. Some scholars today ardently emphasize the racial dynamics at work in this migration system, and in an increasingly familiar gambit, further contend that to do otherwise simply abets the racism they perceive and the culture of silence that purportedly envelops it. Other scholars empha-size other variables—class, religious community, language, nationality, culture, and a host of other such characteristics of the population of foreigners working on the Arabian Peninsula. Moreover, many analyses focus on one or another seg-ment of the foreign workforce—for example, the Indian community in Bah-rain, the Indian middle class in Dubai, the children of unions between citizens and noncitizens in the UAE, second generation migrants in the Emirates, Egyp-tian migrants in Qatar, or Maghrebis in Dubai (Gardner 2010b; Vora 2013; Mahdavi 2016; Akinci 2018; Norbakk 2020; Alloul 2020, 2021). My aspirations are to portray and discuss the population resident in Qatar, and because I seek to avoid an analysis weighted with the categories of the hegemonic American social prism, I consciously opt to use nationality as the primary category by which the various positionalities of the migrant population might be assessed. In the final accounting, this analytic approach emphasizes the determinative role of economic class.[1] Through the now-universal categories of nationality and citizenship—concepts whose meaning is generally agreed upon by the various stakeholders discussed here, and hence comprise what we might call bureaucratic facts—we can glimpse how a constellation of other variables in the subjectivi-ties and identities of the migrant population operate. Via this approach, we can discern how class, ethnicity, caste, religion, sectarian differences, gender, age, various constructions of race, and numerous other features play out in the logic of this migration system.[2]

Hierarchy and Difference in Qatar

Orientalist scholars in the twentieth century took note of the profound sense of religious equality expressed by the community of Muslim believers. From their observations and speculations, those scholars envisioned a broad and founda-tional sort of egalitarianism undergirding Arab societies. That might sound com-plimentary in the contemporary cultural climate, but in proper academic and historical context, that egalitarian ethos was typically posited as the reason for the developmental stasis with which Middle Eastern societies were continually framed—a stasis that purportedly inhibited progress on the path to a Western-styled model of civilization. As André Raymond notes, mistaking this leveling aspect of Islam for a broader social egalitarianism was one of many flaws in the Orientalist paradigm. Instead, in his assessment of the empirical evidence, Ray-mond (2008, 67) concludes that "What is so striking when studying the realities of the social life of Muslim societies in the modern age is, on the contrary, the depth of social inequality" woven into so many different social structures in the

FIGURE 9. Foreign workers gather on the weekend in the commercial plaza at the heart of Al Attiya, or the Industrial Area. After much construction and new developments intended to house the legion of foreign workers, Al Attiya is often referred to as the "old" Industrial Area. Photograph by the author, 2018.

region.[3] In assessing the terrain of that social inequality in Qatar—in explicating the differences it leverages and in portraying the hierarchies that result—I commence with an overview of the forms of hierarchy that we might identify as indigenous to Qatar and to the peoples of the Arabian Peninsula.[4] Subsequently, I turn to an explanation of how hierarchy and difference play out in the various foreign populations now resident in Qatar.

In her seminal work, the anthropologist Anh Longva argued that the principal threshold of difference in Kuwaiti society lay between citizens and foreigners. Although decades have passed since her book's publication, those observations seem equally apropos today.[5] In the social hierarchies characteristic of contemporary Qatar, citizens on the peninsula continue to occupy the apex social position. While we might concur on the positionality of the citizenry as a whole, there is more here than meets the eye: although frequently portrayed as a homogeneous and undifferentiated populace, the citizenry itself is replete with noteworthy differences and fissures. Foremost, the Qatari citizenry remains a population organized principally by tribe. This tribal social form is clearly a vestige of the region's past, but at the same time, its enduring importance—and even the resurgence of this social form in the waning decades of the twentieth century—owes much to the modern Qatari state (Alshawi and Gardner 2014; cooke 2014). Via the tribal mode of social organization, groups of interrelated families comprise what anthropologists refer to as clans, and sets of those clans make up a tribe. Members of the constituent clans and the households that constitute them genealogically trace their lineage to a single ancestor. From one angle, the resurgence of the tribal form affirms Longva's assertion about the primacy of the threshold between citizen and foreigner, for this system of social organization establishes an insurmountable sanguineous firewall between citizens and the many foreigners present on the peninsula. The genealogical calculus of tribal belonging, remapped by the state onto citizenship, provides no quarter for outsiders.

The revitalization of the social tradition of tribalism by the modern state is a complicated feature of contemporary Arabia. On its own, its resurgence is the topic of numerous publications and, indeed, entire books (Al-Mohammed 2011; Alshawi and Gardner 2014; cooke 2014; Samin 2015). In Qatar, the ruling family positions itself as a tribe, for example, and various more marginal communities— such as groups of those Qatari citizens of Yemeni heritage—also present themselves in such form. But these tribes, including the extended urban families who now present themselves as tribes, together articulate a form of difference that is merely one vector of stratification among the Qatari citizenry. Different tribes, for example, may also be seen as more *bedu* or more *hadhar*. These descriptors point to other lines of differentiation among the citizenry: *hadhar* identity has, traditionally, connoted a more urbane and civilized ethos than the rural and formerly nomadic *bedu*. And while some of these vectors of differentiation are ascriptive in nature, other vectors are achieved forms of difference. Education, for example, is another key mechanism by which members of the Qatari citizenry differentiate themselves from one another, and with the unequal distribution of wealth in the rentier system, economic class comprises yet another vector of achieved difference. Altogether, the socioeconomic range of the Qatari citizenry extends from the extraordinary wealth of the ruling family and those other families socially proximate to it all the way to what one might recognize in the global index as a middle-class existence. In the contemporary era, this middle-class position is essentially the socioeconomic floor of the Qatari citizenry: via a robust welfare state and the benefits associated with citizenship, no Qatari citizen would be recognized as belonging to the underclass.

Although citizens occupy the apex of this social hierarchy, they comprise less than 10 percent of the total population on the Qatari Peninsula. At or near the top of the social hierarchy of the foreign communities resident in the GCC are those Arab migrant communities from other nonoil-producing states in the Middle East. The mobilities and migrations that connect Qatar and the other GCC states to these regional neighbors predate most other migratory conduits and, indeed, predate the formation of nation-states altogether. In the twentieth century, this ethnically Arab constituency of foreigners was the primary component of the foreign workforce toiling in Arabia. In the 1970s, Asian workers began to demographically overtake the foreign Arab workforce: in 1975, an estimated 72 percent of the GCC's expatriate workforce were Arabs; by 2009, that percentage had diminished to 23 percent (Kapiszewski 2006; Babar 2017, 3–4; Norbakk 2020, 56–65). The reasons attributed to this shift vary. Scholars have pointed to the perceived threats due to the cultural and linguistic similitude of this Arab migrant population to the host societies; other analyses point more specifically to the Pan-Arabism of the 1970s and the political threat that movement posed to the monarchical leaderships in the GCC. It has also been suggested that the lower costs of Asian migrants, partially a result of their willingness to leave families at home during their time working abroad, helps explain this demographic shift; still other scholars point to the direct competition between Arab migrants and the citizenries of the GCC states who, as they increasingly enter the workforce, begin to compete with Arab migrants for skilled employment (Babar 2017). In Qatar, the foreign Arab workforce currently makes up an estimated 13 percent of the total workforce, and while those Arab migrants come from twenty different sending states, the majority hail from a smaller set of five migrant-sending states: Egypt, Syria, Sudan, Lebanon, and Jordan (Babar 2017, 29).[6] Small portions of the Arab migrant workforce occupy unskilled or low-skill positions in Qatar, but the Arab ethnic component of the migrant workforce predominates in several key high-skill sectors: they are disproportionately represented, for example, in the finance and insurance sectors, as well as in various other professional, scientific, and technical fields, including the education sector. In summary, the cultural, linguistic, and ethnic similitude that the expatriate Arab migrant communities share with the citizenry lodges them near the apex of this social hierarchy. Ironically, those similitudes also help explain their diminishing demographic presence in the region, as well as some of the host states' anxieties around their enduring presence.[7]

Also at or near the top of the social hierarchy of foreign communities resident in Qatar and on the Arabian Peninsula are the foreign professionals and other skilled migrants with passports from the archipelago of developed states mostly found in the planet's northern hemisphere. This set of migrant-sending states includes both Canada and the United States, all of the European countries, both Australia and New Zealand, and a smattering of other smaller nation-states. Japan, Korea, and Singapore might also be placed in this category, but their contributions to this demographic component of the populace of foreign workers in Qatar remain small (see Jones 2019, 12). Altogether, this segment of the foreign workforce can be usefully referred to as a cosmopolitan professional elite. In the nomenclature commonplace on the Arabian Peninsula, these migrants (as well as the Arab migrants previously discussed) are referred to as expatriates, not migrants, a differentiation in nomenclature which signifies the class positionality of this portion of the foreign population, and thereby distinguishes them from the transnational laboring class. Unlike the various Arab migrant communities who occupy the pinnacle position in the social hierarchy of foreign communities present in Qatar, by definition no members of this cosmopolitan professional elite work in the lower economic sectors of the workforce. However, much like many members of the Arab migrant communities described above, members of the cosmopolitan professional elite typically migrate as a nuclear family unit.

Additionally, in newer scholarship the cosmopolitan professional elite is oftentimes essentialized in racial terms and conflated as white. While that conflation has real meaning and symbolic power in the traffic of stereotypes that characterizes social interactions in superdiverse contexts like those found in the Arab Gulf states, those assertions essentially purvey the very racial stereotypes they utilize. Most of the sending states that contribute migrants to the cosmopolitan professional elite present in Arabia are, unlike Qatar, integrationist states, and therefore contribute professional migrants from diverse ethnic ancestries. There is quite a bit of overlap between this cosmopolitan professional elite and other categories of the foreign population described here, including the Arab migrant communities who share the upper echelons of this social hierarchy.[8] For example, there are numerous members of this cosmopolitan professional elite who trace their ancestry to neighboring Middle Eastern states but are citizens of these developed and mostly northern states—a diasporic reality expertly explored by both Jaafar Alloul (2020, 2021) and Mari Norbakk (2020). Similarly, at least a dozen of the scholars cited in this book are precisely defined by this juncture: they trace their ancestral roots to sending states in South Asia, the Middle East, or Africa, but are citizens of developed northern states and should be counted as members of this cosmopolitan professional elite. In summary, while the boundaries between these migrant communities can be blurry, and the communities may overlap, both the cosmopolitan professional elite and the ethnically Arab migrant communities occupy a position of relative privilege when compared to the vast transnational laboring class of foreign migrants at work in Arabia.

Below these groups of foreigners at work in Qatar one finds the vast population of middle and working-class migrants who comprise the majority of the foreign population resident on the Qatari Peninsula. Migrants from South Asia predominate here—men (and some women) from India, Nepal, Sri Lanka, Bangladesh, and Pakistan have a long-standing presence in Qatar and in the neighboring GCC states. In addition to the vast population of South Asian migrants, there are increasing numbers of African migrants visible in Arabia, and notable populations of East Asian and Southeast Asian migrants are present as well. Of the latter regional grouping, both the Philippines and Indonesia have been sending migrants to Qatar for many decades. In the hierarchy of foreign communities under construction here, migrants from African and Southeast Asian nations typically jostle with South Asians for positions near the bottom of this hierarchy. In our 2012 survey of low-income migrants in Qatar, our research team's random sample encountered labor migrants from more than twenty-five different nationalities (Gardner et al. 2013). This number is likely lower than a contemporary assessment of national diversity would find among the resident population in Qatar—first, because new sources of labor are periodically tapped by the migration system described in the previous chapter, and second, because only a subset of the nationalities present in Qatar fall into the low-income category (arbitrarily defined as QAR 2000 for our 2012 survey). Although detailed demographic information about the migrant populations resident in the various Gulf states has long been difficult to access, it is likely that national diversity is even greater among the middle class and professional class of migrants in Arabia.[9] Regardless, the various national groups present in Arabia fall into an established and calcified hierarchy perceptible to most residents of Qatar.[10]

With this broad description of the resident population of Qatar in hand, there are three general points of pertinence here. The first concerns the sexual constitution of these different national communities of migrants. The overall proportion of men to women among the population of foreigners resident in Qatar is highly unequal, as is the case in the neighboring GCC states. In Qatar, there are nearly five men resident on the peninsula for every woman (De Bel-Air 2017, 7). Numerous factors shape this demographic reality, but a migrant's socioeconomic place in the broad hierarchy established above is a key variable: skilled migrants and professionals further up the socioeconomic ladder can bring an accompanying spouse and family to the peninsula. Nonetheless, a trailing spouse or family members in diaspora come with additional costs—school fees, extra vehicles, larger accommodations with sufficient privacy, periodic air transportation costs, and a host of other expenditures are commonly entailed. As a result, only migrants loftily placed in the socioeconomic hierarchy can afford to bring their families to Qatar. This fact is further reinforced by Qatari policy: family visas are available only to migrants who earn more than QR 10,000 (US$2,747) per month.[11] Although many women arrive as trailing spouses, others arrive to work; women are particularly visible elements of the domestic sector, of the commercial service sector, as well as in education, health care, and a handful of other vocations. The overall number of women who reside in labor camps—that is, women employed outside the domestic sector—has been steadily increasing in recent years (De Bel-Air 2017, 8). On occasion, and usually in the wake of a particularly heinous case of exploitation or abuse, migrant-sending states have sought to prohibit women's outmigration to Arabia. This points to a double standard: in most arenas of this mobility, migrants are moving from patriarchal sending states to patriarchal receiving states, and despite the travails of the sponsorship system, men are frequently—and incorrectly—stereotyped as capable stewards of their own fate.

In addition to the differences in the sexual constitution of the various national migrant communities, those communities also occupy different socioeconomic territory.[12] This variability and these differences constitute the second general point to draw from this description of social hierarchy on the Qatari Peninsula. The Lebanese and the Canadian communities present in Qatar, for example, are almost entirely consolidated in the higher socioeconomic echelons, and one would find no members of these national constituencies working as manual laborers. Conversely, other national constituencies are mostly or entirely consigned to lower socioeconomic echelons: almost all Nepalese migrants occupy these lower socioeconomic realms, for example, and the same was true for the Vietnamese contingent of workers present during our survey in 2012.[13] Still other national communities of migrants traverse socioeconomic strata. Many Egyptian migrants, for example, can be found near the top of this social hierarchy, while other Egyptian nationals are employed near the bottom of this hierarchy as low-income workers. The Indian community of migrants is perhaps the quintessential example here: while many Indian nationals toil for Qatar's newly established minimum wage, other members of the Indian diaspora occupy the very highest socioeconomic strata of foreigners in Qatar. The variable socioeconomic footprint of the different migrant communities has a significant impact on their experiences and well-being, for the communities to which migrants in distress often turn have different capacities, different cultural capital, and different visibility in Qatar, all of which impacts members of these communities' ability to resolve the problems and imbroglios they might face on the peninsula.

The third and final point about this social hierarchy concerns the traffic in stereotypes that results from hierarchies that have calcified over time. As I have

noted, my description of hierarchy and difference among the resident population of foreigners in Qatar and the other Gulf states would sometimes truck in the
stereotypes and essentializations that one frequently encounters in the social fields
of contemporary Arabia. From one angle, replicating those stereotypes is analytically treacherous, as these categorizations and observations are oftentimes only
vaguely tethered to any empirical reality, if any at all. At the same time, it should
be recognized that these stereotypes, as an ad hoc social prism for organizing and
sorting through the array of cultural, national, and ethnic diversity one encounters in Arabia, materialize the social reality they purport to describe: over sustained migration, Filipina women become idealized as domestic workers; Nepalese
men are idealized as unskilled laborers; West African men are envisioned as ideal
security personnel. These impressions—the "gender and racial discourses" that Iskander (2021, 14) takes note of, although these "discourses" are commonly deployed via a social prism concerned foremost with nationality—are reinforced in
Qatar by the reality they construct. Through chain migration and employer preferences, these migrant pathways calcify the stereotypes, bigotries, racisms, and
other aspects of the social prism that manifests the reality it purports to represent.
Interestingly, the calcification of these communal identities in the division of labor
in the Gulf states yields a structure of relations that clearly resembles caste
structures in South Asia (Dresch 2006, 208).

This brief and somewhat cursory overview presents the all-encompassing social hierarchy visible in contemporary Qatar. The preservation of cultural
differences—resulting in part from the transnational footprint of the foreign
population, and also from the spatial politics central to the remainder of this
chapter and book—seems to produce a plural society characterized by a form of
hierarchical multiculturalism.

Segregation in Urban Space

In 2009, Divendra had only recently arrived in Qatar, and he resided in the partially finished labor camp at the margins of the Industrial Area. Like me, Divendra sought to explore the city on his days off—we were both eager to see the sights,
gauge the modernity of this new-to-us city, encounter different people from different backgrounds, and experience as much of this strange and unfamiliar cultural
world as possible. He wanted to explore more of the city than the Al Attiya parking
lot, which was thick with low-income migrants on a Friday afternoon (see figure 9). Like neighboring cities on the Arabian Peninsula, Doha is a city replete
with spectacular architecture and urban designs, and there is much to regard
in the urban landscape. Prominent on the list of potential destinations that

garnered Divendra's attention were Doha's numerous shopping malls. In general terms, shopping malls were—and remain—symbolically and socially vital structures in the urban landscape of the Arabian city; they are spaces of high consumerism, oftentimes architecturally spectacular constructions, and function as vibrant air-conditioned social spaces for the resident population of the city. At that time, there were three shopping malls of note in Doha: Landmark Mall, City Centre Mall, and Villaggio Mall. These three malls rose above the city's other malls in the economy of public attention, although their position has since been eclipsed by newer, larger, and more ostentatious malls. In my interviews in the labor camps, these consumerist spaces were a commonplace referent in our conversations. Notably, almost all of the men knew these urban spaces only by reputation: most migrant men of the laboring class were prevented from entering these places by the implementation of a "family day" on Fridays.

Family day was designed and implemented to disallow single migrant men—or "bachelors"—from entering the mall, thereby removing them from these spaces of ostentatious consumption and excising them from some of the most electric quasi-public spaces in the sweltering city. In broader conversations, this policy was justified by the intention of ensuring that women and families (and particularly Qatari women and families) might feel comfortable shopping and consuming in these spaces. To implement this policy, other migrants (typically also South Asian) were stationed outside the entrances to the mall and tasked with the challenging assignment of pulling aside any unaccompanied men and disallowing them from entering the mall. At the same time, these guards were either instructed or otherwise intuited that they should not detain single men from the middle class. I myself—not of the bachelor class of labor migrants—passed through this gauntlet unperturbed on multiple occasions when unaccompanied by my young daughter, and I noted that individuals who appeared Qatari, as well as South Asians perceived as belonging to the middle class, also entered shopping malls on Fridays without issue. The previous section of this chapter concluded with a discussion of the traffic in stereotypes that becomes a quotidian feature of life in a demographically superdiverse context. Those skills—the capacity to initiate a conversation with a stranger amid this superdiversity, and to enter that conversation with an estimate of who the other individual might be—rely on the estimations, assumptions, guesses, and stereotypes that foreigners rapidly develop in the city of Doha. For the guards stationed at the entrance of the shopping mall, their occupation hones this skill to perfection. They must be able to differentiate between foreigners of different classes; they must estimate the migrant's nationality and, if necessary, the language with which to approach him; they must quickly decide which individuals are to be disallowed entrance to the mall; and they must grapple with any consternation or friction that results, particularly in those situations where the individual feels wrongly prohibited from entry.

Divendra was undeterred by these obstacles. A Nepalese friend who worked inside first facilitated Divendra's exploratory entry to Villaggio Mall. Astonished at the interior's decoration and the high-end consumer culture he could glimpse therein, he returned to camp with stories of what he had seen and tales of his adventures inside. His fellow workers were captivated. In later conversations, he confided that his feelings were mixed: although the sights were impressive, the inequality was painfully stark, and in his final estimation he regarded the mall as "a heaven for the rich people and really like a hell for us." Despite these ambivalences, Divendra grew more interested in seeing the other shopping malls in Doha. Compatriots at the camp had suggested that he certainly ought to visit City Center Mall—none of them had ever entered it themselves, but they had all heard that the vertical mall nestled among the skyscrapers of Doha's West Bay was a particularly impressive and spectacular structure. After gauging the Venetian canal and costumed gondoliers at Villaggio, Divendra was ready to make the comparison himself, and he confidently accepted the challenge of finding a way inside yet another forbidden urban space. As this proletarian *boulevardier* later recalled:

> So I went there on the first of May—I think it was a Friday. I took a bus from the Industrial Area—bus 57—to the city center . . . It was afternoon, and it was scorching hot, so I waited outside until evening. I was dressed in my smartest clothes, and I wore my new stylish eyeglasses. At the City Center Mall, I don't have anyone I know, so there were no friends to help get me inside. So I just waited outside. I watched the security guards out there. I saw police vans, also, and I was nervous about trying to enter. What if they catch me and ask me why I am in the mall—don't you know it's family day? Why did you come here? And then I will be in trouble. So I waited outside for ten or fifteen minutes. And then suddenly my mind was made up. I just took out my mobile phone, switched it off, held it up to my ear and, as I walked toward the guards, I loudly said, "Oh, hi Jenny, how are you? Just wait inside—I'm at the entrance now." And then I just went inside—right past the guards. They didn't even bother me!

In Divendra's estimation, City Center Mall was a lesser urban spectacle than Villaggio. Musing over the comparison, he was unimpressed with the former mall, but he noted that still, on his more recent adventures there, he could afford nothing; he had explored the first floor a bit, and then had watched the skaters on the ice rink at the center of the mall. One of the thoughts that crossed his mind there, as he recalled, was that "these Qataris have a lot of money, and they are spending the money blindly." Eventually exiting and returning to camp, the stories of his adventure again captivated his compatriots. And in the coming months, Divendra would continue to explore other parts of the city, including additional areas and urban features where migrants of the laboring class were sometimes prevented from entering. In the months that followed, we would sometimes explore the city together.

But Divendra and the other migrants' active exclusion from the urban spaces I often frequented sat uneasily with me, and his experiences actively circulated in my mind. Moreover, shopping malls were not the only spaces from which these working-class migrants were segregated. I had witnessed numerous instances of this quotidian segregation at shopping malls some ten years ago during my residence in Doha. More recently, in 2018 and 2019 I witnessed working-class migrants being turned away from Souk Waqif by the police that patrol that space, and I have also witnessed them being prevented from entering the Corniche—the long esplanade on the city center's waterfront. The same impulse to sift, sort, and segregate the working class of the migrant population returned in March 2020. Facing some of the highest COVID case rates in the GCC, Qatar established a *cordon sanitaire*—a selective and spatialized quarantine zone—around the Industrial Area: roadblocks, checkpoints, and concrete barriers were the Qatari state's attempt to stem the ongoing spread of the virus (Chandra and Promodh 2020, Iskander 2020).

It was episodes like these—all facets of the same spatial politics, I suggest—that are core concerns of this book and of my analysis of city and society. In the remainder of this chapter, I want to take holistic stock of migrants' experiences with segregation in the urban landscape of the city. By broadening the scope of what drives and constitutes this segregation, I reveal that this sifting and sorting of migrants in the urban landscape of the city is a quotidian feature of labor migrants' experiences in Arabia. There are the notably episodic and occasional forms of active segregation here: preventing these men from entering a shopping mall or being present in various other urban spaces or cordoning off a primary zone of their residence in an attempt to stem the spread of a virus. But these forms of segregation and demographic sorting are, as I hope to demonstrate here, only one manifestation of a broader and more comprehensive spatial politics manifested in the urban landscape of Doha. Building on the empirical foundation of the four migrant synopses presented in an earlier chapter, and drawing more directly from Divendra's experiences described here, I suggest that the forces impelling this segregation in Doha might be conceptualized in four distinct realms.

First, the *kafala* and the broader arrangements of the Gulf migration system play a certain and integral role in the segregation of the transnational proletariat in the urban landscape. For a great majority of the foreign workforce, the location of their residence is assigned by their employer, and its provision is framed as both a benefit and, in the longer tradition of the *kafala*, as an obligation of the sponsor to the foreign worker. Through state-led urban planning efforts, the location of these labor camps has shifted over time; in decades past, the aging and decrepit city center was abandoned to the foreign workforce by a citizenry deeply invested and, suddenly, financially capable of a steady outmigration to the successively new suburban periphery. In the context of this urban history, the location of the Industrial Area at the periphery of the city heralded a reversal; as attention and capital investment began to flow back into the revitalization of the aging urban core, the expansive transnational proletariat long resident there was increasingly relocated to this periphery. First, they were relocated to the Industrial Area, and then subsequently to an array of massive newer developments—like Asian Town and Barwa Al Baraha, also located at the urban fringe. These newer developments gather dormitory-style labor camps and various commercial amenities, all designed to accommodate and service the vast foreign workforce toiling on the peninsula. As these peripheral, planned labor accommodations have proliferated in the urban landscape, the Qatari state has simultaneously implemented a series of prohibitions on the location of labor accommodations (Walker 2015). Altogether, paramount in the causal forces that place foreigners in particular spaces in the urban landscape is the *kafala*, which establishes the unequal, dyadic relationship between foreign workers and the employer-sponsors who must also accommodate them.

A distinctive and second force that results in the spatial segregation of the transnational proletariat in Doha might be summarized most broadly as the result of market forces. Although most transnational migrants are placed in accommodations by their employers, many others are, instead, provided with a housing stipend by their employer, with which they are to arrange and obtain their own accommodation. It is through these market arrangements, for example, that in decades past citizen families relocating to the suburban fringe began to rent their aging houses left behind in the city center to various resident foreigners; in the city center and now at the periphery, foreign migrants frequently advertise shared spaces for rent; and before the Ministry of Municipality and Urban Planning delineated "no bachelor" zones in the urban landscape, my fieldwork oftentimes carried me to aging villas occupied by dozens of transnational labor migrants in residential neighborhoods still predominantly inhabited by middle-class Qatari citizens (Gardner 2010c). These cases exemplify the fact that the *kafala* and the determinative role that it plays in establishing the location of residence for many foreign workers coexists with market forces. And those market forces, operating in the domain of real estate, conjure familiar spatial results: more desirable locations and neighborhoods in the urban landscape are more costly, thereby transposing economic inequality onto urban space. Through the "invisible hand" of the market, we can perceive another segregatory force shaping the circumstances and the location of foreign workers in the urban landscape of Doha.

A third segregational force that we might identify in Doha's urban landscape is the gravity that brings culturally and linguistically similar people together. This gravity is visible at a variety of scales. For example, transnational labor migrants congregate on Friday in the parking lots surrounding Al Attiya Market in the heart of the Industrial Area. In gathering there, workers from the same area of Tamil Nadu commandeer a particular portion of the sidewalk; Nepalis from Chitwan District occupy another. With a few questions to strangers, newly arrived migrants can quickly find their way to familiar compatriots and friends in a faraway land (see figure 9). Similarly, albeit at a different scale, in the dormitory-style labor camps to which many members of the transnational proletariat are assigned, migrant workers typically have the freedom to decide on who will room together in the camp. As a result, Bangladeshi men typically room with other Bangladeshi men; Muslim Indians often room with other Muslim Indians; Sinhalese Sri Lankans seek out other Sinhalese Sri Lankan roommates. This "gravity"—the agentive spatial sorting observable in the labor camps or in the parking lots of Al Attiya—can be extrapolated to the city as a whole: in Doha, and in any city where market forces are at least partially present in the apportionment of real estate, cultures coagulate in the urban landscape.[14] In *Temporary Cities*, Yasser Elsheshtawy (2019b) ruminates at length on "Little Bangladesh," an informal social and commercial space discretely tucked in the urban landscape of Abu Dhabi. Similarly, Americans (and others) are familiar with the "Chinatown" model of urban space that resulted from the rebuilding of San Francisco after the 1906 earthquake and fire. Indeed, this is the same gravity by which Arab tribes, clans, and families first configured Doha's urban landscape in a mosaic of *firjan*. Or consider that Rana AlMutawa (2021, 149) noted that her Emirati interlocutors were drawn to urban spaces that "feature a high proportion of Emiratis relative to other groups." Drawn together by cultural, linguistic, or ancestral similarities, the humans in these examples describe the gravity by which people congeal in the urban landscape. This gravity is another segregatory force in the urban landscape of Doha.

The final set of forces driving the segregation and spatialization of transnational migrant laborers in the urban landscape are those that first drew my attention, the forces centrally visible in the ethnographic description of Divendra's experience with which I commenced this section: the volitional and active segregation of the foreign workforce in the urban landscape of Doha. Members of the transnational proletariat—and particularly male migrants—are oftentimes framed as a pollutive threat to the social integrity of the urban landscape. In tandem with this perception, male migrant workers in the lower economic classes are, in various circumstances, actively prevented from accessing various areas of the city, and particularly those areas of the city frequented by the citizenry and the cosmopolitan elite present on the Qatari Peninsula. Although this set of forces driving the segregation of the transnational migrant population has been a lightning rod for sporadic global attention, I have contended here that this active form of segregation is only one facet of the broader spatial politics at work in the city.

Concluding Thoughts

The four different forces delineated here include several that are imposed on migrants as a condition of their existence in a land foreign to them: when accommodation is provided by their employer, they often have no say at all about their placement in the urban landscape, and at certain times and in certain places, their mobility in the urban landscape is actively inhibited. These forces are oftentimes volitional in nature. Other forces identified here stem directly from migrants' agency: they value and oftentimes need to connect with culturally and linguistically familiar compatriots, and when market forces are at work, their place in the urban landscape is shaped by the economic inequalities that underpin their presence in Qatar. None of these forces typically operates in isolation. Instead, they intersect and overdetermine the resulting spatial segregation and spatial distinction.

In the logic by which these migrants are sorted and segregated in urban space, class seems the most salient variable. By merely presenting himself as a member of the foreign middle class, Divendra passed through the security gauntlet at the entrance of City Center Mall without incident. Other variables and aspects of migrant identity—language, ethnicity, religion, and race—are merely a portion of the lexicon by which the migrant's class might be estimated. And while intrepid and curious migrants might have the capacity to flaunt these strictures, they do so at the risk of garnering the attention of the state, as Divendra described. Moreover, for Divendra, crossing those thresholds was not just a risk to his tenure in Qatar but also a painful confrontation with the inequalities that typify our world and are so visible in a cosmopolitan entrepôt like Doha. While some labor migrants chafe at these restrictions, in my experience most seem to have accepted the world as-it-is, before them, replete with opportunities and challenges. The constraints on their mobility in the city are seen as part and parcel of work in Qatar. In the Gulf city, the segregation of the transnational working class is a social fact.

COMPOUNDS, WALLS, AND CULTURAL SOVEREIGNTY

In the previous chapter, my analytic concern was largely directed at the vast legion of transnational migrant labor residents in Doha—at the men and women who, by definition, comprise the lower echelons in the social hierarchy of Doha's residents. These migrants constitute a transnational proletariat, an underclass imported to Qatar via the migration system with Arabia at its center. As I sought to explicate, this transnational proletariat's experience in the urban landscape of Doha is, essentially, a segregated experience. These migrants' mobility is constrained at various junctures and impeded in particular locations and spaces. Furthermore, the forces impelling this spatial segregation are manifold and varied, and discrimination is merely one ingredient in the segregatory forces perceptible in Doha and in neighboring cities. My understanding of these migrants' experiences was a result, in part, of Friday ethnography and its cadences, conducted foremost during my residence in Doha between 2008 and 2010, and continuing via numerous and periodic returns to Qatar in the subsequent years. As a privileged and professional expatriate, I was able to cross various thresholds and borders in the city to visit migrant residences in the Industrial Area and elsewhere on the peninsula. By night, and oftentimes after a meal with my interlocutor friends, I returned to my residence and sought to digest everything I had heard.

My residence was assigned to me by my employer, Qatar University. Like many migrants of the professional or skilled class—what I have termed the *cosmopolitan professional elite*—my family and I dwelled in a compound (see figure 10). Our residence was one of several options offered to me upon arrival.

FIGURE 10.   A compound in the suburban neighborhood of Al Waab. Photograph by Kristin Giordano 2009.

Although it has since been renamed, at that time the compound's moniker was Al Zuhoor, and it was located in the sea of compounds that sprawled out into the formerly empty desert of the city's suburban periphery. Like other compounds, Al Zuhoor was surrounded by a high wall. Entering the compound required drivers to pass through a gated security checkpoint manned by a guard—yet another foreign worker. My assigned apartment was one of perhaps a hundred different residences behind the high exterior wall. Some of those domiciles were "villas," the Gulf nomenclature for freestanding houses designated for larger families or important personnel. These villas were located in the outer ring of the compound, and from the second story, residents might peer over the compound's exterior wall to the suburban landscape sprawling out to the horizon. Other two-story buildings of multiple apartments occupied the inner region of the compound. My family's second story apartment, located in this inner region, consisted of three bedrooms, a bathroom, a living room, and a kitchen. It was at a desk in the extra bedroom, reconfigured as my home office, that I first began to articulate my frustrations with the segregated experiences of the foreign workers who have long been central to my ethnographic work.

Here one might also recognize how anthropology's foundational concern with otherness, and with other groups of humans' experiences in this world, can sometimes narrow our capacities for reflection and reflexivity. Contemporary American identitarianism and the widespread commitment to the partiality of inquiries framed in terms of social justice seem to have only exacerbated the fettering of the anthropological lens; anthropology's preoccupation with difference, and now foremost with inequality, can eclipse our capacity to recognize similarities and parallels between the anthropological observer and her or his subjects. This blinds us to the common threads woven into the shared essence of the human experience, and the "psychic unity of mankind" that Edward Burnett Tylor first postulated in founding anthropology. To clarify, consider the quotidian features of my ethnographic work at that time: on Friday evenings, after a long day in the labor camps of the Industrial Area or, sometimes, elsewhere in the city, I would eventually depart for home. In my car, I would make my way from the desolate outer fringes of Doha into the vast suburban belt of the city, a landscape characterized by a seemingly endless sea of high exterior walls enclosing compounds much like mine. Arriving then at my compound's entrance, I would make eye contact with the South Asian guard, wait for the gate to be opened, and then proceed into the residential space that was invisible from the street. On those Friday nights, after parking outside the entrance to my second story apartment, I would proceed upstairs to my home. After greeting my wife and daughter, I would retire to my home office to review my fieldnotes and to jot down various reflections and passing thoughts before concluding my workday.

It was not until later that the fundamental irony of my situation first dawned on me. Peering out my home office's window, past the mosque to the compound's outer wall, the parallels between me and my interlocutors in the labor camps suddenly emerged from the analytic fog: was I not writing about my subjects' segregation from behind high compound walls, in an enclave assigned by my employer to accommodate me and others of my class and station? Did I not also occupy another sort of segregated space? That is the fundamental conundrum from which this chapter commences.[1] Borrowing the anthropologist Paul Dresch's concept (2006), I suggest that all kinds of foreign matter fall into the spatial logic that I first sighted in pondering the conditions and the experiences of the transnational proletariat. As I will demonstrate, human beings are only one sort of foreign matter that falls into the segregatory spatial logic of the city.

Compound Life

Scholars' analyses of the housing compounds to which I was assigned by my employer, and those compounds' historical proliferation on the Arabian Peninsula, draw together several different themes and interpretive threads. In 1936, the Arabian American Oil Company (Aramco) constructed the first set of homes at Dhahran to accommodate American employees and their families. Construction of a similar gated community in Manama, Bahrain, commenced the next year (Fuccaro 2009, 191). By 1954, Aramco had built and was operating two additional communities in Saudi Arabia, one at Abqaiq and another at Ras Tanura, altogether with more than 22,000 employees and 3,589 family residents (Lebkicher et al. 1960, 156). Aramco heralded "the creation, in what was open desert country, of modern communities in which employees and their families can live and work, with houses, streets, shops, office buildings, restaurants, hospitals, schools, recreational facilities, lawns, gardens and trees" (Lebkicher et al. 1960, 5–6).[2] In many scholars' work, these enclaved communities were the clear template for urban development and growth in the ensuing decades. Through this lens, compounds are typically framed as a foreign imposition tied to the legacy of American imperialism.

Other scholars, however, see the proliferation of the compound on the Arabian Peninsula as part and parcel of broader global trends. Through this lens, the enclaving of the foreign cosmopolitan professional elite behind compound walls traces its foundations to the neoliberal global moment. These enclaves are emblematic of urban development in the Los Angeles model, where privileged urban denizens retreat to the protection of gated communities, and cities steadily relinquish urban public space to privatized concerns. Yet while most scholars suggest that these new developments were emblematic of American and British employees' wishes to insulate themselves from local society, there is evidence that points to other reasoning. In his book, Nasser Othman quotes Qatari Ibrahim bin Saleh Bu Matar al-Muhannadi, who noted that "The English were not allowed to go to Doha, there was not a single Englishman in the company house. Nor were the English allowed to visit the market without the express permission of Sheikh Hamad (the Heir Apparent). Englishwomen could not enter Doha under any circumstances, and as far as I can remember, even Mrs Dixon, the manager's wife, never went into the capital" (Othman 1984, 52–53).

These observations and the complexities they suggest point to perhaps another analytic thread, albeit one poorly articulated in the literature, that frames these enclaves and compounds as a modernist iteration of deeper patterns in the urban landscapes indigenous to the region. We might even hypothesize that these patterns in the urban landscape are the spatial manifestation of the hierarchical multiculturalism sighted in the previous chapter. Regardless, there are definite parallels between the regional proliferation of the compound in the twentieth century and the various traditions and norms already present on the Arabian Peninsula; in the form of urban development indigenous to the region, the traditional *fareej* already grouped families and tribes together in the urban landscape. In the Kingdom of Bahrain, to the north of Qatar, Fireej Al-Fadhel is the neighborhood in Manama inhabited by the remnant vestiges of the islands' Jewry. Similarly, the millet system, imposed throughout the Middle East under Ottoman imperialism, "allowed for the coexistence of different religious and ethnic communities" while ensuring the boundaries and distinctions between them were maintained (Eldem 2013, 217; see also Barkey 2005; Barkey and Gavrilis 2016). As this suggests, while Aramco may have built the first modern compounds in Arabia, the form of this habitation and the cultural segregation it manifests at least resonate with regional traditions and customary form. Perhaps it even draws upon them.

To some degree or another, these legacies point to the emergence and the proliferation of the compound in the contemporary urban landscapes of Arabia. Prototypical compounds in Doha resemble the Dhahran model first configured by Aramco, and then BAPCO in Bahrain, with a high external wall concealing recreational facilities like swimming pools, exercise gyms, courts, and playgrounds.[3] Streets and, oftentimes, small shops are also frequently found inside these planned communities, and the "lawns, gardens, and trees" therein remind one of the midcentury suburban developments in American cities like Los Angeles, Phoenix, or Las Vegas.[4] In the wake of heavy capital investment in the urban core of Doha that commenced in the early twenty-first century, many of the same features discernible in compounds are also perceptible in the high-rise apartment buildings also constructed to accommodate the cosmopolitan professional elite. Although lacking the landscaping and verdant interior grounds found in many suburban compounds, these high-rise accommodations include many of the compound's other features—swimming pools, recreational facilities, and via verticality rather than compound walls, a private sphere segregated from the public spaces of the city. The homology between compounds and high-rise apartment buildings rests not in any structural parity but rather in the residential enclaving of foreigners of a particular class.

In my experience, life in the compound enclave was memorable, and the social frictions therein point to the tensions inherent in such communal contexts. Canadian and American residents, many of whom traced their ancestry to South Asia or the Middle East, were a small component of the national diversity present there. Perhaps the largest demographic component of my compound's inhabitants was from elsewhere in the Middle East, although many were also from

Africa, and particularly from North Africa. South Asian members of the cosmopolitan professional elite employed by Qatar University were nearly as numerous. Expatriates from other sources—including Europe, East Asia, and elsewhere—were less common. The coherence of residents' position in the social hierarchy of foreign communities in Qatar did little to assuage some of the intercultural frictions that arose in such a communal setting. Compound residents were conflicted about attempts to instigate a "ladies only" period at the communal swimming pool and at the compound's exercise facilities, for example. This conflagration, and numerous others like it, were perhaps exacerbated by the national and cultural diversity of the compound's inhabitants, as Qatar University's employees were much more diverse than many other institutions of higher education in Qatar at the time.

In Doha, a city replete with foreigners, the sea of compounds sprawls to the horizon in many portions of the city's suburban landscape. Another fascinating feature of this suburban belt, however, is the coagulation of Qatari citizens in this same landscape. Migrant workers primarily occupy the Industrial Area and other regions of the urban periphery; the cosmopolitan professional elite dwell in the compounds that comprise much of the suburban belt of the city, or perhaps inhabit an apartment in one of the high-rise apartment buildings closer to the city's central business district. Another vital element of this urban landscape is the domiciles of Qatari citizens. Like the foreign populations they host, citizens reside in particular neighborhoods in the city, and via the state-directed apportionment of land, members of different families, clans, and tribes have configured ways to reside together in the suburban landscape, as best they can, with arrangements akin to the *fareej* of Qatar's recent past (Nagy 2004). Unlike the domiciles gathered together in compounds, however, for the citizenry the prototypical residence is the freestanding villa, surrounded by a high wall that both defines the grounds and yields privacy to inhabitants. Like the city's other inhabitants, Qatari citizens gather in the urban landscape.

In training our attention here on the cosmopolitan professional elite's experience in suburban compounds or in high-rise apartment buildings, and via a brief excursion into the residential geography of citizenship in the urban landscape of Doha, I seek to reinforce the assertion that the segregatory powers delineated in the previous chapter operate on more than just the lowest echelon of migrant workers. Although economic class is the key variable in one's place in the urban landscape, the spatial segregation of the city's many diverse inhabitants transcends the inequalities of class: all of the city's inhabitants—even Qatari citizens—fall into this spatial logic. In addition to the variable luxuriousness of these residential enclaves, what differentiates one urban inhabitant from another is not their segregation in urban space but rather their mobility across the various thresholds and boundaries of difference in the city.

Foreign Matter

In his seminal 2006 essay *Foreign Matter: The Place of Strangers in Gulf Society*, the Oxford anthropologist Paul Dresch considers at some length the impact of the long-standing demographic presence of so many strangers on the structure and shape of Gulf society. In concordance with Longva (1997), Dresch (2006) envisions the distinction between citizen and foreigner as the paramount cleavage in these plural societies (see also Nagy 1997). In Europe and elsewhere, Dresch argues, that same distinction is largely a geographical calculation: noncitizens are primarily identifiable as those located across borders and, hence, outside the polity. In Qatar and in the other Gulf states, however, the citizenry lives in an urban landscape suffused with foreigners, with alien others. As a result, the distinction between citizen and noncitizen is drawn by a constellation of other means. The remainder of his essay is an analytic consideration of the social arrangements that, over decades, have evolved to establish and maintain the distinction between citizen and foreigner. Following Dresch, my emphasis thus far has been on people and their place in the city. Although my attention was first drawn to the experiences of the transnational proletariat, I have now sought to reinforce with evidence my assertion that the sorting, enclaving, and segregation of people into particular urban spaces is a process that transcends the inequalities of class. The transnational proletariat, the cosmopolitan professional elite, and even the citizenry itself—all find themselves either placed in or drawn to particular locations in the urban landscape.

From this analytic waypoint, I now want to contend that while humans are the central subject of this segregational logic, there are other sorts of matter subjected to this same spatial logic, and to the sorting, enclaving, and segregation it entails. By paying attention to space, we can discern how incorporeal foreign matter is also compartmentalized in urban space. Three examples will illuminate my point. The first example concerns gender and the education system in Qatar. As is customary in Qatari tradition, public schools on the peninsula are gender segregated: there are classes designated for girls and other classes designated for boys, and this segregation was extended even into the university system. Qatar University, the national university, remains a gender-segregated campus, as do public schools from the primary level on up. This contrasts sharply with the constellation of private, coeducational schools and universities found in Doha. Many of the coeducational primary and secondary schools were first constructed by different foreign communities of the cosmopolitan professional elite: the various Indian schools, the American school, and an array of other diasporic educational institutions ensure that family members accompanying migrant professionals might remain apace with the national education systems in their respective home states. Similarly, in 2003, the Qatar Foundation—the massively endowed state-funded foundation tasked with stewarding Qatar's development in the realms of education, science, and community development—inaugurated Education City, the twelve-square-kilometer urban campus located at what was once the suburban periphery of the city. Education City contains numerous satellite campuses tethered to world-renowned universities: it is the location of an outpost of Weill Cornell's Medical School, a satellite campus of Georgetown's School of Foreign Service, a soon-to-close manifestation of the University College of London, and an array of other institutions of similar stature. All these campuses are coeducational. In summary, at all levels of the education system, the establishment and proliferation of gender-mixed institutions and campuses are spatially consigned to various exceptional spaces in the urban landscape, of which Education City is the most prominent example.

Alcohol, as another sort of foreign matter, comprises a second illuminating example. Alcohol is generally prohibited in Qatar, as it is in the neighboring Gulf states. For the millions of foreigners at work on the peninsula, however, there are three different ways of accessing alcohol for consumption. Residents may purchase alcohol for personal use at the Qatar Distribution Center (QDC), provided they are not citizens of the GCC, and provided they earn a minimum salary of QAR 3,000 (US $822) per month. Like private schools, the QDC is configured specifically to serve the cosmopolitan professional elite. Second, individuals may purchase alcoholic beverages at one of the numerous four- and five-star hotels built to cater to the same cosmopolitan class of both residents and visitors. Lastly, as both of these points of access are beyond the reach of the transnational proletariat, there is a substantial black market for brewing and selling alcohol in places like the Industrial Area. Leaving aside the final mode of access (which is illegal and renders foreign workers vulnerable to arrest and deportation), the other two modes of accessing alcohol are emblematic of the spatial logic I seek to chart here. Punctuating the urban landscape are designated exceptional spaces—select hotels or a designated distribution center—in which alcohol may be obtained. As Qatar prepares for the World Cup, the strategic enclaving of this foreign matter has been further extrapolated: officials now intend to allow fans to consume alcohol in a variety of designated spaces, sometimes referred to as "wet fan zones" or, alternatively, as "World Cup fan zones."[5]

The third and final case to consider is perhaps the most immaterial of the three examples presented here. As numerous scholars have long noted, the right to own land in Qatar is conferred by citizenship (Dresch 2006, 202; Nagy 2006, 124; Alshehabi 2015). In practice, the legal arrangements prohibiting foreign ownership serve as the keystone in the solidification of the rentier state by ensuring that some Qataris will inevitably profit from the presence of foreigners at work on the peninsula. For example, the owner of the compound in which I was placed received monthly rental payments directly from Qatar University, and hence indirectly from the state. Early in the twenty-first century, however, Qatar began construction of the luxurious residential and commercial development advertised as "The Pearl." An artificial island "reclaimed from the sea," the off-shore development was built to accommodate forty-five thousand residents. Notably, The Pearl is also a freeholder development—an exceptional space in the urban landscape where the regulations prohibiting foreign ownership of property are suspended. In 2019, Qatar heralded plans to expanding the number of freeholder developments on the peninsula, thereby expanding the number of legally exceptional spaces in the urban landscape of Doha (*Gulf Times* 2019). In summary, then, the right to own land is another feature, another sort of foreign matter, that is consigned to designated spaces in the urban landscape.

To recapitulate, in the previous chapter I discerned the spatial segregation of the transnational proletariat as a central feature in the experiences of millions of migrants in Qatar and elsewhere on the Arabian Peninsula. I thought expansively about the forces complicit in that segregation. This chapter commenced with the assertion that the segregational forces I identified in that previous chapter transcend the dynamics of class: while members of the cosmopolitan professional elite—and even Qatari citizens—have greater mobility, the same segregational forces can be discerned in their experiences in the urban landscape. By revisiting Dresch's notion of foreign matter, and bending his conceptualization to include the incorporeal, I have used three examples to suggest that more than just humans are subjected to these spatial politics. With coeducational campuses, we can see that some social relations are enclaved into specific exceptional spaces in the city. With alcohol, we can see how particular commodities and the social results they conjure are consigned to designated zones. And with freeholder developments, we can see how the law itself has been spatially modified to include zones where the otherwise prohibited is allowed.

Cultural Sovereignty

In her influential and highly regarded analysis of Southeast Asian states, the anthropologist Aihwa Ong describes the "fragmentation of the national space into various noncontiguous zones" (Ong 2006, 77). Although scholars had been previously attentive to the impact of globalization (increasingly thought of in terms of neoliberalism at that time), few were attuned to the urban and spatial manifestation of these forces. Ong convincingly argues that the spatial recon-figurations of power she observes in the Asian Tiger states are best conceived as strategic flexibilities by which those states were adapting to the neoliberal do-main.[6] Ong coins the term "graduated sovereignty" to describe these new per-mutations of state power and its evolving footprint in the national space it seeks to govern. Undoubtedly, her ideas map well onto Qatar and the differentiated zones, enclaves, and segregated spaces that I have described in this chapter. And she is correct that the more homogeneous national spaces of the past have given way to new fragmentary topographies of state power. But the empirical founda-tions of her argument are rooted in the Asian Tiger states, and therefore rooted in those states' configuration of the forces of production that are themselves en-sconced in a demographic landscape dominated by citizens. As a result, Ong's notion of graduated sovereignty emphasizes the political and economic goals of the state in the evolving nature of governance she observes.

My reading of the permutations to sovereignty in Qatar points in a different direction. Following Italian philosopher Giorgio Agamben (2005), I understand the state of exception in a dialectic relationship with the powers that grant that exception.[7] Although the political and economic motivations for the segregatory spatial strategies that Ong sees are present in Doha, those explanations fail to grasp the essentially cultural motivations I see permeating the examples con-sidered here. To consign the consumption of alcohol to a small archipelago of designated spaces is, simultaneously, an assertion about its prohibition in the domain punctuated by these exceptional spaces. To allow land ownership in a handful of specified and exceptional locations in Qatar is, simultaneously, an affirmation of its prohibition everywhere else on the peninsula. To cloister for-eigners behind compound walls or in "bachelor cities" at the periphery of the built landscape is to simultaneously convey that those humans are foreign matter—a form of matter that is exceptional in nature, consigned to peripheral and exceptional urban spaces, and therefore out of place elsewhere in the do-main those exceptional zones punctuate. In summary, what Ong portrays as graduated sovereignty is, in my estimation, recognizable more as a form of punc-tuated sovereignty configured to accommodate foreign matter in exceptional spaces, while asserting Qatari cultural sovereignty over the domain punctuated by those spaces.

The city itself is the key mechanism by which this cultural sovereignty is both established and maintained. That tool, and the shape of the city it generates, is the subject to which I turn next.

AN URBAN SPATIAL DISCOURSE

From the contemporary vantage point in American academia, the work of Michel Foucault has had an impact of almost unparalleled significance on the intellectual landscape. In the extraordinary repertoire of concepts that he bequeathed us all, his notion of *discourse* stands squarely among the most influential of his offerings. A standard dictionary definition lodges discourse as something along the lines of "conversation" or "communication through words." Foucault's conceptual coinage ventured well beyond this, and the meaning he attributed to this term was closely aligned with the lodestar to which his work was oriented: like so many other Foucauldian concepts, with discourse he was crafting a tool with which he might analyze the foundational nature of power and its manifold contemporary permutations in Western society. For Foucault, discourse indicated the "practices that systematically form the objects of which they speak" (Foucault 1974, 49). To elaborate, with the concept of discourse Foucault was interested in the a priori rules, the established norms, and the quotidian social practices that inevitably shape what is said, how it is said, and what is left unsaid. For Foucault, discourse is the historically moored set of social practices through which knowledge and meaning are produced. The capillary and quotidian forms of power that were his quarry lay in those a priori forces and norms that shape the very possibilities of our interactions.

I have misgivings about this concept and misgivings about American intelligentsia's seemingly endless preoccupation with Foucault's array of conceptual ingenuities.[1] Setting those misgivings aside, I make use of his conceptualization of discourse. In doing so, my foremost objective is to develop and explicate

FIGURE 11. A computer-generated image of the Lusail Project, the city within a city built for 450,000 inhabitants.

what I call an *urban spatial discourse*. In the same way that Foucault leveled his analytic gaze upon the a priori conditions and relations that shape discursive utterances and interactions, I seek to turn my analytic attention not to the plethora of individual architectural creations and structures that crowd the skyline of Doha and so many cities like it, but instead to the task of discerning the parameters, historical conditions, social forces, and enduring norms that cultivate and shape those architectural instances. In this chapter, I identify something akin to what Keller Easterling (2014, 27, 12) called the "spatial software" that makes up "the very parameters of global urbanism," or at least the portions of it we see on the Arabian Peninsula. Returning to Foucault, then, in a sense I am taking a concept developed around an analysis of language, communication, and the production of knowledge, and transposing it here to the realm of space and urban development. I will leave it to the reader to assess both the efficacy and utility of this gambit.

To convey the essence of this urban spatial discourse, I commence with a discussion of the expanding unit of urban development observable in Doha's recent history. In the substantial scholarship concerning cities and the urban form, there is some precedent to this concern with size and scale. Venturi, Brown, and Izenour (2017, 83) envisioned the growing prevalence of megastructures in the urban landscape as a "distortion of normal city building process" that traced its roots to the circulation of images in a symbolic economy. Similarly, Buras (2019) is concerned with "terrifying bigness," and before him Mumford (1961, 65) had postulated the connection between monumental architecture and expressions of both power and hierarchy. But these urban theorists, and others like them, are foremost concerned with architectural instances and expressions—the actual buildings and forms that constitute the city. As Easterling (2014, 11–12) perceptively noted, "Buildings are often no longer singularly crafted enclosures, uniquely imagined by an architect, but reproducible products set within similar urban arrangements." To grasp the urban spatial discourse itself, we must turn away from the structures that comprise the city, and levy our attention instead on the spaces in which those architectural instances are conceptualized and subsequently built. We must turn our attention to these spatial technologies—to what Kolson (2001, 12) termed the "huge swatches of urban form" by which the city grows (see figure 11).

An empirical assessment of these units of urban development is perhaps the most straightforward way to grasp the abstraction of the urban spatial discourse that I propose here. Those units of urban development can be most readily conveyed via a handful of emblematic examples drawn from Doha's urban landscape. These will allow us to discern some of the key features and recurring qualities of the urban spatial discourse. Then, borrowing another term that Foucault redefined, I will turn to an "archaeology" of that urban spatial discourse—a discussion of the historical conditions and the ideological structures that shaped the emergence of this urban spatial discourse. I continue the elaboration of some of the points that I first broached in the previous chapter. Most directly, I contend that this urban spatial discourse is the template for the governance of the abundant "foreign matter" present in the city.

The Unit of Urban Development

To repeat, the urban spatial discourse that I describe can be first apprehended in the prototypical unit of urban development by which the city grows (see figure 11). That unit of urban development can be illuminated via a few emblematic examples. The Msheireb Project provides a quintessential first example. The urban renewal project is the first effort of Msheireb Properties, the real estate development company that, as a subsidiary of the Qatar Foundation, characteristically blurs the threshold between the public and private spheres in Qatar (Pollalis and Ardalan 2018). In the words of the project's architectural language advisor Tim Makower (2012, 4), the project will result in a "high-density, medium-rise, mixed use, sustainable and pedestrian-friendly urban quarter" built atop a razed central neighborhood abandoned by Qatari homeowners several decades ago. This suburban migration was briefly described in the fourth chapter: as oil profits first began to accrue after World War II, the city began to expand. Although the twenty-first century finds it located squarely in the city's aging urban center, the original Msheireb neighborhood was the city's first suburban development. In the 1970s and 1980s, as citizens departed these residences for tony suburbs further afield in the sprawling urban landscape, Msheireb became one of the numerous neighborhoods in the city's aging center in which properties were rented to the burgeoning transnational workforce from abroad and, in that era, a workforce increasingly drawn from South Asia. With the city's central districts also drifting into abandonment and disrepair, the successful reconstruction and revitalization of the adjacent Souk Waqif—an emblematic urban regeneration project heralded both regionally and globally—reverberated with Qatar's urban planners and power holders. It was in these conditions that the Msheireb Project commenced.

The Msheireb Project occupies a thirty-one-hectare (seventy-seven-acre) parcel in the city's historic center. The project commenced in 2010, and although construction is continuing, the total cost of the project has been estimated at $5.5 billion. The urban tract is conceptually and spatially divided into four quarters: the Diwan Amiri Quarter is a combined civic and heritage area; the Heritage Quarter is the region of the urban redevelopment in which several historic courtyard houses have been preserved and converted into museums; the Retail Quarter, and the Residential (Mixed-Use) Quarter, need no further explanation beyond their titles. Although mathematically impossible, the development's master plan describes a fifth quarter as the "Business Gateway," an area that offers "premium business amenities, supported by a mix of banking, personal and civic services, and ease of access through its convenient location" (Msheireb Properties 2021). The five quarters are intended to accommodate some fifteen thousand residents, and those quarters, already connected by an internal light rail system, also contain numerous LEED-certified buildings. As a result, the whole of the development is framed as an emblematic example of urban sustainability, and advertisements suggest that in addition to tourists and visitors, the luxurious urban redevelopment might entice Qatari citizens to again reside in the city's dense urban center. In the promoter's words: "Msheireb Properties' mission is

to change the way people think about urban living and improve their overall quality of life, through innovations that encourage social interaction, respect for culture, and greater care for the environment . . . Once complete, it will see the oldest
part of Doha transformed into a thriving community, offering residents and visitors all the comforts of a modern lifestyle while incorporating the architectural
techniques of the past to deliver a long-term sustainable environment that cele-
brates the rich Qatari culture and values" (Pollalis and Ardalan 2018, xii).[2]

A second illustrative example of this urban spatial discourse, and one that is
arguably the result of the Msheireb Project and urban redevelopments like it, is
Asian City. Located some fourteen kilometers from the city center, Asian City
is one of seven planned residential "cities" constructed on the outer periphery
of Doha. Altogether, those seven developments will accommodate some 258,000
transnational labor migrants during their time on the Qatari Peninsula. Asian
City consists of 55 residential buildings, each with 312 dormitory rooms designed
to accommodate four men. Residential facilities include, at no cost to workers,
both water and electricity. Housekeeping, pest control, maintenance, and a gym
are also described as free to migrant residents. Asian City includes both a police
station and a help desk, and broadcasts the additional benefit of full-time CCTV
surveillance. In addition to the accommodations located in Asian City, the adjacent Asian Town comprises a constellation of facilities that, as one official
noted, are "meant to provide affordable amenities and services to the country's
low-income workforce close to where they live" (Kovessy 2015). Those facilities
include a cricket stadium, the largest amphitheater in Qatar, a shopping mall
with more than 230 shop spaces, a multiscreen movie theater, and a large su-
permarket. These active and bustling commercial spaces essentially replicate the
areas of the center city that had previously been important commercial districts
for migrant entrepreneurs and their citizen-sponsors.

Originally owned by the Jassim Bin Mohammed Al Thani Social Welfare
Fund, the Asian City project was subsequently passed to Ibn Ajayan Projects for
operation and management. Furthermore, Asian City and the six other "bachelor
cities" were constructed to accommodate the transnational migrant workforce
that would be needed for the spate of construction projects stemming foremost
from the 2022 World Cup. But other forces were also embroiled in these urban
projects. These other forces and pressures included the citizenry's growing concern about foreign men dwelling in rented villas interspersed in neighborhoods
otherwise occupied by Qatari citizens. Additionally, the capital-intensive redevelopment of neighborhoods like Msheireb—neighborhoods that had formerly been
abandoned by Qataris to transnational workers—pushed the growing legion of
working-class foreigners out of the city's center. Moreover, Qatar and all the Gulf
states continue to face an incessant global critique aimed directly at the experi-

ences of migrant workers on the peninsula. This critique periodically turns its gaze to the sometimes-decrepit accommodations found in the older Industrial Area and elsewhere in Doha. Many of these factors are subtly encapsulated in the promotional materials that advertise these facilities: "IAP Real Estate is proud to take part in the operation and management of Asian City to ensure the delivery of high quality and standard accommodation that is especially intended for residing workers to live in harmony and experience the highest levels of both comfort and convenience. At IAP, we continue our best to emphasize and value workers' efforts for taking a big part in building the country and make 2022 World Cup a success story, while staying on course with 2030 Qatar Vision."

The final example is the development known as The Pearl, which is the Qatari example of the offshore residential developments for which the Gulf states are renowned. Developments like The Pearl have a symbolic resonance that is unprecedented, for they are visible from outer space. In local parlance, and as is often repeated in writing, these developments have been "reclaimed from the sea." In this case, The Pearl is a man-made island that occupies the shallow coastal waters once vital to the pearl industry and of great environmental importance (Burt 2014). Construction of The Pearl commenced in 2003. Altogether, the island development contains some 18,831 dwellings intended to accommodate an estimated 45,000 residents. The 400 hectares (985 acres) of reclaimed land are built and arranged to provide more than thirty-two kilometers of new beachfront, and the retail and commercial offerings that suffuse the island development reach for a stylistically cosmopolitan and culturally diverse tenor. Costs for the project were initially estimated at $2.5 billion, but estimates have now ballooned to nearly $15 billion.

The development is connected to the mainland via a two-way, four-lane boulevard, and both its residential and commercial offerings are advertised as elegant, luxurious, and exclusive (Rizzo 2019; Rizzo and Mandal 2021). Like Msheireb, The Pearl is subdivided into districts, or precincts. Porto Arabia, for example, contains the primary harbor and marina as well as many of the development's luxurious restaurants. Qanat Quartier, another of the island's precincts, is replete with canals and various flourishes that reach for a Venetian architectural vernacular. The project was designed and planned by an architectural firm based in Seattle, Washington, and was the flagship project of Qatar's United Development Company (UDC). The UDC is Qatar's leading construction firm, and although described as both a private investment firm and a core listing on Qatar's stock exchange, the UDC remains interconnected with the Qatari state. For example, as a result of the prolonged financial downturn that commenced in 2008, and in combination with the enduring absence of sufficient resident-investors, the Qatari state was left to bail out the UDC in 2011 (Rizzo 2019, 7–8;

Rizzo and Mandal 2021, 81). Perhaps most important, The Pearl was also the first development in Qatar to allow foreigners to purchase and own property.

In addition to these three examples, there are numerous other urban developments that might have also been included here. Education City is a twelve-square-kilometer urban parcel that contains an array of different educational institutions, including numerous American and European satellite university campuses, and some accommodations for students. Lusail, still under construction, is a planned city occupying over thirty-eight square kilometers north of the city, and is being built to accommodate 450,000 people. Its price tag has been estimated at $45 billion dollars. The Aspire Zone is a 2.5 square kilometer development established as an international sports destination. In addition to the Aspire Tower (currently the tallest structure in Qatar) and the adjacent Villaggio Mall and Hyatt Plaza Mall, the Aspire Zone includes stadiums and ancillary sports venues, a sports academy, a sports medicine hospital, significant parkland, various cafes, and a miscellany of other facilities. As yet another example, the Katara Cultural Village is a beachfront elaboration occupying a square kilometer of prime coastal real estate north of Doha. The village includes a beachfront, restaurants, galleries, and other cultural institutions, all arranged in a pedestrian-friendly commercial environment. As a "destination for art, culture, and cuisine," Katara claims to be the "most multidimensional cultural project in Qatar."

Numerous additional examples could readily continue this list. But even with these three examples and the attenuated additions, we might begin to ascertain some of the common threads woven through these projects and the plans behind them, as those threads might help discern the key qualities of the urban spatial discourse I perceive here. Foremost, most of these projects occupy vast parcels of land. The spatial dimensions of these projects are both noteworthy and characteristic. The estimated price tags of these projects are massive, and for the residential projects on this list, the size of the populations they envision serving are equally gargantuan; these projects speak in terms of tens of thousands of humans, even hundreds of thousands of humans. Both the size and the scope of these plans are defining features of the urban spatial discourse I seek to delineate here. Additionally, all of the examples presented here are mixed-use by design; most include residential space, and all of these examples include commercial space as a central feature of their design. From the smattering of promotional descriptions quoted in the examples, one can also perceive that these mixed-use designs often seek to engineer a particular sort of social life—plans and aspirations oftentimes speak directly to the style and the emotional tenor of the lives that designers and promoters envision for residents and visitors. Finally, in these examples one might note the recurring and explicit syncopation of these projects with the state itself: projects oftentimes frame their existence in tandem with the state's Vision 2030 plan, or otherwise highlight fealty to national interests, aspirations, and goals. Altogether, these are at least some of the most significant—and perhaps most obvious—threads that I perceive woven into the fabric of these projects.

Archaeology of an Urban Spatial Discourse

In the Foucauldian sense, an *archaeology* of the urban spatial discourse I describe in this chapter calls for a historical analysis attentive to the systems of thought or other structural forces by which that discourse came into existence. In that vein, I suggest three distinct, interrelated preconditions that explain much about the emergence of this urban spatial discourse. Together, these three preconditions—as an attempt at Foucauldian archaeology—encapsulate many of the characteristics and variables woven through the examples presented in the previous section of this chapter.

The first of those preconditions is perhaps obvious: this particular urban spatial discourse and the expansive unit of urban development by which the city grows is foremost a result of the massive reservoirs of surplus capital that fuel the contemporary Qatari state (Hanieh 2018).[3] The price tags of the individual units of urban development previously described (or "statements" in the linguistically tethered Foucauldian form of discourse analysis) reach well into the billions of dollars—and in some cases, even tens of billions of dollars. The flow of wealth from the state into society typifies the rentier economic system, a much-debated feature of the GCC states: in the rentier arrangement, "the state becomes the origin of all significant economic and social developments, and the determinant of how resources are spread around the population" (Niblock and Malik 2007, 15). In Qatar, the three largest real estate developers—Qatari Diar, Barwa Real Estate, and the United Development Company—are entirely or partially owned by the state (Hanieh 2018, 83–84).[4] These arrangements are not only integral features of the authoritarian rentier arrangements but also evince the blurry thresholds between the public and private economic spheres typical of all the Gulf states.

In his renowned analyses of the city, David Harvey made more insightful claims about the complicated relationship between capital, urbanization, and social relations. In his analysis, Harvey suggests the architecture of spectacle is a gambit for attracting capital in a world comprising neoliberal flows of that capital. Harvey also portrays the city as a mechanism for the absorption of the surpluses that capitalists perpetually generate (Harvey 1989, 90–91; 2008, 25). It is difficult to imagine a more emblematic example of Harvey's assertions than Doha: mostly empty skyscrapers glisten in the skyline, while state-controlled wealth is directed to additional projects like those described above—an island development to accommodate 45,000; seven "bachelor cities" to accommodate the 258,000 workers needed to help construct even more of the city; an entirely new adjacent city that can accommodate nearly half a million people. Perhaps these developments will remain the mostly empty "five-star ghost towns" that Iskander (2021, 91) and Günel (2019) observe. In the subsequent chapter, I will provide a more incisive explanation of these political economic relations in an analysis that suggests the city must continue to grow to appease the key political, economic, and social relations found in Qatari society. Here, however, these details are meant merely to affirm and illustrate the connection between the vast reservoirs of surplus capital and the expansive parcels by which the city grows. Those reservoirs of capital are the first important feature in the archaeology of this urban spatial discourse.

In my estimation, the second feature that helps explain the expansive unit of urban development, and the urban spatial discourse that it indexes, is the largely empty desert surroundings onto which the city continues to grow and expand. In the urban planning and architectural vernacular, the open and mostly empty peripheral lands are referred to as a blank slate—a tabula rasa. This precondition indicates that there was no preexisting patchwork of intricate land tenure or ownership around which the visions of the architects and planners might need to be navigated. In the landscape surrounding Doha, there was no preexisting urban milieu that might shape those plans, or to which those plans might need to be adjusted. Instead, with only the vagaries of tribally conceived tenure and the absence of private property, the expansion of the city faced few social and historical limits. There are exceptions, of course: Msheireb was planned on a mostly razed tract of the city's central business district.[5] Conversely, The Pearl and developments like it elsewhere on the Arabian Peninsula are quintessentially emblematic of the tabula rasa, built as they are on land conjured from the sea. In summary, I suggest that the expansive parcels by which the city's growth is conceived and manifested—the urban spatial discourse that I seek to identify here—are a result of the absence of a preexisting capitalist matrix of private property in Qatar.

There is perhaps more to this aspect of the archaeology of this urban spatial discourse than suggested here. In tandem with the reservoirs of surplus capital, the tabula rasa upon which the expansion of the city was imagined, parcel by parcel, and then manifested in material reality, is a magnetic combination of elements in the realm of architecture and urban planning. These two elements are recurring features in what James Scott (1999) has called *authoritarian high modernism*, the strain of twentieth-century modernism responsible for some of the largest and, in Scott's estimation, most problematic attempts by those in power to engineer society via the built form. As Scott further notes, modernist icon Le Corbusier frequently sought projects and commissions from authoritarians and despots who were almost always insulated from the din of populist tumult. As Le Corbusier exclaimed, reverence to the planner's vision required the sustained conviction these political arrangements allowed: "The despot is not a man. It is the Plan. The correct, realistic, exact plan, the one that will provide your solution once the problem has been posited clearly, in its entirety, in its indispensable harmony. This plan has been drawn up well away from the frenzy of the mayor's office or the town hall, from the cries of the electorate or the laments of society's victims. It has been drawn up by serene and lucid minds. It has taken account of nothing but human truths. It has ignored all current regulations, all existing usages, and channels. It has not considered whether or not it could be carried out with the constitution now in force. *It is a biological creation destined for human beings and capable of realization by modern techniques*" (Le Corbusier 1967, 154).

In this statement, we can see the importance of the tabula rasa as a precondition that might ensure the inconveniences of reality do not sully the purity of the designer's vision. In the context of Qatar and the wealthy Arabian Peninsula, that same combination of elements draws the world's leading starchitects to the region. In the conditions they encounter there, those starchitects' visions can be actualized in the purest form.[6] Similarly, the enduring reverence for the visionary architect and planner, first developed in the Modernist era of the twentieth century with urban planners like Frederick Law Olmsted, Le Corbusier, and Frank Lloyd Wright, remains a central feature of urban development in Qatar and on the Arabian Peninsula.

The third and final element in the archaeology of this urban spatial discourse is equally visible in Le Corbusier's sentiments: the recurring aspirations for a totalistic form of social engineering.[7] These aspirations are evident in many of the plans and their descriptions, and are existentially interwoven with the vast parcels in which those plans are initially envisioned. Consider, for example, just the nomenclature for some of these urban developments—Asian City and Education City are titularly described as cities within the city of Doha itself. Drawing inspiration from the New Urbanist movement that galvanized urban planning over the past three decades, these planned spaces also reject the functional separation that typified twentieth-century modernist urban planning. Instead, these spaces are replete with commercial enterprises, recreational facilities, workplaces, and are oftentimes built foremost to accommodate residents. The tenor of these aspirations to socially engineer the future is perhaps most clearly visible in the computer-generated visions of the forthcoming future that pepper the urban landscape itself (Melhuish, Degen, and Rose 2016; Degen, Melhuish, and Rose 2017; Natasi 2019).

In his book *Non-Places: An Introduction to Supermodernity*, Marc Augé suggests that our contemporary moment is best apprehended as a permutation of twentieth-century modernism rather than a break from it.[8] In building his argument, Augé (2009) is adroitly attentive to space, but like others before him, he is primarily concerned with the compression of space and the withering importance of distance in this era of mobility. I generally concur with these assertions; however, the archaeology of the urban spatial discourse that I have pursued here points to a fundamental conundrum. Although space has been compressed in the sense that distance has been rendered less meaningful and important, there is the paradoxical inflation of the unit of urban development. These inflated units of urban development are symptomatic of what I have termed an urban spatial discourse—the coherent system that shapes and constrains what is built in Doha and cities like it. In this section, I have further contended that the preconditions of this urban spatial discourse might be distilled to a set of three interrelated factors: the abundance of surplus capital, the tabula rasa onto which this growth is first imagined and subsequently materialized, and urban planners' long-standing commitment to socially engineering a particular sort of future. In my estimation, these factors help explain the emergence of that urban spatial discourse and the expansive unit of urban development that it produces.

The City as a Tool of Governance

Here, I want to suggest that the explanation that I have ventured covers some of the necessary ground by which one might explain the emergence of this urban spatial discourse. At the same time, and again somewhat paradoxically, I also think this explanation omits what is perhaps the most fascinating aspect of this urban spatial discourse. In its deployment, this urban spatial discourse satiates the very human need for creating order out of chaos. This is where my analysis diverges from Keller Easterling (2014) and her concern with the contagion of zoning technologies that proliferate in the global urban form today. In my analysis, this urban spatial discourse is, foremost, a tool of governance wielded by the state. While there are economic and political effects to be reckoned with, others seem largely inattentive to the compartmentalization of culture and of difference that results. In the context of Qatar and the city of Doha, that human impetus to create order out of chaos might be most clearly glimpsed in the compartmentalization of the foreign matter that suffuses the Qatari Peninsula in the contemporary era. This impulse to compartmentalize and organize that foreign matter begins with making that matter legible. Let me try to explain.

Many decades ago, the anthropologist Mary Douglas (1966) turned her attention to the categories of food that different cultures either prohibit or deem edible (see also Norbakk 2020, 226–228). In articulating these cultural constructions in terms of a deep structural polarity of purity and danger, Douglas makes perhaps the most compelling argument for a symbolic approach to culture. Sifting through the complexities of prohibitions, commands, and proclamations in the books of Deuteronomy and Leviticus from the Christian Bible, Douglas discerns a fundamental symbolic logic to the ancient Hebrew system for classifying the possibilities of human consumption, or more clearly, for navigating what Michael Pollan (2006) called the omnivore's dilemma—the dilemma faced by creatures, like us humans, who can eat just about anything. Douglas argues that the camel, the rock badger, the hare, and the pig were forbidden foods to the ancient Hebrews because those creatures possess categorically anomalous characteristics. Perhaps they have cloven hooves but fail to chew the cud, or something like that. For ancient pastoralist Hebrews, therefore, those animals fell out of the categories of creatures culturally defined as edible. Additional details aside, Douglas argues that culture is a symbolic system for making order from chaos, for building coherence from the disorder, and from the blurry boundaries that we humans readily encounter in our world. Categories and classifications are how humans make the world understandable.

I see parallels between Douglas's structural analysis and the urban landscape produced by the spatial discourse I have described in this chapter. In 2014, for example, I contended that we might best understand the Msheireb Project as the spatial repository for both the idea and the practice of sustainability, and that we might understand that rendition of sustainability primarily for its symbolic resonance in a global index of modernity (Gardner 2014). Similarly, consider some of the other instances of the urban spatial discourse described in this chapter, and in doing so, remain attentive to the ideas and practices they seek to spatially consolidate: Energy City will "centralize real estate and services for oil and gas companies," for example. Education City spatially consolidates many foreign higher education facilities in a single urban parcel and establishes a space where the gender-segregated educational norms of Qatar are excepted. Katara envisions itself as the central hub for institutions and commercial enterprises in the ambit of the arts and congeals a variety of related cultural institutions in a singular urban space. Aspire Zone gathers the state's spectacular commitment to sports and athletics. Asian City is a totalistic location where portions of the gargantuan foreign workforce necessary to construct and service the growing city can be enclaved in the urban landscape. Similarly, The Pearl is an exceptional space where foreigners can purchase property. The same enclaves are commonplace elsewhere on the Arabian Peninsula. To the south, for example, Dubai Media City advertises itself as the "region's largest Media and Content Hub," while Dubai Healthcare City, as the "world's first enabling healthcare and wellness free zone ecosystem," spatially consolidates the institutions and enterprises of that ilk. Masdar City, outside of Abu Dhabi, is a zero-carbon enclave that is, as Gökçe Günel (2019) suggests, essentially a "spaceship in the desert." Indeed, Saudi Arabia established the Economic Cities and Special Zones Authority to govern the ongoing proliferation of these exceptional spaces; that is, spaces that have arisen to govern foreign matter.

To recapitulate, in Doha and elsewhere on the Arabian Peninsula the urban spatial discourse I have sought to delineate in this chapter shapes urban growth and the spatial extrapolation of the urban landscape. The expansive unit of urban development that this urban spatial discourse evokes is a product of the vast reservoirs of capital at hand, of the tabula rasa on which those visions are materialized, and of the totalistic vision of the future those designs seek to engineer. Following Augé (2009), we might also see this urban spatial discourse not as a departure from twentieth-century modernism but rather as an evolutionary permutation of that paradigm. I have further suggested that we might grapple with this urban spatial discourse's cultural and symbolic utility. Amid the contemporary era of mobility, and with the doors to Qatar flung open to a chaotic blizzard of neoliberal flows, the urban landscape of the city is suffused with foreign matter. That neoliberal chaos is the juncture where I see parallels with Douglas's symbolic analysis: the urban developments, various enclaves, elite spaces, special zones, and cities within cities are, among other things, tools by which the disordered nature of this neoliberal ecosystem is conceptually ordered and spatially governed.

This line of thinking has been previously broached. I, for example, analyzed the layout of a merchant's aging house in Manama, Bahrain (Gardner 2010b, 137–140). The spatial separation of the *majlis* and an altogether separate apartment in which visiting merchants and traders might temporarily reside were central features of my analysis. These were spatial, structural, and historical manifestations of the social capacity to accommodate strangers and outsiders, while simultaneously maintaining a cohesive private, domestic space. The layout of this house was a spatial metaphor for a national identity built around the idea of hospitality: Bahraini society was culturally configured to host a diversity of people from around the world yet did so without the compulsion to integrate and homogenize that difference. I observed the cultural tradition of accommodating difference might be read into the aging structure of the merchant's house I visited. Similarly, miriam cooke (2014) more eloquently articulates a strikingly similar point. In her book *Tribal Modern*, cooke revisits the Qur'anic term *barzakh*, and draws great analytic inspiration from the concept. Tussling with its meaning and connotations, she settles on a definition that balances both togetherness and difference: *barzakh* "divides and defines differences in mutually constitutive and newly productive ways" (cooke 2014, 76). As she contends, this balanced and comfortable approach to difference and otherness is a key feature of the Arabian cultures one encounters on the peninsula today. I would add that the urban spatial discourse I have described in this chapter is one of the tools by which that tolerance and balance—despite its limitations—have been achieved.

While cooke's emphasis is on the balance required for differences to coexist, I conclude with one more observation about this urban spatial discourse. As noted in the closing sentiments of the previous chapter, to consign foreign matter to spaces and zones in the urban landscape is, simultaneously, an assertion about the exceptionality of the foreign matter consigned to those spaces. In drawing inspiration from theorists like Giorgio Agamben and Aihwa Ong, I suggested that we might also recognize that the delineation of exceptional urban spaces is dialectically entwined with an assertion of cultural sovereignty, and this mosaic of spatialized difference is integral to the hierarchical multiculturalism that I see in the urban landscape of Doha. That hierarchical multiculturalism incorporates distinction and difference and proffers no impulse for integration or homogenization. That multiculturalism is also hierarchical—in the same sense that, for Longva, Kuwaiti society was most recognizable as an ethnocracy. I have sought to portray how the urban spatial discourse underlying the growth of the city has helped concretize these social relations in the city.

CEASELESS GROWTH AND THE URBAN TROPHY CASE

A second New York is being built
a little west of the old one
Why another, no one asks
just build it, and they do

—David Berman (*Actual Air*, 1999)

Just a few years ago, I brought a group of students to Doha for a week. The city was one of two worlding cities in our focus, each of which students would explore during the field-based portion of the course. The opportunity to engage these cities firsthand was, obviously, an integral feature and prime attraction for a course titled Migration and the Global City. In the schedule I established for our week in Doha, I had set aside Wednesday afternoon for an exploration of West Bay, the dense accumulation of skyscrapers perched over the turquoise waters of the sea (see figure 1). Those skyscrapers include several notable structures and awe-inspiring towers, including the French starchitect Jean Nouvel's stunning and graceful creation, as well as William Pereira's iconic pyramidical Sheraton Hotel, constructed in 1978. These architectural trophies are gathered around City Center Mall, the beating commercial heart of West Bay. On this afternoon, the mall would serve as our destination—the point at which our class would eventually reconvene. After breaking the students into small groups, their assignment for the afternoon was merely to explore and experience this portion of the city: via a *dérive*, or an urban drift, students might encounter the unexpected, perhaps see the unforeseen, or maybe meander into some pocket of the urban landscape just off the beaten path. Ideally, such a drift through the forest of skyscrapers might yield some experiential insight into the essence of this city, and perhaps into the lives of those who build and inhabit this urban trophy case. At least that was the idea.

I joined the students in this exercise, as is my custom. My urban drift through West Bay began to coalesce around photographing the adornment of the urban landscape with images of the Emir, a feature of the city that had grown particu-

larly commonplace during the economic and social "blockade" of Qatar insti-
gated by several neighboring states on the Arabian Peninsula. My newfound
thematic interest guided me to potentially ideal vantage points for photographs.
Clambering about this portion of the city eventually brought me into contact
with the security personnel who policed the grounds of one of the many skyscrapers now occupied by government ministries. Photography is not allowed, I
was warned, and was then directed to move along. In compliance, I dove back
into the forest of skyscrapers. The whole of West Bay seems to be in a perpetual
state of construction, and as a result, its streets can be particularly unfriendly to
pedestrians. As I would later discover, one of the small groups of students that I
had released into the city—a posse of intrepid young women, armored by their
American privilege and displaying their typical charisma and politesse—had a

FIGURE 12.   A migrant worker sweeps the central walkway of Souk Waqif early
in the morning. Photograph by the author, 2021

much different experience that afternoon. The young women persuaded a migrant security guard to show them the empty floors high in one of the most iconic buildings gathered in this urban trophy case. This building had garnered much attention upon its completion in 2009, and here, a decade later, many of its floors remained unfinished and unoccupied. I was envious of their experience and transfixed by the details they later provided to me and the class.

What explains the presence of those empty floors in an iconic skyscraper designed by a globally renowned architect? In part, that explanation is the central objective of this chapter. But let me fuel that question with a bit more empirical detail. The security guards that I encountered in my drift through West Bay were present as the direct result of the steady relocation of government ministries to these empty buildings, as those ministries were seemingly the only significant tenants who might occupy portions of the metastasizing surplus of office space in Doha. Consider also that scholar and researcher Steffen Hertog (2019, 293) reported that, as of 2011, only sixty-two apartments of the thousands available in Qatar's free zones had been sold. Similarly, in a recent conversation I had in Doha, a Qatari friend employed in Msheireb reported that prices for the apartments there had been slashed and leases shortened, seemingly to no avail. The streets of Msheireb remained desolately unpeopled, with public spaces occasionally occupied by a construction worker heading from one place to another, a store clerk on break, or a groundskeeper tending to the urban space itself. Most residents of Doha are familiar with the sight of a forlorn migrant-clerk manning the counter of an empty global franchise, or minding the entrance to some minor spectacle of consumption that lacks any customers at all, or maybe tending to some other urban space of negligible use. All visitors to Doha are accustomed to encountering members of the veritable army of migrant workers who service the city (see figure 12).

In this chapter, I hope to provide an answer to the conundrum buried in the heart of these examples. Why is this city being built? Who is all of this for? How might we describe the engines of urban growth that course beneath the surface of the incessant construction of more and more Doha? Why, with such an evident surplus of commercial office space and a definite surplus of shopping malls in the urban landscape of the city, is more of both under construction? Or think of this conundrum in more precise terms: when The Pearl continues to struggle to find sufficient buyers in an infrastructural setting designed for forty-five thousand inhabitants, why is Qatar nonetheless pushing ahead with the construction of Lusail, the new city-within-the-city designed for four hundred fifty thousand more inhabitants? In summary, the question guiding this chapter is very basic and straightforward: by what logic does the city continue to grow?

In attempting to answer those questions, we might begin with Natasha Iskander's observation (2021, 84) that "Doha and its opulent satellites grew not in response to the needs of its residents but rather in fulfillment of the modernist dream that the emir and his government had for what the city should become." Her pithy statement appropriately conveys the central role that those who sit atop the sociopolitical hierarchy of the contemporary Qatari nation-state have played in the growth, development, and form of the city. I will return to the subject of elite agency and the shape of the city in the concluding segments of this chapter; however, I commence with David Harvey's basic observation that cities have long provided an integral repository for the reservoirs of surplus capital generated by capitalist relations. In this chapter, I explore the relationship between those two explanatory paths and suggest that the social and political hierarchies characteristic of contemporary Qatar have grown in dialectic with the economy of urban growth and development that solidified in the late twentieth century. Indeed, Lewis Mumford (1961, 545), writing in that same era, observed that "once an economy is geared to expansion, the means rapidly turn into an end, and 'the going becomes the goal.'" Along those same lines, I suggest that Doha's ongoing urban development—or the process of constructing the urban future envisioned by Qatar's leaders—has emerged as the keystone in social, political, and economic arrangements on the peninsula.

The Configuration of Arabian Modernity

The task of summarizing the essence of Arabian modernity is, of course, a fool's errand in the grandiosity of its aspirations. But to move a bit closer to some modicum of a holistic understanding of the society responsible for the ongoing production of this city, I point to a set of foundational themes that have long percolated through scholarship concerned with the Arabian Peninsula and the peoples who reside there.

The first of those themes concerns the historical transition away from what Onley and Khalaf termed "shaikhly authority" (Onley and Khalaf 2006). In alignment with the social traditions of the region, authority was traditionally vested in tribal leaders, and was therefore personal, hereditary, and patrimonial in nature. When the wealth from hydrocarbon resources first began to accrue, it was controlled by each country's singular leader, and by the mostly British and American corporations that had facilitated their rise to power. From that centralized point of a personified state, wealth was distributed through the networks and hierarchies typical of Arabian societies on the peninsula at the beginning of the twentieth century. These relations remained in place as oil wealth slowly began to accrue. As the Saudi anthropologist Madawi al-Rasheed (1997, 81–82) described it, in that era rulers subsidized tribal shaikhs "through the continuous distribution of rice, coffee, sugar, camels, and weapons." But with the arrival of hydrocarbon wealth, money replaced almost everything on that list. Outsiders' perceptions of these relations and these arrangements should be understood in the ideological context of the mid-twentieth century. In an era characterized by the paradigmatic and global crescendo of modernity and by the hegemony of modernization theory on the tenor and shape of international relations, the distribution of hydrocarbon wealth through the traditional hierarchies of personal and tribal relations appeared premodern and uncivilized to many. Those critiques might be understood as one facet of the broader Orientalist discourse by which Middle Eastern societies were sometimes framed.

What eventually emerged from that shaikhly system was superficially different from the traditional arrangements typical of Arabian societies. Yet the emergent and modern relations that evolved in the twentieth century, while more closely aligned with international norms, remained structurally akin to the traditional relations that preceded them. In new and modern arrangements, powerful tribes and merchant families positioned themselves not to receive cash infusions via the ancestral calculus of tribal relations but instead to receive contracts to build, manage, or develop some part of the city or some capacity of the state. The budding sense of nationalism in the GCC states congealed around the vision statements and policy frameworks that established growth and development as the twin lodestars by which the nation might navigate its path to a modernist future. In this reconfiguration of Arabian societies around the objectives of growth and development, certain portions of Qatari society prospered and advanced, while others' power was diminished and marginalized. But the distribution of wealth remained largely guided by relations that were tribal, personal, hereditary, and patrimonial in nature, as it was in the preoil era. And those objectives—growth and development—are nowhere more manifest than the urban landscape itself.

An array of other themes pertinent to the configuration of Arabian modernity orbit around the conceptual gravity of the rentier state. In contemporary academia, rentier state theory seems somewhat embattled.[1] In my estimation, the energies of that scholarly consternation might be best recognized as a signal of rentier state theory's enduring value and utility. In the wake of American academia's postmodern turn, it's not misguided ideas or faulty concepts that garner critique from many academics today; rather, ideas and concepts that have explanatory power, proven utility, or a common-sensical appeal seem to attract the most virulent critique.[2] Rentier state theory describes the economic arrangements of those states in which the wealth of the nation is derived externally (for example, by the sale of hydrocarbon energy on the global marketplace), in which that wealth is first controlled and managed by the state itself, and in which that wealth is subsequently distributed through the state institutions to the citizenry (Beblawi 1987). This is in stark contrast to state-society arrangements elsewhere, in which wealth flows from the citizenry to the state, typically via taxes. As this summary suggests, rentier state theory points to the exceptional nature of these economic arrangements. Although always grounded in that economic logic, the ensuing scholarly conversations concerning rentier state theory also provide insights into the political, social, and cultural ramifications of these arrangements.

One result of the rentier system is the centralization of the state in these economies and, more broadly, in the societies of the Arabian Peninsula. As discussed in previous chapters, many of the gargantuan urban projects by which the city grows are entirely or partially funded by the state. This basic fact exemplifies the rentier system. At a more microcosmic level, the rentier state offers citizens a comprehensive cradle-to-grave safety net, often including land grants, low-interest loans, free education, free health care, free or subsidized utilities, and quite a bit more. These economic arrangements, and the social and political epiphenomena they produce, simultaneously affirm the tribal form of authoritarian hierarchy found in countries like Qatar. The substantial safety net for citizens is also hypothesized to essentially quell political consternation by establishing the citizenry's patrimonial dependence on the state.

Another key feature of the rentier system is public sector employment. In Qatar, nearly all employed citizens work in the public sector.[3] In financial and economic terms, public sector employment functions as the keystone to contemporary state-citizen relations. As many scholars have noted, employment in the public sector serves as the primary mechanism for the transfer of wealth from the state to the citizenry, and vast portions of the aforementioned safety net are delivered primarily through public sector employment. The social and cultural results of these arrangements will be further explored in the subsequent chapter, but in addition to the enclaving and spatial segregation of citizens from foreigners in the urban landscape, these employment patterns comprise another mechanism for the preservation of Qatari distinction amid the sea of foreigners resident on the small peninsula. Moreover, with nearly all citizens employed directly by the state, scholars have yet to ponder the cultural footprint of these arrangements on the social and political identity of the citizenry. The fact that nearly all citizens are, in some way or another, involved in the incremental management of the state itself seems both exceptional and remarkable in global history.

The rentier system, in tandem with the *kafala*, also clearly privileges citizenship in exceptional ways, foremost via policies and laws concerning ownership.

Owning land and owning businesses, for example, are both delimited partially or entirely to citizens, albeit with notable exceptions consigned to special zones and districts.⁴ In the ownership of businesses, these rules and regulations not only privilege citizens by ensuring all businesses include a citizen as majority-owned but also establish the viability of sponsorship itself as a financially lucrative vocation. Sporadic scholarly attention has portrayed how foreign entrepreneurship is harnessed (Choudhury 1998; Gardner 2008b; Khalaf 2010). For example, throughout the Arabian Peninsula, the term "sleeping partner" has been used for decades to describe the citizen majority-owner of businesses, large and small. That partner and majority owner is, stereotypically, uninvolved in the day-to-day operations of the business and is oftentimes the business's primary financier. In the rentier arrangements codified by these policies and laws, that partner derives profit from the migrant-partner's entrepreneurship and labor. These sorts of arrangements underpin most of the small businesses that energize this worlding city, and can also be framed as a reverberation of the rentier system: Qatari citizens remain deeply reliant on the state and on the external creation of wealth.

This is only a partial glimpse of the structures and relations by which Arabian modernity has been configured in the twentieth century. But this system's coherence might be better conveyed with an example. In 2008 I began teaching on the women's campus of Qatar University. Flying back and forth between Seattle and Doha—first for job interviews, and then later for periodic trips to return home, attend international conferences, or pursue various research endeavors—large sums of money flowed from Qatar University to Qatar Airways in my name. My family and I were given an apartment in a compound in the Al Waab neighborhood. Somewhat exorbitant monthly rental payments went from my employer to the owner of the compound, a prominent Qatari citizen. We purchased one car upon arrival, and a second in the following year, with monies again traveling from Qatar University, passing through my accounts, and then on to the car dealerships owned, at least in part, by Qatari citizens. Portions of the school fees paid for my daughter's preschool similarly circled back to a citizen-sponsor. In addition to these major expenditures, there is the plethora of quotidian expenditures that, in part, all percolated back to sleeping partners and citizen-sponsors: every flat tire fixed by a migrant mechanic, every item purchased at a cold store, the entirety of the furnishings and decorations for our apartment, all of these purchases fall into the logic of the rentier economy. Moreover, migrants and their citizen-sponsors are essential features in the construction of all these places—my compound, the shopping malls, and the university at which I taught. Only select economic activities, such as remittances to migrants' homes, or perhaps the purchase of materials abroad, escape this gravity. The rest circulates in Qatar through the vast migrant workforce present on the peninsula. By the logic of these arrangements, the foundation of the economy is expenditures by the state. Central to those expenditures is the construction of the city itself.

The Justification of Urban Growth

In the basic outline of Arabian modernity provided in the first portion of this chapter, I have emphasized the political-economic arrangements that evolved in the postoil era. I recognize these material relations as the foundation of contemporary societies on the Arabian Peninsula, and therefore as deeply implicated in the astonishing cities that have also arisen and in the complicated societies that have erected those cities. In passing, I also mentioned the collective ambitions of growth and development, concepts that, in my estimation, function as the motherboard by which these increasingly complex societies—now nations—are coordinated. Later on in this chapter, I turn to the discourses, ideas, and narratives by which these objectives are justified and enabled in the competitive discourse between neighbors on the Arabian Peninsula. First, however, I address how the penchant for ceaseless urban growth is cultivated, framed, and justified within Qatari society and to the various constituencies present there.

Essential to the coordination of these increasingly complex societies are the national vision statements that are periodically crafted by these wealthy states, then broadcasted to the citizenry, to the residential populations in Arabia, and to the global public. As we embark on the third decade of the new millennium, the operative vision statement in Qatar is the document entitled Qatar National Vision 2030, published in 2008 by the General Secretariat for Development Planning. As the document states, "The national vision aims to transform Qatar into an advanced country by 2030, capable of sustaining its own development and providing a high standard of living for its population and future generations." That transformation can be understood as a top-down mandate for growth and development. That development is further articulated in four domains requiring careful stewardship: the human, social, economic, and environmental realms of development. In articulating these aspirations in more detail, the document also sketches the knowledge-based society that is vaguely discerned as the destination of the growth and development codified in the vision statement. The tidy and coherent document also mentions "world-class infrastructure" several times in explicating a national vision of the future.

The basic premises of this vision statement are noteworthy. Growth and urban development are taken for granted as the obvious objectives of the Qatari state. The role of the nation's leader is to steward that growth and development with all available wisdom and foresight. The document mentions the careful "balancing" of these various objectives and pressures, and the document stresses the capacities of the nation's leadership to "choose and manage a pathway that delivers prosperity yet avoids economic imbalances." In the context of contemporary Qatar, fragments and portions of this vision statement are publicly brandished in the public-facing materials produced by numerous other institutions, ministries, programs, and by corporations with active projects on the peninsula. As an impressive and notably holistic articulation of the future envisioned by the state, the *Qatar National Vision 2030* document seems integral to the coordination of so many different institutions and interests. Most significantly for our purposes here, however, the document clearly promotes a vision of the future that will be achieved through urban development. Urban growth is the path to the future envisioned and portrayed here.

Another key ingredient in the recipe for urban growth are mega-events. These events are particularly commonplace in Qatar and the United Arab Emirates, and sometimes are hosted elsewhere in the GCC. The 2006 Asian Games, the 2022 FIFA World Cup, and the failed bid for the 2020 Summer Olympics are several of the most notable mega-events pertaining to Qatar. In addition to those veritable mega-events, however, Qatar hosts a steady regimen of tennis tournaments, hydrofoil races, film festivals, expositions, lesser football tournaments, and numerous other gatherings of all sorts. Portions of this list fit into what some economists now refer to as the MICE industry, with the acronym representing meetings, incentives, conferences, and exhibitions. Considered altogether, we might usefully differentiate two aspects of these activities and commitments. In part, these mega-events and the constellation of other activities hosted by the state, including all of what is referred to as the MICE industry, are intended to draw tourists and visitors to the city. This traffic captures neoliberal flows of money and people in the form of tourists, while simultaneously making use of the emergent urban infrastructure called forth by the Qatar National Vision 2030 document. The MICE industry folds neatly into the idea of a transition to a knowledge-based economy and society, which is also briefly articulated in the document. While these activities and commitments may be oriented toward bringing outsiders to the city, there is another aspect to the elements on this list; many of these events also require massive additions to the urban infrastructure of the city. The successful bid for hosting the 2022 FIFA World Cup, for example, required eight gargantuan stadiums, all serviced by the new Metro system tunneled under the city. These mega-events spur urban growth, underpin the economy, and thereby fuel the distributional logic of this rentier system.

An additional aspect by which urban development and growth are enabled is the mirage-like quality of the urban future broadcasted to both Qatari citizens and outsiders. This quality is captured by the transitive nature of the Qatar National Vision 2030 document: the promise of the city always resides in the future. That urban future is perpetually forthcoming. When new hotels or posh new restaurants open in Doha, when new projects near completion and the ribbons welcoming the public are finally cut, when new shopping malls are completed and doors swing open for the first time, or when entire new districts of the city announce themselves as open for visitors and investors, the city's inhabitants briefly flock to these spaces. In my years of residence there, we, too, were part of this flock. Perhaps these clamorous crowds yearn for the city of the future and all it seems to promise. That same mirage of the forthcoming city is also discernible in the proliferation of computer-generated images, scale models, and dioramas portraying the soon-to-arrive urban future (see figure 11). They are quintessential examples of the domain of the imagined urban future the theorist Edward Soja (1996) called secondspace.[5] These images circulate widely, and in the form of billboards and construction blockades in the urban landscape, they even clad the city itself. The vision of the forthcoming urban future presented in this imagery, or encountered firsthand in the new urban spaces to which the city's elite inhabitants briefly flock, reveals an urban future shorn of the frictions and problems anchored in reality. Absent in those images is the legion of foreign workers who still reside, offstage, in the city; missing is the seemingly endless construction and reconstruction of a churning economy premised upon urban growth and development. Instead, in those images Qatari families mingle with a cosmopolitan stew of foreign professionals and content consumers. How could any commercial image convey the alienation and the ennui that accompanies a visit to yet another new luxury enclave, or to another architecturally stunning and opulently magnificent hotel, or to an even larger shopping mall replete with the same ostentatious commercial junkspace as others? Perhaps this is why Guy Debord (1983, 63) concluded that "the spectacle is nothing more than an image of happy unification surrounded by desolation and fear at the tranquil center of misery."

Architectural Trophies, Mega-Events, and the Symbolic Economy

The architectural trophies that crowd Doha's skyline, and the mega-events that call forth even more urban growth, also function in the symbolic vernacular.[6] An explanation of the prevalence of trophy architecture and mega-events in Qatar would be incomplete without reference to this global symbolic economy. One might agree with the vociferous urban critics that the burgeoning skylines of the Gulf are simply the result of an astoundingly wealthy people, under the sway of a Western modernity, with an unprecedented surplus of money to spend. That line of thinking affirms Harvey's contentions (1989, 92) from three decades ago—that the spectacular urban spaces are, foremost, a means of attracting capital and the right sorts of people. While those explanations certainly apply to the city, I instead point to an altogether different logic to this symbolic economy—a logic intricately connected to the political-economic relations I have already described in this chapter.

When thinking about the prevalence of trophy architecture and monumental structures in Doha, I think it is important to detach any analysis of the city from the normative analytic frame derived from scholarship concerning large and heterogeneous nations like the United States. Unlike the developed states of North America and Western Europe, most of the cities in the Gulf states are combined primate/capital cities. In some cases, these cities are the only significant urban agglomerations in small states (Kuwait City, Kuwait; Manama, Bahrain; Muscat, Oman; Doha, Qatar). In other cases, they represent the primate cities of somewhat autonomous emirates (Abu Dhabi, Sharjah, Dubai). As such, the appropriate comparative frame for these cities does not include Los Angeles, Kyoto, Marseilles, or Rio de Janeiro, but rather Washington DC, Tokyo, Paris, and Brasilia, for all these Gulf cities are capital cities. In relation to their context, by design these cities represent a nation to the world. These cities are the nations' trophy cases, and are so in a sense that is more than figurative.[7] These cities are a stage for the nation.

The predominance of cosmopolitan starchitects in Doha's architectural constructions (with past and ongoing projects from I. M. Pei, Arata Isozaki, Jean Nouvel, Santiago Calatrava, and Zaha Hadid, for example) is also suggestive and yields some clue as to the symbolic register indexed by these projects. Many such constructions—for example, the convention center, the hotels, the Pearl, and the museums—are projects that explicitly cater to a foreign audience: the museums function as locations where Qatari culture is defined and distilled for a predominantly foreign audience; the Pearl is a freeholder zone in which foreigners can (and, from Qatar's perspective, hopefully will) purchase property, thereby capturing some of the capital flows that now exit the Qatari economy. And many of the events that occurred in Doha—a professional women's tennis match in which Venus and Serena Williams played in the final match, the Doha Tribeca International Film Festival attended by Martin Scorsese, Robert De Niro, and Ben Kingsley; the Oryx Cup hydroplane boat races held on Doha Bay; the England/Brazil friendly football match; the 2022 FIFA World Cup—all can be understood by the particularly cosmopolitan brand of cultural capital they exemplify.

In interviews with Qataris I was initially surprised by their evaluations of these monumental projects and events that accompany them. With the Pearl, for example, three young women quickly responded to my inquiries by noting that "Oh, the Pearl isn't for us. We would never live there. It's a place for the foreigners, for people like you, Professor." At the same time, they expressed their pride in that project, noting that it would be one of the most beautiful places in all of the Gulf, a fine place to represent Qatar to the outside world, and an excellent place for them to shop should they ever desire. Or, at the 2010 Qatar ExxonMobil Open in Doha, I was surprised by the extraordinary paucity of Qataris at the final matches: international tennis stars competed in front of an audience largely comprised of foreigners, and in a stadium with a significant number of very expensive empty seats. One way to understand these events is as advertised: with the historically insular nature of Qatari society, there is a general and widespread interest in bringing the outside world to Qatar. To restate that claim in the parlance of Villaggio Mall's advertising campaign from that same period, "Venice is now in Doha." Yet these mega-events and architectural trophies are also part of what Michael Rustin (2008) called a symbolic economy. As this conceptualization suggests, these buildings and the events they are constructed to host have meanings that transcend their function and utility.

My understanding of that symbolic economy in Doha is straightforward. Scholars working in the neo-Marxist tradition have long pointed to consumerism as the most observable facet of the culture of capitalism (e.g., Robbins 2005; Broswimmer 2002). According to their analysis, this cultural system has fundamentally reshaped societies and cultures around the world. It strips individuals from other and prior collective forms of meaning and belonging, and it places them in a world in which identity is authored, in part, by the things one chooses to purchase and, in part, by the producers who help invest those commodities with particular meanings. From an anthropological point of view, it is particularly noteworthy that this cultural system highlights the individual and individual choice over other collective social aspects of human existence. Through the grand scale of consumption in the Gulf states, however, we can see how this consumer ethic does something quite different from highlighting the individual and her identity. Once we comprehend Doha's museums, shopping malls, sporting events, stadia, universities, and trophy skyscrapers for their symbolic value, one can easily perceive how collective notions of belonging, and particularly nationalism, are reinforced by a sort of collective consumption. Much like a young Qatari woman at the mall trying to decide which purse best represents her individuality, style, and taste, the Qatari state purchases items of symbolic importance to project a refined, cosmopolitan, and thoroughly modern national image to a global audience, an ongoing act that simultaneously asserts the benevolent leadership of the ruling family and its cohort, whose role in this system is to choose tastefully and to choose well. The city, as a trophy case to both that leadership and its citizen-subjects, functions as the material form around which nationalism congeals. The city thereby reinforces a unified sense of belonging over the heterogeneity of preexisting interests and diverse social communities among the citizenry. Mega-projects and trophy architecture are the means by which this can be achieved.

Concluding Thoughts

In conclusion, there are a handful of themes that I would like to highlight from this chapter's explication of the forces underpinning Doha's urban growth. In the analysis presented here I contend that urban growth and development are instrumental in the distribution of wealth from the state to the citizenry. In building an economy largely centered on the expansion of the city itself, the Qatari people have been able to maintain a set of hierarchical relations and tribal affiliations that, together, preserve significant aspects of traditional social organization. As a product of the preservation of these traditional aspects of Qatari social organization, we can also see how the political legitimacy of monarchical power in Qatar depends on continued and sustained urban growth. The urbanists Harvey Molotch and Davide Ponzini (2019, 5) contend that the monarchical states of the region assert their sovereignty with "colossal structures and symbolic showiness." In the analysis provided in this chapter, I would concur with the interconnection they establish between the urban landscape and monarchical sovereignty. To that observation, I would add that these states, and the elite members at the apex of those societies, are also politically dependent on the logic of distribution that urban development calls forth.

Another thread in this chapter that might be usefully highlighted here is reflected in the analytic importance of what Steffen Hertog (2019) termed "elite agency." This elite agency was central to Onley's portrayal (2007) of the region's history and interaction with empires of the nineteenth century. Others have added to the small chorus of scholars who point to the primacy of elite agency in shaping *khaleeji* state, city, and society (Batty 2012; Exell and Rico 2014; Jones 2019; Iskander 2021, 84–85; Rizzo and Mandal 2021, 77). Over several academic generations, led largely by European and American scholars, the historian's lens has increasingly moved away from its focus on great men, great events, and the narratives constructed around those at the helm of the nation-state. Instead, contemporary scholars and historians seek to redress the omissions and exclusions of these approaches by exploring "other" histories. Although there is much to laud with this enduring corrective, it seems a reflection of academic concerns that were primarily distilled in the democratic context of Western academia, and one tethered to the social and academic relations of the previous century. After decades spent pursuing yet another omission or exclusion in one national narrative or another, contemporary scholars today seem poorly attuned to the power and the agency of the elite themselves. In this chapter, I have consciously sought to explore the connections between the Qatari elite and the urban landscape of the city. The preferences and tastes of that elite have shaped the city itself, and it is that same stratum of the citizenry that benefits the most from the ceaseless urban growth that results.

CULTURE AND LIFE IN A FRAGMENTED CITY

The previous chapters have assembled the various understandings of Doha that, in summation, help illuminate the idea of a fragmentary city. The city can be conceptualized as an urban node in a global and neoliberal network of connections and mobilities that incorporate all sorts of matter—human beings, ideas, invisible gas, social practices, spirituality, financial capital, styles and fashions, and more. The demography of the city is extraordinarily diverse and varied in ways that are unusual in comparison to most of the developed nations of the Northern Hemisphere. Much of that diversity and varied forms of difference are present in the city. This mosaic of difference in the urban landscape is governed by an urban spatial discourse that shapes the ongoing growth of the city and produces an urban social fabric that I have referred to as a form of hierarchical multiculturalism. The ongoing growth of the city is fueled by the vast reservoirs of surplus capital generated by the hydrocarbon wealth energizing the contemporary era of mobility. And the city must continue to grow; the social relations I have described are held in place by the production of the urban landscape itself. In the fragmentary social terrain that results, various forms of social and cultural difference are both welcome and ever-present. Citizens and foreigners alike inhabit enclaves, pockets, and segregated spaces in the city, and oftentimes move between an archipelago of similar spaces cast across the urban landscape. These arrangements help maintain cultural difference amid the transnational mobilities that characterize the contemporary era. Simultaneously, those arrangements reinforce the hierarchical aspect of the multiculturalism that characterizes the city of Doha.

FIGURE 13.   Nepalese migrants play cricket in a stretch of interstitial urban space near the Industrial Area. Photograph by the author, 2018.

That is a complicated portrayal of a city and its social fabric. It is also a portrayal that incorporates features and attributes seen in other cities of the world and in other historical eras. I suggest these features and attributes signal a new frontier in the planetary urban form. In this chapter, I turn my attention to topics at the heart of the social and cultural anthropologist's inquiry—what is life like in the city that I have described? What social and cultural manifestations result from the urban spatial discourse by which the city has grown? In an attempt to illuminate some of the social and cultural features unique to the global frontiers of urban modernity found on the Arabian Peninsula, I provide three vista points on urban life in Doha. From the first of those vista points, I explore the positionality of citizens relative to foreign matter, and convey how the relations between citizens and everything they host reflect this patchworked urban landscape. In the second of those vista points, I identify a social role particular to this urban spatial discourse—the men and women I call *imagineers* are go-betweens, cultural brokers of a sort, who thrive in the exchange of information and the flows of power between enclaves, and therefore across thresholds of cultural difference. Finally, in the third ethnographic sojourn presented here, I speak to the social vitality of the spaces in between the units of development characteristic of Doha and the urban spatial discourse shaping its growth. I trace the importance of this interstitial urban space to the whole of society, and particularly to the more marginal elements of Qatari society. Although these three vista points are inevitably partial in nature, together they help elucidate new and emergent social features encountered in Doha and, by proxy, in the other worlding cities of the Arabian Peninsula.

Lazy Arabs

In the two years I spent teaching at Qatar University, the institution was undergoing a period of rapid and wholesale change.[1] Nonetheless, over that period of time I developed a deep affection for the university, for my students, and for my colleagues in the Department of Social Sciences. But that affection ought not to obscure the everyday challenges encountered in trying to function as an academic researcher, a teacher, and a productive scholar while employed there. Those challenges occasionally took comic form. For example, although Qatar was (and remains) one of the wealthiest nations in the world on a per capita basis, in my experience the supply of paper at the university was unpredictable and itinerant. Indeed, in that institutional ecosystem it often seemed easier to procure a new US$2,000 printer than a ream of paper needed for making use of that printer. So mid-morning one day in 2009, with a set of in-class exercises needed in a matter of hours, I hopped into my Honda Civic and headed for nearby Landmark Mall to purchase a few reams of paper with money from my own pocket. On this particular day more than a decade ago, I entered the air-conditioned Landmark Mall and encountered an array of coffee shops crowded with Qatari men. As my fieldnotes from later that night suggest, the men were in conversations, reading the newspaper, talking with each other, or perhaps talking on their mobile phones. Many were smoking cigarettes—a newly prohibited behavior in these quasi-public spaces, and at that time, a difficult transgression for the legion of migrant service workers and security guards to attempt to address. In my fieldnotes, I considered why, in the middle of a workday morning, were so many Qatari men not at work. Although it sounds stereotypical and cliché to say it, at that hour in an American mall I would expect to see housewives with infants and, perhaps, a fair number of retirees out for a stroll in a climate-controlled environment. In Qatar, however, the workday shopping mall is full of able-bodied men in their prime. Why were they not at work?

There is nothing particularly adroit about my observational capacities, and indeed, many other expats in the region have made similar observations—sometimes in writing, and more frequently in person—to me and to other expatriates with whom they share some sort of comforting affiliation. At social gatherings among these expats, I frequently encountered a discourse portraying Arab laziness. This discourse is empirically tethered to numerous observations and anecdotal experiences like the one I have described. In stereotypical expatriate sentiment, Arab lassitude is linked to the hydrocarbon-derived wealth of the nation; rather than earning that wealth, Qatar and the other *khaleeji* states benefitted from the happenstance location of vast hydrocarbon reserves within their borders. These interpretations also reflect the enduring Orientalist discourse so potently identified by

FIGURE 14.   A crosswalk in Msheireb. Photography by the author, 2020.

Edward Said (1978), who discerned a European tradition that contrasted its own progress with the irrational, lazy, uncivilized, and crude character of the "oriental" (see also Alatas 1977). Nor, in my own experience and research, are these Orientalist perspectives consigned to European and American sources, but are also shared by the many diasporas and various foreign communities who reside in Arabia. Sometimes these sentiments even characterize citizens' critical assessments of their own society—a notable permutation of what William Mazzarella (2003, 138–141) once referred to as auto-orientalism.[2]

While the discriminatory logic of Orientalism lodges this purported lassitude as a flaw endemic to some cultural or racial essence of the Arab people, rentier state theory reaches a similar endpoint via a different line of reasoning. Although rentier theory is in the first accounting an economic theory, its extrapolation oftentimes carries analysis into terrain that is clearly sociological in nature and scope. For example, in addition to the other descriptive features of the rentier economy, Hazem Beblawi (1987, 385–386)—one of the theory's progenitors—also suggested that these economic arrangements produce a rentier mentality, a state of mind premised on, "a break in the work-reward causation. Reward—income or wealth—is not related to work or risk bearing, rather to chance or situation." In this line of analysis, Arab lassitude is a result of a changing system of incentives manifested in the rentier state. My interests here are in unpacking what Beblawi might have meant by the "situation" that he concludes his assertion with.

First, although there is a thread of reasonable coherence to this explanation, I think it demands reframing. The majority of Qatari citizens work in the public sector. Although the workforce is burgeoning with foreigners, many of those public sector workplaces remain primarily Qatari and operate in Arabic. Workdays in the public sector usually conclude early in the afternoon, while the private sector continues until 5:00 p.m., if not later. For Qataris, time in the afternoons, evenings, and portions of the workday are often devoted to social networking or to time with family. This might include visiting and connecting with friends or colleagues; one might conceive of this time in terms of the accumulation of *wasta*, the Arabic term for social capital; one might also envision this time in terms of the maintenance of relations with tribe and family. Most modern Qatari households contain a *majlis*, a room designed specifically for male versions of this social function (Nagy 1997; Al-Mohannadi and Furlan 2022). Although nearly nine of every ten humans on the Qatari Peninsula are foreigners, after their day concludes Qatari citizens most typically return to neighborhoods largely segregated from the foreign population. Some of those suburban neighborhoods are still vaguely organized by kin and extended family, like the *fareej* of yesteryear that many Qataris now nostalgically idealize (Nagy 2006). In summary, the segmentation of the workforce and the spatial segregation of Qataris from foreign matter in the city together index a different sort of social logic that I am seeking to discern here. What expatriates might read as lassitude is, an active investment in a set of traditional social relations that, in some form, persevere in the modern city.

The men at the shopping mall that I encountered were busy with a different sort of work than I was able to recognize. Through an urban spatial discourse that enclaves foreign matter, and through the self-segregation of the Qatari citizenry to both public sector employment and residential districts in the urban landscape, Qataris have been able to retain some semblance of traditional social relations amid a sea of foreign influence. In the logic of the Qatari domain, tribal affiliation, family reputation, and the *wasta* an individual has been able to accumulate as a social creature are the currency by which one advances in society. Much of this happens in decidedly Qatari spaces in the city. Notably, this calculus indexes a social logic in which foreigners—as outsiders—are poorly positioned to compete. Qataris' retention of some modicum of traditional social relations despite such a comprehensive and wholesale embrace of global, neoliberal forces, much of which is close at hand in the city, and in consideration of Qataris' standing as an outright minority in their city and country—all this suggests that the maintenance of Qatari social coherence is a notable anthropological fact. To see tradition persevere, rather than erode or disappear, suggests that there are mechanisms by which cultural diversity and difference might be retained, even amid the increasing tide of global interconnection that characterizes the contemporary era of mobility. Qatar, and the Qatari people, face demographic circumstances at the frontiers of the global condition. The city itself seems to be an integral tool in this notable achievement. Urban theorists, and those anthropologists who remain committed to social and cultural diversity, should perhaps take note.

Information Brokers in the Fragmented Cultural Landscape

In 2008, I began meeting with Divendra at his labor camp in Doha's Industrial Area.[3] His experiences and perspectives have featured centrally in several of my previously published pieces, and they also commenced this book. Consider another one of those experiences, drawn from a scenario he faced in 2009. In his first stint as a transnational migrant in Qatar, Divendra and the other South Asian laborers at his company faced all sorts of serious problems at the hands of their Palestinian employers. Their problems included the poor conditions of the labor camp to which they were assigned, the nonpayment of promised wages, the extraction of various fees from what salary they did receive, and the stress of navigating several different lawsuits filed by their employers as part of an attempt to discipline the exploited South Asian workforce. Early in these difficulties, Divendra and several fellow workers were able to meet face-to-face with their Qatari sponsor to explain their situation and plead their case to him. After that meeting with him, the worker's sponsor communicated with the brothers—their employers (whom he also sponsored)—and most of the workers' problems were quickly resolved. Within months, however, the same issues returned. In this second manifestation, their employers ensured the South Asian workers had no access to their mutual sponsor: they refused to facilitate such contact, and they discontinued the workers' transportation services. As a result, the workers' problems endured for the remainder of Divendra's time in Qatar.

Next, consider a seemingly unrelated experience from that same period. In 2009, I was midway through my service as an assistant professor at Qatar University (see figure 15). In addition to teaching classes, that year I began to work with an institution in Doha on a research project focused on Gulf migration and its impact on the family.[4] The director and a handful of other personnel at this institute were American, and the draft of my paper was circulated among them for comment and review. Overall, this was a painless process, but eventually my draft's circulation stopped at the desk of one of the highest-ranking Americans in the institution's hierarchy. His concerns were manifold. He criticized my use of the term "exploitation" to describe the circumstances some migrants face in the region, for example. After relaying a constellation of other concerns, he warned that a paper of this sort would most certainly raise the ire of "the Qataris." A series of internal discussions ensued, to which I was not privy, and although the working paper eventually reached publication, it did so under a cloud of his warnings.[5] As an anthropologist with a particularly long record of researching the lower strata of the migrant workforce present on the Arabian Peninsula, I had heard these sorts of concerns and warnings before. The nature of my research agenda will be unwelcome, I have been told, and over many years, I would need more hands than my own to count the number of people who felt compelled to inform me of the risks I would face. In 2021, I conveyed the essence of this experience to a fellow researcher and colleague of African descent. Despite our different backgrounds, and despite the notably different institutional ecosystems we occupy, he reported a variety of similar interactions over a decade of research focused on transnational labor migration. We laughed and concurred on one other important point: those warnings always came from other foreigners.

My experience as a privileged foreign professor at Qatar University and Divendra's experience as a labor migrant in Doha's Industrial Area were extraordinarily different. But these vignettes also share some ground, and there are

FIGURE 15.   Qatar University's old campus, designed by Kamal El-Kafrawi, an Egyptian architect based in Paris. Constructed of precast concrete plates, the building featured octagonal classrooms topped with Arabic-styled wind catchers. The university is one of many nodes in the knowledge-based economy where information brokerage is active. Photograph by Kristin Giordano, 2011.

two aspects therein that help illuminate the social and cultural terrain of urban Arabia. First, both of these scenarios reflect the segmented and segregated social terrain of the city. Differences—in class, culture, nationality, race, and language—are maintained and reinforced by the enclaves, the compartmentalization of foreign matter, and, broadly, the segregation resulting from the urban spatial discourse I have described. Moreover, these differences are arranged hierarchically, and the quotidian tasks of life in this social terrain require frequent communication across those thresholds of difference. Divendra reported his challenges to his Palestinian employers, for example, and eventually pleaded his fellow workers' concerns to his Qatari sponsor. In my case, the mostly American institutional sponsors of my research were speculatively concerned with what the Qataris who funded their institution might think, or perhaps more precisely, what they imagined that they might think about my research agenda.

Here I want to point to the dominant role that the human imagination plays in this social terrain. In a short paper published several years later, for example, I collated and analyzed a set of urban legends that I had heard in my many conversations with migrant workers in their labor camps (Gardner 2012a). The tall tales and the worrisome stories that proliferated among working-class migrants there were often about Qataris and the mysteries of Qatari culture. In my analysis, I suggested that the proliferation of these myths and legends, and the often-preposterous falsehoods that they trucked in, were premised on the fact that none of the migrants retelling these urban legends had any firsthand knowledge or experience with the Qatari citizenry. The things they imagined about Qataris reflected the fact that they knew no Qataris. Similarly, most of the Americans evaluating my draft paper had little firsthand contact with any Qataris. Instead, they were left to speculate about that mysterious Qatari otherness from afar, from across the thresholds of cultural difference instantiated in the urban landscape. Qatari preferences, concerns, and attitudes were not something most of these foreigners frequently encountered or with which they commonly engaged. Rather, they were left to imagine the cultural terrain beyond the thresholds that separated them.

My point here should be clear. In the insular social terrain fostered by the city, and by the urban spatial discourse underpinning it, this is to be expected. In this superdiverse city, the absence of sustained cultural interaction with otherness is often the norm.[6] But this description also points to the second thesis threaded through these vignettes. The insular, segregated, segmented social terrain described here cultivates a particular sort of social entrepreneur—a go-between, a gatekeeper of sorts. In the ethnographic canon, these social actors are commonly referred to as brokers. These social actors received a spate of attention linked to the vast decolonization projects around the world. For example, Eric Wolf's illuminating work (1956, 1076–1077) described brokers as Janus-like—turned in two directions at once—and readily identifiable for their capacity to "stand guard over the crucial junctures or synapses of the relationships which connect the local system to the larger whole." Johan Lindquist (2015, 2) revisited this lost strand of the ethnographic canon and provided a revised and updated definition of the broker: "a specific type of middleman, mediator, or intermediary . . . the broker is a human actor who gains something from the mediation of valued resources that he or she does not directly control, which shall be distinguished from a patron who controls valued resources, and a go-between or a messenger, who does not affect the transaction." In the fragmented city, a legion of foreigners has arisen around the exchange of valuable information across the thresholds of cultural difference that comprise the social terrain of the city.

But there is more to this. The experiences I have related here point not only to these foreigners' roles as gatekeepers or brokers—whose powers are built on governing the movement of information across these thresholds of difference and, inevitably amid this multicultural hierarchy, up and down the hierarchies of power—but also to their function as imagineers.[7] At key junctures of communication and in the exchange of information up and down the social hierarchies characteristic of these plural and superdiverse societies, brokers not only regulate the communication of information for their own personal gain (as in Divendra's case) but are also continually engaged in estimating, guessing, evaluating, and portraying what might be culturally or socially appropriate to those atop this social hierarchy. This assertion rests on the social fact that while these brokers may or may not share ethnicity, class, and/or religion with their hierarchical superiors, they often have little substantial insight or contact with the inner workings of Qatari society, or with others above them this social hierarchy. This, in turn, is a result of the urban spatial discourse, the segregation it encourages, and the insularity that predominates in this social terrain.[8] It is in the gap between reality and its representation that the power of the human imagination takes form.

In my experience, it is often an imagined set of interests, aspirations, and concerns that characterizes these imagineers' portrayal of *khaleeji* society. In the scenarios that commenced this section, the imagined interests and concerns of Qataris presented by these gatekeeping imagineers were disabused by Qataris themselves—by the citizen-colleagues I collaborated with at Qatar University, for example, or by the Qatari sponsor who fielded and momentarily resolved Divendra's concerns. To be clear: these brokers' portrayals of Qatari (or other Gulf nationals') concerns with my research agenda were, almost always, starkly different from the tenor of my own encounters and interactions with Qatari citizens, in both official and unofficial capacities. What this points to is the often-significant difference between Qatari interests and their portrayal by these imagineers. Behind those boundaries and thresholds of difference are humans in all their social complexity. But the terrain of this imaginary can compound and exaggerate those differences. As I speculated years ago, this imagineering opens the door for a host of stereotypes, essentializations, and the zombie Orientalisms that still stagger through great swaths of contemporary analysis, often in disguise.[9] Speculation aside, we might conclude more straightforwardly that, in this fragmented and hierarchical social milieu, prone as it is to insularity, and configured to maintain cultural difference, the social imaginary seems to play an outsized role. This condition seems rooted in the urban landscape of the city itself.

Interstitial Urban Space

My goal for this chapter is to illuminate noteworthy aspects of the social and cultural assemblages that arise in the urban landscape that I have sought to describe in this book. I now turn my attention to the urban spaces of the city, and to a particular sort of urban space that I believe merits attention. What I term *interstitial urban space* is a form of what Barron (2014) has called "terrains vagues"—the loose spaces, abandoned parcels, uncertain properties, and other tracts of urban space into which urban social life inevitably spills (see figure 13 and figure 16). I use interstitial urban space to describe the margins and seams of the urban spatial discourse described in previous chapters.

My interest in this sort of space traces back more than a decade (Gardner 2009). In my first year of residence in Doha, my notebook began to steadily accumulate an increasing number of fieldnotes concerned with the city itself. Notably, at that juncture the city was still new to me, and as a result, features of urban life that would soon become everyday, commonplace, and quotidian—and thereby slip past my notice—still caught my attention. One of the threads woven through many of these experiential jottings concerned moving about the city, and my various attempts to grapple with the peculiarities of my experiences. Although this fieldnote is somewhat exemplary, it is also a jotting in which time is askew; in its iteration, the fieldnote was a retrospective recollection of an experience I had earlier in my family's residence in Doha. But, with that caveat in mind, the fieldnote also conveys a key aspect of life in the fragmented and complicated urban landscape of contemporary Doha.

Like many other transnational families of Qatar's upper middle class, during our residence in Doha my small family and I sometimes spend our weekend mornings at one of the brunches offered by the numerous hotels recently constructed in the city. Early in our stay in what was still a new city to us, we selected the Mövenpick hotel for what we hoped would become part of a weekly ritual. One might be hard-pressed to distinguish the new Mövenpick amid the sprouting skyline in the city center—after all, it is merely one astonishing postmodern building among many in the opulent junkspace of contemporary Arabia. Our trip to the hotel involved several detours through the city center's streets, nearly all of which were under construction. We finally made our way to a hardpan dirt parking lot adjacent to the hotel. With our young daughter in tow and a steep wind blowing dust in all directions, we encountered minor difficulties in traversing a short chain fence, heaps of discarded cinder blocks, an abandoned pile of sand, and a miscellany of construction debris and garbage on our journey from the car to the hotel's front door.

In terms of the human senses, the inside of the hotel presented a stark contrast to our experiences outside. The air was frigid. The lobby was sleek and modern, sparsely furnished, with clean lines and contemporary art, and we were quickly guided to an elevator that whisked us to the child-friendly and ostentatious brunch that had attracted us in the first place. Since that time, I've come to pay more and more attention to these thresholds, and to the sloppy and difficult interstitial spaces in this city and the other cities of the Arabian Peninsula—to the piles of cinder blocks, construction debris, abandoned vehicles, sidewalks that meander to no-

FIGURE 16.   Food preparation, as informal urbanism, at a "Friday market." Note the piles of garbage and debris in the background of this interstitial urban space. Photograph by the author, 2020.

where, and to the forgotten in-between spaces of the Gulf city. In part, it's because as a denizen of Doha one spends so much time passing back and forth across thresholds dividing the polished, stylized, and antiseptic modernity that is de rigueur in the contemporary Gulf, and the chaotic dishevelment that seems to occupy these interstitial spaces. The contrast is stark. If one simply pays attention, one realizes how common this experience is in all the cities of the Gulf.

Over more than a century, urban theorists have described cities in terms of the wondrous social fabric that results from the density of our urban inhabitations.[10] That density—our togetherness with strangers and the various bonuses of proximity—are the gravitational core of the urban milieu. But the urban social fabric that results from those milieux is a variable to be analyzed and explored.

From one angle, this fieldnote helps clarify the paramount and significant presence of thresholds and boundaries of difference in Doha's urban landscape. In a city replete with foreigners and with foreign matter; in a city that has grown by a capital-intensive urban spatial discourse and the expansive units of urban development that fuel it; in a city in which unfettered access to the internet, or alcoholic beverages, or coeducational classrooms, or the ownership of property, or Christian churches, or vast contingents of fellow migrant countrymen are consigned to specific enclaves and designated urban spaces—in this city, that social fabric is disjointed and fragmentary. It is a mosaic of difference, akin to patterns we might discern in other urban landscapes, perhaps. But Doha is also unlike those other cities in terms of the prominence and proliferation of these enclaved spaces in the urban landscape. In the enclaves and planned spaces that make up this urban landscape, the attention—of planners, inhabitants, officials, visitors, and others—is perennially directed inward, and there is little attention to how a parcel or building "in fact connects (or fails to connect) with other buildings and populations" (Nastasi 2019, 100). At the margins of the computer-generated images that promote the plethora of Doha's urban projects, for example, the landscape becomes foggy and indistinct, and typically fades into nothingness. Those spaces at the margins of projects and plans are my quarry here.

In the fieldnote, what caught my attention for the first time was the space just outside the boundaries of those parcels, enclaves, and urban spaces—the foggy nothingness visible at the margins of many promotional images and scale models of the city (see figure 11). From then forward, I began to pay attention to those spaces in between other things in the urban landscape. In the original fieldnote, I mentioned detritus, garbage, and construction debris; in the ensuing years, using my camera and my notebook, I began to expand the list of what one might encounter just outside compound walls, or just beyond the boundaries of a property, or past the last building on the last block. That list came to include abandoned vehicles; a plethora of tires and all sorts of assorted garbage; abandoned watercraft; numerous signs, including many that explicitly prohibit dumping, trespassing, or lingering; graffiti, recorded by my camera with notable frequency; and quite a bit more. Carrying this idea from Doha back to Tacoma, Washington (the city in which I make my home), I also came to recognize that these interstitial urban spaces were locations where invasive plant species also seemed to flourish. In Tacoma, these invasive species included scotch broom (*cytisus scoparius*) and the himalaya blackberry (*rubus armeniacus*), the latter of which produces an edible and sometimes-welcome fruit. Regardless, in my thinking, this rambunctious list of miscellany and whatnot eventually coalesced as a list of indicators—indicators that signaled the presence of interstitial urban space.

To better document this sort of space and to better grapple with its significance, I began to devote more time to these urban explorations—to dérives that might help me better experientially engage these spaces and perhaps better understand them. In Tacoma, those endeavors carried me under freeways, along the margins of property lines near the historic waterfront, and to the seams and interstices of tenure interlacing the urban landscape. I became increasingly aware that this interstitial urban space was entering a period of intensifying use in America. As economic inequality in the United States increased, society's most marginal elements—the homeless American *lumpenproletariat*—slowly began to accumulate in these interstitial urban spaces. In cities on America's West Coast, many of these interstitial urban spaces became, essentially, busy urban camps. In Doha, I also noticed the intensifying use of interstitial urban space, albeit by different sorts of people. For example, in 2019 I visited one of the bachelor cities on the periphery of Doha. One portion of the empty stretch of the desert beyond its walls was piled high with garbage and detritus—indicative of interstitial urban space, in my calculus. On that particular Friday, it was also crowded with thousands of migrant men (see figure 16). They were cooking, drinking, cutting hair, selling this and that, gambling, and socializing, all in what is popularly called the "Friday Market" that takes shape once a week in this interstitial urban space. Beyond the densely packed market area, various groups of men played cricket on other parcels, in the spaces beyond the walls of the bachelor city and whatever comes next on the desert's near horizon, be it a road, a factory, a construction site, or another bachelor city (see figure 13).

In both Doha and Tacoma, this interstitial urban space had clear and observable social utility. In neither case was the whole of society present. Rather, in both cases it was marginal and disenfranchised social elements that seemed to make use of this interstitial urban space. This resonated with other familiar ethnographic work. In 1989, the anthropologist James Holston published his heralded ethnography of Brasilia, titled *The Modernist City*. Holston documents the construction of Brazil's new capital in the 1960s. The city, constructed on a parcel carved from the forest, was an attempt at a whole planned city, the grandest feat of social engineering, and in the context of that era, a tabula rasa for the monumental ambitions of modernist urban planners at the apex of the twentieth-century high modernism. Despite the steady hand of several of the world's leading urban planners, and despite the intricate and detailed energies that were devoted to erecting the new capital city, Holston's ethnography helps the reader take stock of the human incapacity to socially engineer and implement such a comprehensive urban whole. Even before Brasilia was complete, for example, unplanned shantytowns had formed at its periphery. Informal markets blossomed on street corners, people took to park squares and other urban spaces, and commercial districts sprouted outside the city. Informal, irregular, and unplanned activity was a constant. Here we might take note: various urban inhabitants, many of whom were not stakeholders in the original plans, engaged in unplanned activities in spaces planned for other uses. In Brasilia, it was perhaps inevitable that real urban social life proved too liquid and too unruly for the city envisioned and erected in the high modernist image. That is at least one lesson we might take from Holston's ethnography.

As another insightful urbanist, Marc Augé (2009), suggested, what we see in contemporary cities like Doha—what he termed "supermodernism"—appears to be a continuation of the patterns and the penchants of twentieth-century high modernism. That is the postmodern conundrum—that the past, and its problems, are endlessly recycled and forever with us. Gargantuan urban parcels are the planning norm in Doha, and whatever those urban spaces' flaws may be, those gargantuan urban parcels are accompanied by gargantuan swaths of interstitial urban space. In Doha, as well as in other cities I have investigated, this form of urban space seems to be under frequent and steady social use. Numerous ethnographic cases suggest it is the more marginal elements of society that utilize this interstitial urban space (Constable 1997; Wu and Canham 2008; Bourgois and Schonberg 2009; Menoret 2014; Elsheshtawy 2019b). As others suggested, good urban planning works best when the results are organic and flexible enough to accommodate the unforeseen (Scott 1999; Kolson 2001). Richard Sennett (1970) wrote that only by abandoning the penchant for preplanning, control, and our ongoing attempts to socially engineer life in the city might we meaningfully engage our human capacities and become fully aware of each other.[11]

The informal urbanism that spills into the interstitial urban spaces described here is a testament to the incapacity of supermodernist urban planning to encompass the unruly realities of human social life. In the capital-intensive and tribal authoritarian context of the Arabian Peninsula, it seems likely that the tensions between the energies devoted to urban planning and the unruly realities of human social life will remain defining elements of these cities' futures.

Concluding Thoughts

The three ethnographic excursions that make up this chapter were intended to help readers better glimpse the social and cultural terrain of life in the city of Doha. They are partial glimpses, of course, but each of them speaks to the unique social fabric one encounters in the city. On the one hand, the patterns of this social fabric resemble the city that the urban theorist Christopher Alexander (1977, 44) envisioned many decades ago—"a city made up of a large number of subcultures relatively small in size, each occupying an identifiable place and separated from other subcultures by a boundary of nonresidential land"—a pattern that he termed a "mosaic of subcultures." Harvey (1989, 87) added that these cultural enclaves, zones, and quarters were often associated with strong migration streams, which Doha's experience seems to corroborate. On the other hand, the pattern of the social fabric I have described seems akin to the technoburbs that Robert Fishman (1987, 203) first described just a decade after Alexander. Fishman saw an urban landscape that was little more than a haphazardly planned jumble of discordant urban elements, "fragments in a fragmented environment," as he phrased it. The urban character of Doha, I suggest, lies somewhere between the polarity of Alexander's urban mosaic and this Fishman's fragmentation.

CONCLUSION

A City I Will Never See

The intricate connections between religion and the urban form are fascinating and varied features of human history (Mumford 1961; Buras 2019; Kotkin 2005). Take, for example, the case of Kumbh Mela. In India, huge numbers of people come together every twelve years in a periodic gathering at a major juncture of rivers. There, tens of millions of Hindu devotees bathe in the river waters and celebrate their religious community. A vast temporary city, much of it on poles suspended above the rivers, arises to serve what has been labeled the largest congregation of religious pilgrims in the world (Mehta et al. 2015). Kumbh Mela is a fascinating example of the interplay between religious aspects of culture and the urban forms that grow from human congregation.

In a similar vein, some eight hundred miles to the west of Doha is Mecca, another city whose history is deeply entwined with religious pilgrimage and, more broadly, with human mobility. On the outskirts of Mecca is Mina, the "City of Tents," another sort of ephemeral city. Unlike Kumbh Mela, of course, the remainder of Mecca is not a coagulation of tents and temporary structures but rather a permanent feature of the fantastically beautiful Saudi desert landscape. With all Muslims compelled to attempt, if possible, at least one pilgrimage during the brief flicker of the human lifespan, the whole of the city has expanded in dramatic fashion to accommodate more and more pilgrims. Like Doha and the other cities of the Arabian Peninsula, Mecca has grown in tandem with an array of different mobilities, regional interconnections, and capital accumulations. In the case of Mecca, those mobilities and connections are all tethered to the Kaaba, the elegant holy cubic structure toward which all Muslims pray, and to

FIGURE 17. A traffic sign on approach to Mecca and Medina. Photograph from Wikimedia Commons.

the Grand Mosque that surrounds it. The Saudi King's official title is the "Keeper of the Two Holy Mosques," a testament to the symbolic centrality of the city in Saudi society. This is the city that once enchanted Malcolm X on his pilgrimage in 1964, a year in which Mecca attracted an estimated two hundred thousand pilgrims. Today, that number has ballooned into the millions, and plans are now afoot for the city's infrastructure to accommodate tens of millions of annual pilgrims in the decade to come (Nagraj 2020).

The evolutions of Mecca place it in the ambit of other cities on the Arabian Peninsula. In my analysis of Doha, I have endeavored to discern and identify some of the patterns, attributes, and social relations that might connect Doha's experience with those other cities. Concerning Mecca, however, the parallels with Doha are striking: the ancient neighborhood around the Grand Mosque was mostly bulldozed in past decades, and the Ottoman citadel dating to the eighteenth century—a vestige of previous imperialism—was quietly razed to make way for something new. Mecca is a highly edited urban palimpsest. The financing of Mecca's recent urban redevelopments also blurs the division between the public and private sectors, as seen in Qatar and elsewhere in the GCC and previously discussed in this book. The mountainous amphitheater that once surrounded the holiest of Muslim spaces has been forever altered, with ancient peaks flattened to accommodate new hotels and constructions. The Binladen International Holding Group, the largest of the Kingdom's construction companies and a name familiar to most, completed the US$15 billion Abraj Al Bait project in 2011. Also known as the Golden Clocktower Complex, it is the third tallest building in the world by current measure. The hotel portion of the project includes thousands of luxurious rooms. Those with direct views of the Grand Mosque might readily cost more than US$3,000 per night. The same complex includes a five-story shopping mall with some four thousand retail spaces. This puts Starbucks, Sbarro, Pizza Hut, Burger King, Krispy Kreme, H&M, Cartier, Tiffany, and countless other commercial outposts typical of the planet's commercial junkspace steps away from the holiest of Muslim sites (Koolhaas 2002; Augé 2009).

After viewing the city from a helicopter, Saudi artist and photographer Ahmed Mater remarked that Mecca now seems bathed in green, fluorescent light. He and others now compare Islam's holiest city to Las Vegas (Hubbard 2016). In his explorations of Mecca and with his camera in tow, Mater even spent time in the labor camps of the transnational migrant worker population that resides in Mecca, a workforce present there to help to erect a mostly new city atop the remnants and vestiges of the old. Like Doha, many of those workers dwell in camps now located at the periphery of the city. And in Mecca, even bigger urban changes are afoot: the Kingdom recently announced a truly massive new urban project intended to reshape much of the city. Named Masar, the urban project includes retail, commercial, cultural, and government centers. The plan also calls for tens of thousands of hotel rooms and residences to be added to the city's current stock. The planners, financiers, and the array of corporate partners they have assembled promote the Mecca-to-come with the generic language of cosmopolitan marketing—as "a modern landmark and cultural destination with multiple features" (Arab News, 2020). The recipe for urban development described here, as well as the grandiose unit of urban redevelopment with which these changes have been conceptualized, closely resembles the case of Doha and its growth, as I've presented in this book.

When it comes to Mecca, critics continue to vociferously point to what will be lost with the changes afoot, if they have not been lost already. Ziauddin Sardar first began to witness the ongoing destruction of the city in the 1970s, and had this to say on the topic: "It is through the effort of traveling to Mecca, walking from one ritual site to another, finding and engaging with people from different cultures and sects, and soaking in the history of Islam that the pilgrims acquired knowledge as well as spiritual fulfillment." Or consider the sentiments of Sami Angawi, the founder and former director of the Hajj Research Center: "Races, nationalities and customs, professions and trades and even languages and dialects have all mingled in the crucible of Mecca" (quoted in Mater 2016, 595). Both of these remarks seem eloquent and concise summarizations of the value of diversity long fostered by the pilgrimage to Mecca. But those sentiments also speak to the vitality of the urban milieu more broadly, and are strikingly similar in their phrasing to the value attributed to the cosmopolitan ethos of the city—the value in encountering difference and in engagements with otherness. Yet while cities and spaces can foster these interactions, they can also impede them. Sardar (2014) pointed to the changing nature of Mecca: "Today, hajj is a packaged tour, where you move, tied to your group, from hotel to hotel, and seldom encounter people of different cultures and ethnicities. Drained of history and religious and cultural plurality, hajj is no longer a transforming, once-in-a-lifetime spiritual experience. It has been reduced to a mundane exercise in rituals and shopping."

When it comes to the city of Mecca, there is even more of interest that I can point to here. A quick perusal of the city's recent history points to an alarming legacy of danger. One year, 107 people were killed by a collapsing crane. Another year, 2,236 humans perished in a stampede. Yet another year, that number was 1,426. In 1979, some 50,000 pilgrims were held hostage by a band of Saudi insurgents, and the subsequent battle to control the Grand Mosque lasted nearly two months. Hundreds died, and sixty-three militants were later beheaded. Setting these violences aside, we can continue in another direction, for there is even more here. In Mecca, numerous diasporic communities have long been woven into the fabric of the city. Can we apprehend Mecca, in part, as a city of diasporic refuge? By what arrangements have these communities inhabited the urban landscape for so long? Or, pushing in yet another direction: what is the impact of the closure of the city's famous night market, where religious pilgrims brought their various wares to sell? Have these activities moved to other spaces in the city? And are interstitial urban spaces at play here? I could readily continue, but let me suggest what seems obvious—that Mecca is perhaps the most interesting of the worlding cities on the whole of the Arabian Peninsula and merits the attention of the many diverse urbanists thinking about humanity's urban future.

But this long excursion into the fascinating aspects of contemporary Mecca is intended to preface an altogether different point in the conclusion of this book. Mecca is a city I will never see. The visceral and embodied experience of this urban landscape, and the inherently social aspect of our human collectivity that coalesces in Mecca's streets, all of it drawn to the sacred gravity of the Kaaba at the center of that ancient city—these are features of Mecca I will never experientially know. It is a city and an urban experience from which I am excluded (see figure 17). Knowing it only from afar, peering over the shoulders of this cultural text's authors, and grasping it only through the curated experiences of others, I nonetheless think there is even more of an analytic import here. Does not the *hajj* and the experience of Mecca that I am straining to glimpse gain meaning and vitality through my exclusion? It seems obvious to me that the sacredness at the heart of this city—the essence of the "once-in-a-lifetime spiritual experience" that Sardar described—is a result of the common bond of faith shared by the diversity of pilgrims who annually trek to the city. That common bond and the urban social fabric manifested in Mecca are a product of my exclusion. I see no reason to lament my exclusion other than the unsatiated curiosity of an urbanist, I suppose. For me to lament my exclusion would smack of an American sort of entitlement, would it not?

It is in this sustained musing about Mecca that readers might be able to first intuit the value of exclusion that I wish to assert here. Drawing again on Douglas (1966) and the tradition of structural anthropology, it seems clear that exclusion, meaning, and urbanists' sense of place are all intricately entwined. Another place I think we can see the same value to exclusion is in the Qatari experience that I have sought to portray in this book. In my analysis, the most important mechanism by which the Qataris have managed and shaped that experience is the city itself. In more specificity: through the segmentation of the workforce and the consolidation of Qatari citizens in the public sector; by insulating themselves in neighborhoods clustered in the urban landscape; by the maintenance of some approximation of endogamy; by continuing to speak Arabic in those spaces and to each other; by tending to and maintaining social relations we might recognize as "traditional"; and foremost, by building an archipelago of discrete urban spaces in which all of it might take shape—all of this helps explain the prominence of Qatari social distinction and its enduring definition. This perseverance is all the more remarkable in light of the sea of foreigners that inhabit the Qatari Peninsula, and the preponderance of foreign matter in the urban landscape constructed there. The perseverance of Qatari society, and the coherence of the culture that emanates from it, is an anthropologically noteworthy fact.

Imagine if this book had been framed differently and had commenced with a different core assertion: This ethnography tells the story of a small set of Arab tribes and the society that congealed around them in history. Under the seemingly incessant siege of the forces of modernity, constantly reckoning with the impending possibilities of cultural change, growing increasingly interconnected with the capitalist world system, and navigating overlapping and complicated relations with a sequence of powerful imperial forces all the while, Qatari social and cultural distinction has somehow persevered into the contemporary era. Again: this assertion is all the more astonishing when one considers the super-diverse demographics of the city, and the Qatari people's fragmentary portion of that demographic whole. And also again: as this book suggests, the city itself has a lot to do with the preservation and the perseverance of the Qatari way of life. With the central role of the city in the calculus of my argument, I think another point merits even further emphasis here: the perseverance of Qatari social and cultural distinction requires space, and in this case, urban space.

The same is true, I suggest, for many other residents of Doha in this era of mobility. A legion of foreign workers has been attracted to the peninsula and to the opportunities available there. Almost none of them wish to integrate into Qatari society nor remain on the peninsula in old age. In an era that seems to demand mobility and to compel their migration away from their homes, most of those foreign workers keep their gaze steadily trained on their faraway homes, at least in part. The major portion of migrants' paychecks are regularly remitted to those households in distant lands, and a transnational migrant worker's savings, modest as it may be, is commonly earmarked for the maintenance of those other ways of life. Through their earnings and energies, migrants seek to remain a part of a society grounded in another place, to buy land or build a better home there, to pay for children's education or for a daughter's dowry, to save enough to return home and eventually retire. Their aspirations are territorialized. In the interim, migrants' contractual vacation months—time to be spent at home every year or two—are anticipated with great energy and planning. In summary, the many and diverse foreigners present in Qatar are quintessentially transnational creatures, as are the livelihood systems they build and to which they contribute.

All of this is to say that the spatial segregation of various communities in the urban landscape of Doha has some positive aspects and features with which we need to reckon. Those urban spaces and places in the city often have a cultural gravity, of which we should take note.

Urban Space and the Territorial Gravity of Culture

To assess the enclaves, zones, and precincts produced by the urban spatial discourse undergirding Doha's growth and to take measure of the cultural gravity I see in those enclaves and spaces, we might commence with an assessment of the practical utility of these arrangements. Many of the enclaves, compounds,

camps, and zones encountered in Doha's urban landscape provide linguistic, cultural, and culinarily familiar spaces for humans borne on the tides of this era of
mobility. Those spaces and places are where transnational migrants might land
upon arrival, assess the horizons before them, where they might gather information from others, glean advice from veteran migrants, and take a deep breath
as they gird themselves for whatever challenges they face next. Those enclaves,
compounds, camps, and zones—also those neighborhoods, districts, precincts,
and various other urban spaces—are the spaces where culture, always a collective endeavor, might take root and perhaps even flourish. It is the abstract relationship between culture and space that is my eventual destination here, but I
want to linger for a moment more on the recurring practical utility of this cohesion and the segregation of difference.

In 1992, after four years of college, I moved to New York City. My first apartment there was on 6th Street on the Lower East Side, just a block off Tompkins
Square Park. With a close friend, I shared an overpriced studio located on the
same block as nearly a dozen Indian restaurants. There were no Indian restaurants on the next street over nor two blocks east past Avenue A. Rather those
restaurants gathered together in the urban landscape by choice. Similarly, after
the conflict in Indochina was finally quelled and the Americans were expelled,
Vietnamese immigrants to the United States began to remake the neighborhood
up the hill from Seattle's International District. With an evident abundance of
entrepreneurial energy, this resulted in a busy neighborhood referred to as Little
Saigon. We see the same cultural gravity in the urban landscapes of Arabia. Indian restaurants, businesses, and residences gather in the urban space around
the century-old Indian Club of Bahrain. Bangladeshi migrant entrepreneurs
commandeer an abandoned superblock in the urban heart of Abu Dhabi, and it
becomes ephemerally refashioned as Little Bangladesh (Elsheshtawy 2017). Villages and regions from throughout South Asia stake out geographical claims in
the parking lots surrounding the Al Attiyah market on a Friday afternoon in
Doha (see figure 9).[1] Similarly, although usually assigned to their labor camps
by their employers, transnational labor migrants commonly sort themselves into
rooms within those camps, and cohabit with roommates similar in terms nationality, language, religion, style, and various other facets of human existence
that fall under the umbrella of culture. Even more examples are possible here,
but all of this charts the cultural gravity that I discern as a recurring social feature of the urban landscape. Humans are social creatures, and culture is oftentimes the core element of the gravity that pulls us together in space. In a world
where hundreds of millions of people are on the move—the defining feature of
the era of mobility, as I have termed it—our cohesion in urban space around this
gravity has a practical utility.

In addition to the practical facets of the cultural gravity that I have described, there is also a more philosophical angle on the separation, segregation, and maintenance of cultural distinction that merits articulation here. This justification begins with the value of cultural diversity and difference—a value long perceived as integral to the urban milieu. Like many urbanists before her, for example, Jane Jacobs (1961) praised the diversity of the urban environment and dedicated her life to its protection. In New York City, Jacobs saw neighbors and strangers woven together in an urban social fabric that she praised. There she took note of what she called "sidewalk ballet," the subconscious order beneath the veneer of disorder and chaos that one might first perceive in the city. Similarly, Lewis Mumford spoke glowingly of the special quality of life in the city. From his vantage point, "only in a city can the full cast of characters for the human drama be assembled." In dialogue with those who are different from us, we might take "the first step out of that tribal conformity which is an obstacle to self-consciousness and to development," Mumford (1961, 116–117) concluded. These sentiments sound strikingly similar to Ziauddin Sardar's remarks about the *hajj*; it is through the engagement with difference that we humans might find spiritual enlightenment.

The enduring value of diversity to the urban milieu is a correlation that many would agree is now axiomatic. And as previously noted, estimations of the value of urban diversity tread essentially the same ground as those theorists concerned with cosmopolitanism and the cosmopolitan ethos. The anthropologist Ulf Hannerz (2005, 200) defined cosmopolitanism as "an intellectual and aesthetic openness toward divergent cultural experiences." That definition will suffice for our purposes here, but the reader might note that matters of cosmopolitanism's definition preoccupy much of the concept's elaboration over the last two decades. With Hannerz's basic definition in hand one can at least perceive the proximity of the cosmopolitan ethos to urbanists' praise of diversity in the city.[2] Those two conversations come together in Elijah Anderson's (2011, 276) conceptualization of the urban spaces he identifies as "cosmopolitan canopies." Drawing from his observations of Philadelphia, the city that is his home, Anderson theorizes the functional value of urban spaces in fostering this cosmopolitan ethos. These spaces convene various inhabitants of the city, and, as he states, "provide an opportunity for diverse strangers to become better acquainted with people they otherwise seldom observe up close." A historic market in Philadelphia serves as Anderson's prototypical example. Continuing, Anderson adds that "when people exposed to all this return to their own neighborhoods, they may do so with a more grounded knowledge of the other than was possible without such experience."

What initially caught my attention in this assertion, and what remains vital to the argument I am assembling in this conclusion, is not the places in the city where differences come together and interact, although those spaces are a welcome addition to our urban landscapes. Rather, I think our attention should be levied at the places to which people return, as Anderson passingly describes. I am interested in the implications of this return to one's "own neighborhood" in the city. The value that Anderson perceives in the cosmopolitan canopy is the value of diversity and the positive benefits of engagement with difference. The differences of importance here are not individuals' many differences—for example, that I met a particularly tall woman at the market, or that a red-headed server publicly berated me in the food court. Rather, the "grounded knowledge" of otherness, as Anderson describes it, and what one "brings back" to one's neighborhood are experiential understandings most conveniently glossed by the concept of culture. And here, then, is the key point: the magic that Anderson perceives in these cosmopolitan canopies is a magic premised on the cultural differences between the individuals in interaction. To continue to benefit from the energy of these interactions, the cultural differences involved need to be maintained.

The urban theorist Christopher Alexander intuited this fact many decades ago. He argued that the preservation of subcultures in the urban landscape was an ecological matter—"that distinct subcultures will only survive, as distinct subcultures, if they are physically separated in space" (Alexander 1977, 49).[3] Doha seems noteworthy for achieving this outcome: squarely amid the era of mobility as we humans are, facing an urban future that will seemingly contain larger and larger waves of people pulled, impelled, forced, or drawn from their homes to a life on the move, the preservation of human diversity is a more pressing issue than ever. Without the urban ecology to preserve those differences, those differences will eventually blend together, and what "appears heterogeneous turns out to be homogenous and dull" (Alexander 1977, 43). From this angle, we might appreciate the city of Doha and the urban spatial discourse that shapes the experiences of the many different peoples who inhabit it.

The constraints, exclusions, segregations, borders, zonings, and various limitations on human mobility have proven to be dangerous tools in human history.[4] But as Frank Furedi (2020, 11) contended, "humanity has always been in the business of drawing lines," and the simplistic and often wholesale indictment of borders and boundaries currently fashionable in American academia purveys a perspective deeply ignorant of the spatial foundations of public life and the spatial dimension of human culture. As this book has sought to demonstrate, Qatar is an exceptionally busy and notably diverse urban juncture in the contemporary world. Despite the plural and heterogeneous nature of this urban juncture, Qatari distinction and social cohesion remain strong. For the many others who work for the Qataris, also, Doha seems to allow those inhabitants to maintain their cultural and social distinction. Is it possible that they, too, gain something from Qatari exclusion? Regardless: this diversity and its maintenance is pinned to the organization of urban space in Doha, and to the enduring truth that culture is a collective project that requires a territorial footprint. In *barzakh*, in the Ottoman millet system, in the arrangements of the historical port cities that emerged in tandem with the circuits of trade in the Indian Ocean World—the intricate balance of togetherness, distinction, and difference have, for centuries, been managed and maintained in ways that are unfamiliar to Western cities and to most American thinkers (Barkey 2005; Gupta 2008; Eldem 2013; cooke 2014; Barkey and Gravilis 2014; Roberts 2021). As anthropologists have argued for more than a century, our cultural diversity is perhaps humankind's greatest achievement and asset. The preservation of that diversity in the era of mobility is an objective that merits our collective attention and our energies.

The Antipathy for Exclusion

In closing, I want to begin with the sentiments of the anthropologist Marc Augé, from his introduction to the second edition of *Non-Places*. Augé (2009, ix) says: "The ideal, egalitarian world may come not through the abolition of frontiers, but through their recognition." In my estimation, the task to which our species should aspire is to aptly manage this planet and its resources and to manage its various frontiers as best we can, starting now, if not earlier. As we navigate new policy realms in the governance of human mobility, we will do so with the nation-states, the borders, and the legal regimes that currently occupy our maps. Scholars, researchers, and policymakers need to maintain a level-headed and evidence-based conversation about the preservation of human diversity in navigating our challenging global future. As an anthropologist, I am particularly concerned with the differences between humans that take social and cultural forms. The premise of this needed conversation about the maintenance of human cultural diversity should be the very same premise upon which the whole of anthropology was built long ago—that human diversity has an inherent and strategic value. As Augé (2009, xv) continued: "our ideal ought not to be a world without frontiers, but one where all frontiers are recognized, respected and permeable; a world, in fact, where respect for differences would start with the equality of all individuals, independent of their origin or gender."

This ethnography is offered as an empirical contribution that might help inform that conversation. As I noted in the preface of this book, I believe there is so very much for us to learn from the Qatari experience and from the city they have constructed in the desert. This book is offered as an addition to the ethnographic canon. In recent years, I have returned to the depths of that canon with great energy, and with a growing admiration for the commitment to impartiality typical of my many predecessors' ethnographic engagements with social and cultural otherness. I have tried to replicate their commitment here, although this book has the added complexity of being not just about otherness but about others' engagement with otherness. In plumbing the depths of the ethnographic canon, however, it has also dawned on me that readers of this book—should there be any at all—will likely mine this ethnography for details and threads that I cannot perceive from my vista point in the present. It seems likely that a level-headed and evidence-based conversation about the preservation of cultural diversity during this era of mobility will be a difficult conversation to properly cultivate. With the impending and more immediate future in mind, I see numerous challenges and impediments to the conversation that we must have about the maintenance of cultural diversity in this era.

First, the neoliberal capitalist world system is now clearly in full possession of the entire planet. That economic system and the social relations it conjures continue to generate inequalities that are deeply woven into capitalism's DNA. The permutations and evolutions of state, society, and city emanating from the common foundation of global capitalism are one of the themes to which this ethnography might speak. But in the contemporary era, the energies with which some academicians seek to combat the production of that global inequality are frequently misdirected against the very nature of difference itself. The expression of difference, and particularly its manifestation in the form of culture, should not be misapprehended as a proxy for economic inequality. Nor should the ethnographer's interest (or the cosmopolitan's interest) in engaging that difference be mistaken for political or moral support for the underlying engines of economic inequality. The economic inequalities generated by capitalist relations are quintessentially problems of a global scope, and are thus shared by all. In the endeavor to redress that inequality—an endeavor shared by some—we must not sacrifice our commitment to diversity and to the value of human difference.

A second point of potential friction, and a challenge to any level-headed conversation about the preservation of cultural diversity, concerns the nation-state and the policy environment constructed around it. Anthropologists see the world as a mosaic of social and cultural differences accumulated over the longue durée of human history. Boundaries and the borders of nation-states were somewhat recently erected atop this mosaic of difference, and therefore imposed on the blurry continuum of human variability. There is much to both understand and lament in the excavation of this history of the present. But we must attempt to set those lamentations aside, difficult as that may be; the best tools with which we might navigate our impending global future are those of the nation-state and the various political regimes that lay before us today. It is worth adding that, in addition to being the best tools for the planetary challenges at hand, they are also the only tools appropriate to global governance that we possess unless one maintains some glimmer of hope for the boisterous populism of the social mediasphere, now more carefully curated than ever by the planet's largest profit-seeking corporations, most of which are based in America. Suffice it to say, as flawed as they are, I perceive the apparatuses of the nation-state as integral to our collective path forward.

The third potential friction I see concerns the dire need to maintain an inclusive and diverse scholarly conversation about the urban future that lies ahead for our species. Taking stock of where we commenced the twentieth century, our progress on this front has been extraordinarily immense. Our ongoing conversation about our planetary future—a future that also seems inevitably urban—must embrace the scope of human diversity, and must continue to plunder the depths of our understandings of that diversity as we seek guidance and wisdom on the journey ahead. Despite the fireworks and various performative confrontations to the contrary, however, I believe the American dominion over this conversation remains stronger than ever, and movements to decolonize those conversations are oftentimes nothing more than a charade in subconscious fealty to American hegemony. In light of this book's sustained consideration of migration, the city, and difference, I suggest that we can see that American dominion at a few key junctures.

Foremost, that American dominion is the taproot of the deep antipathy for boundaries, segregation, and borders of any form. In part, that antipathy is a projection of American privilege, and the planetary command of the American ethos that grew from the collapse of the Cold War and the full extension of neoliberal conditions to all corners of the globe. But that antipathy also projects the privileges integral to American citizenship and the domain of the American national container to the global ecumene; it transposes the rights of mobility configured in the national container to the domain of the entire planet. In both senses, we can take stock of America's durable hegemony in the global ideoscape, and then perhaps recognize what this antipathy to boundaries, segregation, and borders eclipses in our assessment of city and society. The histories of other places and other cities—including Qatar—are replete with divisions, segmentations, segregations, and limitations on human mobility and movement. The Ottoman Empire's millet system is just one example, albeit a pertinent example to the region. The broader Indian Ocean World provides a host of other examples in its multifaceted history, and the contemporary permutations of space and distinction in Doha echo aspects and portions of those historical arrangements. In more fairly assessing the arrangements and exclusions orchestrated by the city of Doha, we need to better apprehend the positive qualities rendered by these spatializations and their value to people on the move.

Another place where we might take an estimate of this American hegemony and its occlusion of our capacity to grapple with the value of cultural difference is the mirror image of the point above. Along with the antipathy for boundaries, segregation, and borders, the fetishization of integration and inclusion permeates many global scholarly conversations today. Similarly, it suffuses the conceptual tools with which those conversations are commonly articulated. Here, again, we see the distillation of objectives that were tailored in various long-standing conversations about the American national container being projected upon the whole of the global ecumene and upon various states in that domain. In Qatar, few citizens wish for the legion of foreign workers to integrate into their society. Likewise, few of the foreign workers present on the peninsula and in the city wish to remain in Doha or, more specifically, wish to integrate into Qatari society. To appropriately take stock of the city, migration, and mobilities characteristic of the contemporary era, we must dethrone the American penchant for inclusion, and we must undermine the centrality of the aspiration for integration in our social world. Conversely, the capacity for distinction and the maintenance of difference should be promoted where possible.

Yet another locus for this American hegemony is in the referential centrality of the United States and its cities in those global scholarly conversations. In a previous era of scholarship, American centrality was typically ensconced in various assertions of progress and civilizational stature, for which the United States served as a model in many estimations. In the contemporary era, the United States remains a central reference point, albeit now more often encountered as the negative space promulgated by a bursting legion of academic guilt-mongers. These tactics inhibit meaningful engagement with difference and otherness. To foster an inclusive and diverse scholarly conversation about our planetary future and the cities that will comprise it, we need to open the scholarly conversation to other values, other experiences, and to a discussion of other configurations of city and society. Over more than a century, anthropology and its ethnographic toolkit have been configured precisely to this purpose. Perhaps anthropology's holistic grasp of otherness might provide some antidote to the epistemological and ontological infrastructure of American hegemony. As I have sought to portray in this book foremost with the concept of a social prism, portions of that hegemony lie in the concepts and categories by which we assemble our understandings of difference and distinction and by which various social movements then congeal. I offer this ethnography of city, space, and people in an attempt to spark a conversation removed from the ambit of that hegemony.

Postscript

This is a strange time to be an American scholar. It is perhaps an even stranger time to be an anthropologist. In this era, the roving and mercurial gaze of others in the intellectual ecosystem I inhabit oftentimes disregards arguments, evidence, reason, and logic. Instead, critics seem more concerned with who has the right to speak, and how the perceived moral code conveyed by the speaker's ideas might or might not be construed. For an anthropologist whose intent is to talk about the noteworthy, troubling, fascinating, and sometimes captivating aspects of other places, other cities, and the other people who occupy those locations, these conditions have resulted in a particularly perplexing moment to have offered readers this book.

At this perplexing historical moment, the objectives and analytic themes I describe are oftentimes eclipsed by a set of issues that present themselves as more pressing and immediate than those that preoccupy me here. In their American iteration, those more pressing issues mostly orbit around what we now refer to as identity, around the American iteration of the socially constructed idea of race, and around the enduring landscape of inequality that continues to characterize the human world, as it always has. In the projection of those issues upon the disciplinary heart of contemporary anthropology, and upon the simple act of someone like me offering the book you have just read, two sets of concerns have arisen that seem necessary to address in this postscript. They are necessary in the sense that they matter so dearly to disciples of the paradigm that currently dominates my discipline and all of the American academia in the early decades of the twenty-first century.

The first tier of those concerns is about who is speaking. In essence, there is concern about me, the author of this text. For the record, I am a white, middle-aged American male who commenced life in America's lower middle class. Through my parents' effort and success, I entered adulthood with a family solidly (if briefly) lodged in America's upper middle class. Significant portions of my childhood and my adulthood were spent living outside the United States. In childhood, I was first outside the United States as my parents chased opportunity. In adulthood, I was outside the United States as I chased my own opportunities, most of which concerned ethnographic fieldwork and the pursuit of my PhD. In the context of that fieldwork and the research projects underpinning the analyses presented in this book, those qualities of mine—my whiteness, my

American passport, and my male gender—opened many doors for me. Simultaneously, and obvious to anyone familiar with the societies present on the Arabian Peninsula, those same qualities also closed other doors to me, including some that are of great interest to anthropology.[1] Notably, these particular aspects of one's identity—and here, also take note of the departure of "subjectivity" from our conceptual vocabulary—increasingly typify how we Americans gauge one another.[2] Regardless, I am unsure if these basic and personal details will satiate readers who bring these sorts of concerns to their engagement with a text like this. I suspect they will not.

Although much of American academia is brightly concerned with these aspects of human identity, anthropology actually digested many of these concerns several decades ago in the discipline's "reflexive turn." A by-product of the rise of postmodernism, in the early 1990s anthropologists began to focus intently on the ethical implications of our capacity to portray otherness in this world, and more broadly, on our long-standing intellectual commitment to grappling with the social and cultural forms that comprise human diversity. These concerns were magnified by the fact that, via the method and craft of ethnography, the anthropologist's persona and character are, simultaneously, her or his primary research instrument. We anthropologists immerse ourselves in other cultural worlds, and in doing so, we seek to learn, to holistically describe, and to impartially analyze what we see and what we encounter. We do so from whatever vista point we are able to establish therein. With anthropology's "reflexive turn" now entering its fourth decade, its various frictions and polemics strangely endure and abound.[3] In recognition of those seemingly endless frictions, this book has taken the pathway that Nancy Scheper-Hughes (1992) discerned long ago with her conceptualization of "good-enough ethnography." Anthropologists should feel compelled to remain attentive to the reflexive issues described above and to the politics of representation at their heart. But that attentiveness should never be allowed to compromise our interest and our proven capacity to conduct meaningful ethnographic work about others. Our long-standing objective as anthropologists—to cross thresholds of cultural difference with empathy on a mission of understanding—should endure.

A second tier of concerns, beyond the ad hominem aspects detailed above, inquire about my beliefs, my ideals, and the ideological commitments I have brought to the authorship of this text, and thereby imply that the objective of impartiality is a mirage. While attacks on the objective of impartial assessment are both preposterous and debilitating, here I will turn to those beliefs, ideals, and commitments, although I suspect they are already apparent. Where shall I start? Perhaps I should start with some caveats. Like Peter Zeihan (2022, 471), who I was reading as this manuscript went through its penultimate edit, I am a student of history, an internationalist, a long-standing environmentalist, and a democrat (that's a small d). But unlike many others who may share some of that ground, my beliefs and ideals are tempered by a scientific commitment to impartiality and an anthropological commitment to a form of cultural relativism. What I think, believe, and what I might wish the world (or Qatar) to look like is less important to what you have encountered in this book than it is for many of my contemporary colleagues. That is the strange and interesting overlapping space between scientific impartiality and anthropological relativism—and the essence of the objectivity that Lévi-Strauss envisioned for anthropology in the quote I presented in the preface to this book.

Let me attempt to be even more specific. If it is not already evident, I am deeply committed to understanding the world as it is, and from the waning privilege of my American positionality, to improving that world for others as best I can. Those twin commitments, in varying proportions, characterize most of my work as a scholar, a researcher, a teacher, and an academician. This book has been more directed at explanation and understanding and less at the objective of improving or reshaping the world in some manner or other.[4] In addition to those fundamental ideological commitments, I have further allegiances that might be of interest. I believe the most significant event in recent human history is the global expansion of the capitalist system over the last five centuries, a historical expansion so magisterially illuminated by anthropologists Eric Wolf (1982) and Sidney Mintz (1986). This expansion was a stunning human achievement that is deeply implicated in almost all of the human achievements we venerate today, and also the culprit behind many of humankind's most significant challenges we face. And in terms of my allegiances and beliefs, there is even more, much of which might also already be apparent to readers. Along with Marvin Harris, I believe that the values we hold dear, and the system in which those values cohere, is a collective adaptation to human existence that we usefully term *culture*. To summarize Harris's pithy phrasing (1979, ix): "human social life is a response to the practical problems of earthly existence."

Additionally, like the generations of anthropologists before me, I am fascinated by the many different ways that humans distinguish and categorize both others and themselves—caste, class, tribe, age set, clan, race, religion, ancestry, moiety, gender, ethnicity, and a dozen other cultural ingenuities that pepper the ethnographic canon. I have termed those culturally different ways of categorizing difference a *social prism*—a concept I have coined for the culturally specific and clearly differentiable modes for subdividing the blurry terrain of human difference. I sought to explain my conceptualization of the social prism at some length in the earliest chapters of this book, but that blurry continuum of human difference merits one additional point here. I share Paul Gilroy's conviction

(2000) that science points to a planetary humanism, and to the foundational equality that underpins anthropology's long exploration of cultural difference. As anthropologists have been arguing for over a century, we human beings are all cut from the same cloth.

I believe both of the questions I have endeavored to answer in this postscript—who is this author and what does he believe—are symptomatic of deeper problems with intellectual discourse in American academia today. I hope that my evidence and my analysis of it were gauged on its own merit. But let me clarify this point even further: while a part of me chafes at the questions I have addressed here, I recognize those answers do have a particular value to anthropology, for again, in ethnography *we ourselves are the research instrument*. Despite those reservations about questions that seem personal, I am more broadly supportive of inquiries and transparency around funding. As we all know, or at least ought to know, following the money is oftentimes key.

In building this book, sustained financial support for the research underpinning it resulted foremost from my job as a tenured professor at a private liberal arts college in the United States, a vocation squarely premised on the steep slope of American inequality.[5] The research monies underpinning the sequence of projects I have conducted over two decades include funding from the Qatar National Research Fund, Qatar University, the Fulbright Foundation, with support from the Bahrain Training Institute, and with additional funding from the Wenner-Gren Foundation, from the REALM research unit at Columbia University, from George Soros' Open Society Foundation, and from a few other sources. I also received research monies and other forms of support from my employer, the University of Puget Sound. As you should expect, however, the words, ideas, and analyses I have presented here are entirely my responsibility, although they are a bricolage of others' ideas, works, and creativity. All said, in the two decades of work underpinning this monograph, the most intense pressures I have felt concerning the explication of my analyses and findings have been from the intentions and preferences that other foreign colleagues, acquaintances, and supervisors imagine the Qataris to possess, something I discussed in more detail in the penultimate chapter of the book. Notably, I have encountered equally intense pressures emanating from the campus culture in which I exist and from American academia more broadly. Via those pressures, hegemonic forces seek to govern analytic trajectories and delimit scholarly conversations at both the conceptual and discursive levels.[6] In this book, I have tried to disregard those pressures as best I can, albeit with the result of an analysis that is seemingly out of alignment with the dominant American paradigm of the day and with the crusaders in its vanguard.

But there is more to this issue. From my vantage point, many of these contemporary American academic concerns and pressures have coalesced in the increasingly thin ethnographic portrayals of the people who occupy other cultural realms in the contemporary world. Complexities, ambivalences, compromises, contingencies, certainly joy, and countless other aspects of the endlessly mercurial human soul were always essential features of the humanity that anthropology found in all of the many peoples it has considered so far. These threads and nuances are long-standing features in the discipline's impressive ethnographic canon—an encyclopedia of cultural diversity that is unparalleled in human history. In an intellectual era preoccupied almost entirely with power and inequality, and endlessly fixated on the shifting therapeutic terrain of how people feel, anthropology's portrayals of otherness (however the anthropologist might construe that otherness) seem increasingly desiccated, sadly pessimistic, and so thoroughly American in terms of the social prism those analyses typically purvey.[7] This ethnography has searched for some oxygen beyond the bounds of that hegemony.

To return to the framing with which the book commenced, I hope that this text has productively contributed to the growing ethnographic canon that will inform how we humans might cohabitate in the cities that will carry us into our planetary future. And I hope that it might contribute in some small way to the preservation of cultural diversity and the veneration of difference on our tumultuous planet.

Notes

PREFACE

1. I myself conformed to this practice in my previous books.

2. This is akin to what Molotch and Ponzini (2019, 3) describe as the objective of "restraining judgement." It is interesting that they come to that conclusion amid a discussion of the book *Learning from Las Vegas* (Venturi, Scott, and Izenour 1972)—the visually intensive tome that was, arguably, the watershed moment in ushering postmodernist concerns into architecture, urban planning, and urban studies. Notably, those postmodernist concerns are equally implicated in the long and sustained indictment of the impartiality underpinning the objective of "restraining judgement."

INTRODUCTION

1. Divendra and all the names of migrants and other interlocutors that appear in this book are pseudonyms. Portions of Divendra's story, utilizing the same pseudonym, are further elucidated elsewhere (Gardner 2012, 2015a).

2. It was in stories like these that I envisioned the fact that many of these migrants were dreaming of a meritocracy of sorts—a place where their achieved capacities might meet with opportunity.

3. Kathiravelu (2016, 10–12) makes this same point and contends that migrants' omission is a result of the national identity projects underway on the Arabian Peninsula. While this is certainly astute, her emphasis is on the omission of their contribution rather than their mere presence. That logic also pardons the successive waves of scholars and academics who have sought to address the busy juncture of city and society in Arabia.

4. For example, Buras (2019) sees the legacy of good planning everywhere in human history. In summary, the diversity and differences that Rudofsky (1964) helped us glimpse are now fully digested and central to our thinking about the city.

5. Kolson (2001) provides an insightful overview of the pre-Columbian urban history of North America, and one that is particularly attentive to hierarchy, differences, and the remnants of the built form. Some phrases gleaned from his captivating chapter on the topic include aspects of urban societies in North America that were "minutely ranked," "highly regimented," clearly prone to "endemic warfare," driven by "extraordinary competition," forged via "intense warfare," manifesting "social differentiation" and a "powerful centralized authority," with signs of "apparent cannibalism" in places, and mostly consisting of "ranked societies" with clear evidence of the "division of labor."

6. Speaking particularly to inequality in the Arab world, Raymond describes the deep history of inequality in the social structure underpinning Arab cities and points to the good historical evidence of that inequality. More than just an enduring form of inequality, Raymond (2008, 68) also takes note of the scale of this inequality, and at one point describes it as "an inequality so huge."

7. Here I am struck by the parallels with Orlando Patterson's assertion (2018, xxix) that freedom, and our understanding of it, are intricately tied to the human history of slavery in all of its global manifestations. As he explains: "Before slavery people simply could not have conceived of the thing we call freedom. Men and women in premodern, non-slaveholding societies did not, could not, value the removal of restraint as an ideal"

157

(Patterson 2018, 340). Similarly, one might contend that only amid the various landscapes of inequality, and the various despotisms that emerged in tandem with them, did the democratic idea of sharing power come into vision as a desirable possibility.

8. Fine examples would include Friedrich Engels (1993), Mike Davis (1990), and W. E. B. DuBois (2010), but many others would fit on this list as well.

9. Mumford was clearly also a proponent of this broader estimation of difference and the value of the diversities that coalesced the city. For Mumford (1961, 34), "The city was the container that brought about this implosion, and through its very form held together the new forces, intensified their internal reactions, and raised the whole level of achievement."

10. Lewis Mumford (1961, 34) again: "As with a gas, the very pressure of the molecules within that limited space produced more social collisions and interactions within a generation than would have occurred in many centuries if still isolated in their native habitats, without boundaries."

11. As McDonough (2009, 11) notes, "For the [French] Situationists, cities were profoundly historical landscapes, whose current appearances were shaped . . . by the successive events that time has buried, though never completely effaced." Interestingly, Kolson (2001, 184) carries this point even further in suggesting that great urban spaces, by definition, are those that willingly accommodate the cultural detritus of the past. A decade earlier, however, Harvey (1989) was careful to note that this palimpsest was certainly a text edited by the political-economic forces that are at the center of his focus.

12. See Dresch (2006) and (Salama and Wiedmann 2013, 20), for example. I found Al-Nakib's explication (2016, 58–69) to be particularly insightful and clear.

13. This is a widely purveyed reading of Boas. Several of the memorable works in my own digestion of this critique include Gupta and Ferguson (1997), Marcus and Fischer (1986), and Moore (1999). Eric Wolf (1982, 6) noted that in the aftermath of Boas, cultures were too often envisioned as bounded objects, "like so many hard and round billiard balls."

14. Perhaps it is also not a coincidence that these critiques arrived in the aftermath of the postmodern turn, a philosophical conglomeration of ideas that draw their principal energies from the task of destabilizing and deconstructing any coherent knowledge structures inherited from the past.

15. Molotch and Ponzini (2019, 26) make a similar and general point about the dominance of the Western city in our understanding of the urban processes endemic to all global cities.

16. See Bashkow (2004, 445) for an excellent discussion of Lowie.

17. When chronologically framed by the longue durée, claims to have been in some place for "time immemorial" often morph into more pedestrian claims—to have been some place just prior to more recent arrivals, or perhaps to have been in some place for a longer period than those newer arrivals.

18. We might also recognize the *bedu/hadhar* bifurcation of Arabian societies' tradition as a social prism reified by generations of social scientists. See both Longva (2006) and Al-Nakib (2014) for particularly illuminating discussions of this aspect of the Kuwaiti social prism.

1. FRIDAY ETHNOGRAPHY AND THE CITY

1. Caroline Osella via personal communication.

2. Seth Holmes (2013) provides a fine example of that anthropological intrepidity in his journey with undocumented migrants across the Mexican-American border.

3. I conducted fieldwork in Saudi Arabia for two months in 1999. I later resided in Al Ain (in the United Arab Emirates) for three months in the summer of 2002. Later in 2002

and for much of 2003, I resided in Bahrain, where I conducted ethnographic fieldwork for my dissertation. Subsequently, between 2008 and 2010 my family and I resided in Doha during my employment at Qatar University. Finally, in addition to these periods of residence in Arabia, a series of projects commencing in 2010 allowed for periodic visits for work and research, resulting in numerous years in which I spent more than a month on the ground in Qatar.

4. Don Stull, who was at the time the editor of *Human Organization*, once pointed out to me that "lived experience" seems to be the only sort of experience available to us humans.

5. In reflection of this fact, I have also left out the denotation of [*sic*] in the various verbatim quotes in this text. That denotation, signifying "as written," connotes an error or a recognizable grammatical mistake. These denotations would unnecessarily clutter the analyses presented here, particularly given that English is a second or third language for many of my informants.

6. See Walter Benjamin (1999, 443) not only for this quote but also for a broader discussion of Baudelaire's articulation of an early idea of modernity, a conceptualization entwined with life in the urban metropolis.

7. Yasser Elsheshtawy (2022, 178–180) provides a clear overview of drifting, its history, and pedestrian-focused approaches to the city.

8. See also Wolfe (2016) and his notion of the "urban diary"; Brogden (2019, 13) and his conviction that "walking provides an important slowing-down encounter with the urban landscape, as part of an essential phenomenological element within 'lived experience;'" or Klinenberg's intuition (2018, 4) that by being there, "at ground level I would observe certain neighborhood conditions that aren't visible in quantitative data." Similarly, see Elsheshtawy 2010, 60.

9. In addition to those described here, see Buras (2019), Elsheshtawy (2022), Gehl (2011), Koolhaas (1995), Mater (2016), Mehrotra and Vera (2015), Rudofsky (1964). See Natasi (2019) for a discussion specific to the role and circulation of images of Arabian cities.

2. INVISIBLE GAS

1. As Hopper (2015, 9) reports, slaves comprised an estimated 22 percent of Qatar's population in 1905, a result of the increasing global demand for dates and pearls, the two primary exports of that era. While the slaves of African descent remain of central focus, European-led abolishment and interference with the African source countries shifted the Middle Eastern slave trade to Baluchistan, and "by the 1920s had replaced East Africa as the main source of new labor for eastern Arabian markets" (Hopper 2015, 203).

2. See Geertz (1973) and Anderson (2006). If you have not spent time with Anderson's footnotes in *Imagined Communities*, I would highly recommend their perusal, particularly in consideration of the fact that your curiosity evidently brought you here.

3. See Hewison (1987, 45–47). Dresch (2006, 206) perceived the "industry of nostalgia" that developed around notions of authenticity and the neighborhoods the Gulf Arabs collectively imagined in their past.

4. There are plenty of examples, but I am struck by the words of Ibrahim bin Saleh Bu Matar al-Muhannadi: "We were much better off in those days, believe me. Don't be deceived by appearances. In those days, people were more generous and sincere . . . they were honest with each other" (quoted in Othman 1984, 49).

5. Here again, I am drawing on the image of the state and the society provided by Onley and Khalaf (2006).

6. See Samin (2017, 149–153) for a similar description of Saudi Arabia.

7. Alshehabi (2019) sees four key characteristics to the petro-modernist state: ensuring the centrality of the ruling families at the apex of the state's political structure; to

produce a population loyal to the ruling families and committed to the petri-nationalist state; the establishment of a vast welfare state to care for the citizenry; and to carefully and adroitly deploy contemporary technological advances while simultaneously preserving traditional premodern relations.

8. Consider other perspectives on the rentier state as well: before his killing in 2004, one of the founding leaders of al-Qaeda on the Arabian Peninsula, 'Abd al-'Aziz al-Muqrin, exclaimed that Saudi "people have begun to imagine that making a living can only be accomplished by securing a government job. This is a vulgar notion that the apostate traitorous rulers have planted in people's heads. They also planted in their minds the notion that you will not be able to eat or drink until they control you and you become their employee" (quoted in Samin 2015, 202).

9. While oftentimes portraying that chaos, those scholars, like von Grunebaum (1955), took it as their mission to discern patterns and characteristics underpinning urban agglomerations across the whole of the Middle East and North Africa.

10. Fletcher and Carter (2017) delineate a set of "structural principles" that extrapolate ideas first ventured by Raymond (2008), whose principles serve as a starting point for their analysis.

11. In her descriptions of Manama, Fuccaro (2009, 9) contends that "The mixed ethnic and sectarian composition of the urban population reflected a long history of immigration associated with trade, pearling, pilgrimage and military conquest."

12. This seems to be one of the many points where scholarly narratives and common sense seem to be at odds.

13. Notably, Hay (1959, 110) commences his assessment by exclaiming that "Development has been carried out in a controlled and orderly manner and the haste which produced such chaotic conditions at Kuwait has been avoided."

14. In their detailed ethnographic assessment of the Saudi Arabian city of 'Unayzah, based on their fieldwork there in 1986 and 1987, Soraya Altorki and Donald Cole (1989, 128–129) note a strikingly similar situation: "many of those [foreign workers] who work in the city reside in the old mud-brick part of the town which has been abandoned by most 'Unayzah people for new housing in other areas."

3. THE JOURNEY TO ARABIA

1. Divendra would pull a similar maneuver in the years to come as he sought to extract himself from this particular job.

4. THE GULF MIGRATION SYSTEM

1. The Gulf Cooperation Council is also referred to as the Cooperation Council for the Arab States of the Gulf.

2. Note that those migrants who do express a desire to remain in the Gulf states are the most accessible population to visiting academics and journalists, and also occupy an outsized space in the collective attention directed at the migrant population residing on the Arabian Peninsula. For instances of this broader concern with ideas of belonging, the reproduction of these various diasporas, and the messy social realities therein, see Gardner (2010b); Mahdavi (2016); Babar (2017); Norbakk (2020); Alloul (2020, 2021).

3. Two decades ago, Karen Leonard (2002, 214) framed it thusly: "As trans-status subjects caught up in the processes of globalization in the Gulf, professional men and women find themselves displaced from their homelands and pushed to consider migration to the West, while working-class men and their wives at home focus more strongly on the homeland and their place in it."

4. Iskander (2021) convincingly argues that this turnover is an integral feature of a migration system that exploits the unskilled.

5. Elsewhere (Gardner 2021b), my back-of-the-napkin estimates look something like this: twenty-five million migrants on the Arabian Peninsula, multiplied by four to account for migrant comings and goings over a decade, and then multiply that figure by five to underestimate the members of the households those migrants represent and support. This yields an estimated five hundred million people embroiled in this migration system.

6. Steven Vertovec (2007, 1024) conceptualized superdiversity to describe the increasingly familiar demographies comprising "small and scattered, multiple-origin, transnationally connected, socioeconomically differentiated and legally stratified immigrants who have arrived over the last decade." The Eurocentricity of this definition is betrayed by his use of the term "immigrant," which is mostly inapplicable in the GCC, but the conceptualization remains valuable here.

7. The basic infrastructure of this process is perhaps most clearly visible in Tristan Bruslé's work (2009/2010, 158–159).

8. I suspect there may be some places where this is also true for young women, but I have no firsthand knowledge of that.

9. For more detail, see Gardner et al. (2013). Several members of the research team assembled for the project detailed in this paper hope for an opportunity to soon update these figures and to measure changes to these costs over the last decade. It also merits mention here that these averages obscure the variability between sending countries: costs are much higher in some sending locations than in others. We noted extraordinary variation in these costs between sending states, with Bangladeshi migrants reporting the highest costs and the migrants from the Philippines reporting the lowest costs in our sample (Gardner et al. 2013, 11–12).

10. Although there are notable parallels in other migration systems and their histories: the US Bracero Program, for example, also locked migrant workers to their employers, and the Gastarbeiter program in Germany (also from the 1960s) did the same.

11. The emphasis on the social and cultural roots of the *kafala* is discussed by a variety of scholars, including Beaugé (1986), Longva (1997), Gardner (2010b), Frantz (2011), Lori (2012), Diop, Johnston, and Trung Le (2015), and perhaps most comprehensively, by Jureidini and Hassan (2020). Alshehabi (2019) strongly emphasizes the British colonial legacy of the *kafala*, and Iskander (2021, 32) rejects explanations tied to the cultural legacy of the region. In their assessment, Jureidini and Hassan (2020) perceive more substantial ties between the *kafala* and Islamic tradition.

12. The distribution of authority was also clearly described by Jill Crystal (2005, 168–170).

13. This certainly reinforces the value of systematic and quantitative research, and this very argument was central to our research team's successful 2010 proposal to the Qatar National Research Fund. This anecdotal cherry-picking is perhaps responsible for the negative reputation that clings to the migrant-heavy Gulf states, despite outward-bound wealth transfers that surpass those of most other wealthy regions of the world.

14. See Gardner (2018) for a longer discussion of the symbolic role of law on the Arabian Peninsula.

15. The impact of the changes was perceived as largely ineffective. See Gardner (2010b) and Lori (2012, note 16) for more detail.

16. For example, see "Reform the Kafala System," Migrant-Rights.org, https://www.migrant-rights.org/campaign/end-the-kafala-system/. These critiques reliably come from institutions whose raison d'être (and funding streams) are tied to the ongoing critique of

the Gulf migration system. See Iskander (2021, 69–71) for a particularly even-handed discussion of these reforms.

17. See the ILO report from August 20, 2020: "Qatar Adopts a Non-discriminatory Minimum Wage," International Labour Organization, https://www.ilo.org/beirut/countries /qatar/WCMS_753583/lang--en/index.htm.

18. For example, see "Saudi Arabia Announces Change to Kafala System," Al Jazeera, https://www.aljazeera.com/news/2021/3/14/saudi-arabias-long-awaited-kafala-reform -goes-into-effect.

19. Albeit often via decisions reached in the complicated social contexts that I have described in this chapter, and also, oftentimes, through a blizzard of misinformation and disinformation that I explicate in detail elsewhere (Gardner 2012b).

20. Appiah (2018, 86) speaks of a man "always betraying his ideals, and forever scrutinizing his own prejudices and preferences like a quizzical ethnographer."

5. SEGREGATION AND SPACE IN THE MODERNIST CITY

1. In part, this was inspired by a similar analysis by Matsuo and his coauthors in the introduction to their edited volume (Ishii 2020), and Alloul (2020, 2021) seems dedicated to something along these same lines, but see also Kanna (2011, 30–31) for a typically eloquent explication of the same analytic tactic. Abdoulaye Diop and his coauthors' findings in their study (2017) also support the utility of an approach that, in the superdiverse context of Qatar, emphasizes class foremost as a categorical demographic frame.

2. Ho and Kathiravelu (2020) move toward a "more than race" analytic frame as well. In recognition of the power invested in the various schema for classifying and organizing human diversity, my emphasis on nationality is merely an entry point for a consideration of the intersections between the many other variables that have long interested anthropologists.

3. He subsequently notes that "When compared to those for other societies and other periods, these figures point to an inequality so huge that it is hardly surprising it should find expression in the spatial structure of the city" (Raymond 2008, 67).

4. Indigeneity is an inherently flawed concept to any anthropologist or scholar who approaches human history via the longue durée, as I have sought to do in this book, but I will leave these arguments dormant at this point.

5. "In Kuwait, we find three overarching categorical dichotomies in terms of which persons were identified and classified: Kuwaiti—non-Kuwaiti, Arab—non-Arab, and Muslim—non-Muslim. These are categories that were officially acknowledged in the public discourse of social life, universally understood, and, in principle, purely descriptive and value-neutral. In reality, given the Kuwaiti context, they were loaded with a wide range of connotations, and the definitely of at least one of them ('Kuwaiti') was hotly disputed among the Kuwaitis themselves . . . Undoubtedly the most outstanding among the three, this dichotomy was based the critical criterion of *citizenship*" (Longva 1997, 45). Her ideas are of enduring value. This is all the more surprising with the intellectual deforestation typically levied at any and all thinking from the past. In the long wake of the postmodern turn, older ideas and previous thinking are oftentimes only useful as foils for establishing the new and novel.

6. These data are from 2013.

7. Dakkak's fascinating PhD dissertation explores the Arab migrant experience in great detail through fictional accounts that portray those experiences. Dakkak (2020) sees gargantuan differences between migration experiences from earlier eras and more recent migration experiences, and suggests that those early migrant encounters were vital in setting the tone by which all migration experiences are interpreted to this day.

8. This is also characteristically true of the Indian communities in the various GCC states, all of which stretch from the lowest economic stratum of manual laborers into the cosmopolitan elite described here.

9. The difficulty of accessing data is widely commented on in scholarship; for example, Babar (2017, 11, 26).

10. All of this is strikingly evident in a description of the Qatar-based portion of the team associated with the Msheireb Project, as described by Melhuish and her coauthors (2016, 234–235): "The client team based in Doha comprised a mixed group of mostly American, some British and Australian, and some Egyptian and Lebanese development directors and managers, many of whom had previous experience in Dubai and the region, notably Kuwait and Beirut. However the senior executive level was made up of Qataris from the civil service and ministries, answerable ultimately to the Chairperson of the Qatar Foundation, Sheikha Moza. Also on the development team were a handful of Qataris with training (commonly in Britain or the US) and some experience of working in architecture or urban and interior design, in line with state directives on Qatarization. At a more technical level, particularly IT support, roles were mainly filled by male employees form the Indian subcontinent, while female PAs included a mix of nationalities (e.g. Russian, Indian), front-of-house receptionists were often Filipina women, and tea-boys south Indians."

11. Or QR 7,000 (US$1923) with free accommodations from an employer.

12. See Hosoda (2020) for a clear articulation of a similar point in relation to the Filipino community in the United Arab Emirates.

13. See also Bruslé (2009/2010) for an insightful analysis of the socioeconomically bottom-heavy Nepalese community in Qatar.

14. For example, in 1992 I moved to New York City and shared a studio on 6th Street on the lower east side—a street entirely dominated by perhaps fifteen different Indian restaurants. The gravity that brings these different entrepreneurs together in urban space is what I am interested in here.

6. COMPOUNDS, WALLS, AND CULTURAL SOVEREIGNTY

1. Notably, Kathiravelu (2016, 134–180) explores these same parallels in her book.

2. Alsayer (2019a, 2) sees these same constructions as an attempt "to transform society and its built environment."

3. As Fuccaro (2009, 205) notes, the phase of urban development that commenced in the 1960s was "inspired by Western concepts of urban planning," and the enclaves constructed by BAPCO in Manama provided a model for new neighborhoods and construction.

4. Alsayer (2019a, 6) describes how "The systematic transformation of Dhahran from portable homes to a U.S. suburb complete with green landscapes was celebrated as the U.S. triumph over the desert." In its 1960 handbook, for example, Aramco boasts of the "creation, in what was open desert country, of modern communities in which employees and their families can live and work, with houses, streets, shops, office buildings, restaurants, hospitals, schools, recreational facilities, lawns, gardens and trees" (Lebkicher et al. 1960, 5–6).

5. Rule eleven from the document titled "A Code of Conduct for Tourists Visiting Qatar for the World Cup 2022" states that "A tourist is prohibited from consuming alcohol in stadiums or outside the specified areas." From another angle, this is a form of the "morality zoning" that Fuccaro describes (2009, 231) in her historical analysis of Manama.

6. These parallels are perhaps most clear in some of the examples I have not presented here, such as the Special Economic Zones. See Oxford Business Group (2015).

7. At the same time, for Agamben (2005) these "states of exception" arise foremost during crisis—during purported extraordinary circumstances or their conjuring. In Qatar, the state of exception seems to arise from the quotidian tumult of development and urban growth.

7. AN URBAN SPATIAL DISCOURSE

1. Those misgivings include a concern with Foucault's overwhelming preoccupation with power such that, in the final accounting, that preoccupation seems to eclipse as much as it reveals about human nature. I am also wary of the stasis of the American distillation of "French Theory," which has changed little since it first coalesced in the 1980s. And one might also lament Foucault's penchant for concept inflation by which discourse suddenly means something other than discourse, and archaeology suddenly means something other than archaeology. Most scholars today are essentially inured to this last feature of the contemporary ideoscape.

2. See also Msheireb Properties (2021), where the development is trumpeted for providing "an intrinsic mix of hospitality, retail, residential, commercial and civic offerings. Designed to have everything close and convenient enough to walk to, each quarter caters to every need of an urban dweller. The five quarters comprise offices, the city's key extended government area, luxurious residential units, green spaces, an international academy, community mosques, state-of-the-art retail spaces, treasured cultural offerings, an extensive café culture and world-class dining and hotel options—all within minutes of one another. With an intrinsic mix so diverse, Msheireb Downtown Doha will truly be a place like no other."

3. Hanieh (2018) further articulates that these surpluses are vital not just to the cities of the Arabian Peninsula but to the whole of the global financial system.

4. Hanieh (2018, 83–84) provides useful and detailed data concerning ownership in his assessment of the ten largest developers in the GCC, three of which are Qatari: the Qatari Diar, as a sovereign wealth fund, is entirely owned by the state; the Qatari Diar also owns 45 percent of Barwa Real Estate, alongside private investors; the United Development Company is listed as a private business, but various state-controlled funds hold an estimated 34 percent of the firm.

5. Kolson (2001, 184) argues that "great urban space begins with a willingness to accommodate, rather than obliterate, the culture detritus of the past . . . this is the secret of some of the world's most beautiful and successful cities." Perhaps this helps explain why the Msheireb Project and the adjacent Souk Waqif—both of which had to accommodate a preexisting urban landscape, remain some of the most popular urban spaces in Doha. See also Elsheshtawy (2019a, 244).

6. As Molotch and Ponzini (2019, 6) claim, those "grand plans are only loosely followed; they get replaced at fairly short intervals."

7. Kolson (2001, 125–127) traces this feature of urban planning to Haussmann and his service to Napoleon III. See also Melhuish, Degen, and Rose (2016) and Degen, Melhuish, and Rose (2017) for a discussion of the process by which representations of these atmospherics are crafted.

8. Conversely, David Harvey (2008, 60) suggests that postmodernism signified a break with "the modernist idea that planning and development should focus on large-scale, metropolitan-wide, technologically rational and efficient urban plans."

8. CEASELESS GROWTH AND THE URBAN TROPHY CASE

1. The keystone to this sustained scholarly conversation is Hazem Beblawi (1987). In the postmodern tradition, critiques of his ideas typically treat rentier state theory as a

narrative rather than a theory, thereby shifting the terms of the critique from an assessment of the evidence in support of that theory to an indictment of the implications that such a narrative might be imagined to connote.

2. Again, this seems to be the result of the seemingly endless and analytically simplistic Foucauldian preoccupation with power.

3. Although precise and up-to-date figures can be difficult to obtain, Gengler (2021, 242), referring to data from the Global Labour Markets and Migration, notes that in Qatar, "nine out of ten employed citizens work in the public sector."

4. Paul Dresch (2006, 202) remarked that because citizens are "privileged landholders" in the Gulf, real estate serves as another conduit for the transfer of wealth from the state to the citizen. See also Iskander (2021, 57) for a discussion of the competitive advantages conferred to citizens by law.

5. For Soja (1996), *secondspace* is the space of the city as it is represented and imagined, the very domain in which CGI images seek to intervene. See also Melhuish, Degen, and Rose (2016) and Degen, Melhuish, and Rose (2017).

6. I first articulated these ideas in Gardner (2008a).

7. In a conference paper (Gardner 2008b), I sought to grapple with the collective aspect of the consumerist ethic manifest in the cities of Arabia—with the "collective consumerism that predominates in the region."

9. CULTURE AND LIFE IN A FRAGMENTED CITY

1. These ideas and this argument were first broached in a conference paper I delivered (Gardner 2011b).

2. See also Gardner (2010a). During my fieldwork in Bahrain in 2002 and 2003, I interviewed numerous Indian business owners who collectively portrayed the Bahraini worker as indolent, spoiled, lazy, and unreliable. One business owner noted to me that "the effort that they [Bahrainis] would normally put in is half as much as an expatriate. When you think about wanting to put a Bahraini in [a job], well, they're so lazy. They just don't do as much." Another suggested that "the basic problem is with their attitude. They're just not used to working—especially hard work. They've taken it very easy all these years, and that has passed on to the younger generation." Some Bahraini interlocutors concurred. As one young Bahraini man noted, "The things people say about the Bahraini work ethic—well, I agree with it in general. [Bahrainis] feel like they're entitled to more than what they're getting, and they feel like they shouldn't be doing as much as they are for it. A lot of people criticize Bahrainis for not performing as well as Indian workers . . . You can see it firsthand. Just go into any place. Go to Jasmis [a fast-food restaurant that had begun to employ Bahrainis at the time] or any retail place. See how the Bahraini man or lady behind the counter treats you. They'll be talking to a coworker or on the mobile, or they'll yell to the person behind you." When forced to hire Bahrainis under a state-mandated quota system, many business owners and managers would simply pay these employees and ask them to stay home.

3. Portions of this chapter draw on Gardner (2015a, 2015b).

4. See Gardner (2011a).

5. I encountered similar experiences with a photography exhibit and with various other projects at the American satellite campuses located in the region.

6. In her insightful analysis of experts, consultants, and power holders in the GCC, Calvert Jones (2019, 16) quotes a foreign expert who emphasized that the ruling elites are oftentimes out of touch with local realities and contexts.

7. This term, originally coined by the American aluminum manufacturer Alcoa in the 1940s and popularized by Walt Disney, is also the name of a Japanese entertainment company.

8. What I am suggesting here is that the sociocultural tradition of insularity perceptible in the social traditions of the region is enhanced by the enclaving proclivities common to authoritarian high modernism (Scott 1999).

9. These ideas were first broached in Gardner (2015b).

10. Jane Jacobs (1961) is perhaps the most notable example, but we might also add Gehl (2011) and Klinenberg (2017) to this list.

11. In concluding his book, Sennett (1970, 198) suggests that "in extricating the city from preplanned control, men will become more in control of themselves and more aware of each other. That is the promise, and the justification, of disorder."

CONCLUSION: A CITY I WILL NEVER SEE

1. The social topography of this parking lot is discussed at more length in Gardner (2023).

2. In addition to Hannerz's 2005 piece, see also Gardner (2023).

3. Excellent scholars of the urban form in the Gulf disagree with this reading. Al-Nakib (2016, 205), for example, contends that separation and segregation inhibit contact with difference in the city.

4. Although a legion of scholars and academics seem to have built careers on the assumption that this debate is ongoing.

POSTSCRIPT

1. For example, in the context of Arabia, women's activities and their friendship were often out of bounds for me. Only foreign women have the ethnographic privilege in Arabia of working closely with both men and women. As a result, ethnographic assessment of migrant domestic workers, for example, was mostly out of reach for me.

2. The turn from *subjectivity* to *identity* is a conceptual shift of recent provenance. Our ongoing conceptual reliance on identity is, I suggest, a measure of the American dominance of the global intellectual conversation and, more directly, over the conceptual toolbox on which that conversation draws. Unlike subjectivity, the concept of identity shears the individual from the social contexts into which she was born, and pays little attention to the coconstruction of our individuality in dialectic with those social forces and social forms. Identity is a concept vastly more amendable to the neoliberal ideology and privileged consumerist ethic that America continues to promote, despite the superficial political dramas of our past decade.

3. Or was Mark Fisher (2009, 2014) correct in his assertion that postmodernism corrupts the very possibility of any future?

4. Although several of the research projects underlying this book were clearly of an applied nature—those projects explicitly sought to enable, foster, or inform change via the policy environment. See, for example, Gardner (2010b); Pessoa, Harkness, and Gardner (2014); and Gardner, Pessoa, and Harkness (2014).

5. Remember, this tenure purportedly offers me some insulation from forces that might influence my analyses and interpretations.

6. Many of my colleagues (and, probably, some of the people evaluating this manuscript as experts, publishers, editors, or gatekeepers of some sort) are often now concerned a priori with a moral assessment of the author, even before their work is digested. A colleague of mine in political science, for example, conveyed to me that I might perhaps not be "on his team." Similarly, in nascent form, one chapter of this book was rejected by the journal *City: Analysis of Urban Change, Theory, Action*, with the admonition from an anonymous editor that my attempted revisions demonstrated "a lack of commitment to a wider emancipatory project which are part of critical theory and contributions to

City" (email December 2, 2020). These sorts of exchanges leave me puzzled. What is the nature of this project, exactly? Is this the same "sacred project" that Smith (2014) described nearly a decade ago? And what are these teams of which my colleague spoke?

7. For readers interested in discerning or assessing the therapeutic terrain of our concerns, I suggest Lasch (1979), Moskowitz (2001), Furedi (2003), Smith (2014), Bloom (2016), and Lukianoff and Haidt (2019).

References

Agamben, Giorgio. 2005. *States of Exception*. Chicago: University of Chicago Press.

Akinci, Idil. 2018. "Being Emirati: National Identity Construction among Young Dubai Citizens and Second-Generation Arab Migrants in Dubai." PhD diss., University of Sussex.

Alatas, Syed Hussein. 1977. *The Myth of the Lazy Native: A Study of the Image of Malays, Filipinos and Javanese from the 16th to the 20th Century and Its Function in the Ideology of Colonial Capitalism*. London: Frank Cass.

Alexander, Christopher. 1977. *A Pattern Language: Towns, Buildings, Construction*. New York: Oxford University Press.

Alloul, Jaafar. 2020. "Leaving Europe, Aspiring Access: Racial Capital and Its Spatial Discontents among the Euro-Maghrebi Minority." *Journal of Immigrant & Refugee Studies* 18 (3): 313–325.

Alloul, Jaafar. 2021. "'Traveling Habitus' and the New Anthropology of Class: Proposing a Transitive Tool for Analyzing Social Mobility in Global Migration." *Mobilities* 16 (2): 178–193.

Al-Mohammed, Hayder. 2011. "'You Have Car Insurance, We Have Tribes': Negotiating Everyday Life in Basra and the Re-Emergence of Tribalism." *Anthropology of the Middle East* 6 (1): 18–34.

Al-Mohannadi, Asmaa S., and Raffaello Furlan. 2022. "The Syntax of the Qatari Traditional House: Privacy, Gender Segregation and Hospitality Constructing Qatar Architectural Identity." *Journal of Asian Architecture and Building Engineering* 21 (2): 263–283.

AlMutawa, Rana. 2021. "Everyday Life in the 'glitzy' City: Navigating Belonging and Exclusion in Dubai." PhD diss., University of Oxford.

Al-Nakib, Farah. 2014. "Revising Hadar and Badu in Kuwait: Citizenship, Housing, and the Construction of a Dichotomy." *International Journal of Middle East Studies* 46 (1): 5–30.

Al-Nakib, Farah. 2016. *Kuwait Transformed: A History of Oil and Urban Life*. Stanford: Stanford University Press.

Al-Naqeeb, Khaldoun Hasan. 1990. *Society and State in the Gulf and Arab Peninsula: A Different Perspective*. Translated by L. M. Kenny. London: Routledge.

Al-Rasheed, Madawi. 1997. *Politics in an Arabian Oasis: The Rashidi Tribal Dynasty*. London: I.B. Tauris.

Alsayer, Dalal M. 2019a. Architecture, Environment, Development: The United States and the Making of Modern Arabia, 1949–1961." PhD diss., University of Pennsylvania.

Alsayer, Dalal M. 2019b. "The 'Right to the City' in the Landscapes of Servitude and Migration, from the Philippines to the Arabian Gulf, and Back." In *Mapping Migration, Identity, and Space*, edited by Tabea Linhard and Timothy H. Parsons, 283–309. Cham: Palgrave Macmillan.

Alshawi, Ali, and Andrew Gardner. 2014. "Tribalism, Identity and Citizenship in Contemporary Qatar." *Anthropology of the Middle East* 8 (2): 46–59.

Alshehabi, Omar H. 2015. "Rootless Hubs: Migration, Urban Commodification and the 'Right to the City' in the GCC." In *Transit States*, edited by Abdulhadi Khalaf, Omar Alshehabi, and Adam Hanieh, 101–131. London: Pluto Press.

Alshehabi, Omar H. 2019. *Contested Modernity: Sectarianism, Nationalism, and Colonialism in Bahrain*. London: OneWorld Academic.

Altorki, Soraya, and Donald P. Cole. 1989. *Arabian Oasis City: The Transformation of 'Unayzah*. Austin: University of Texas Press.

Anderson, Benedict. 2006. *Imagined Communities: Reflections on the Origin and Spread of Nationalism*. London: Verso Books.

Anderson, Elijah. 2011. *The Cosmopolitan Canopy: Race and Civility in Everyday Life*. New York: W. W. Norton.

Appadurai, Arjun. 1996. *Modernity at Large: Cultural Dimensions of Globalization*. Minneapolis: University of Minnesota Press.

Appiah, Kwame A. 2018. *The Lies That Bind: Rethinking Identity*. New York: W. W. Norton.

Arab News. 2020. "Umm Alqura Unveils Masar, a New Culture Destination in Makkah." July 1. https://www.arabnews.com/node/1697921/corporate-news

Augé, Marc. 2009. *Non-Places: An Introduction to Supermodernity*. 2nd ed. London: Verso.

Babar, Zahra, ed. 2017. *Arab Migrant Communities in the GCC*. Oxford: Oxford University Press.

Babar, Zahra, and Andrew Gardner. 2016. "Circular Migration and the Gulf States." In *Impact of Circular Migration on Human, Political and Civil Rights*. United Nations Series of Regionalism (Vol. 12). Switzerland: Springer.

Banta, Melissa, and Curtis M. Hinsley with Joan Kathryn O'Donnell. 2017. *From Site to Sight: Anthropology, Photography, and the Power of Imagery*. Cambridge, MA: Peabody Museum Press.

Barkey, Karen. 2005. "Islam and Toleration: Studying the Ottoman Imperial Model." *International Journal of Politics, Culture, and Society* 19 (1–2): 5–19.

Barkey, Karen, and George Gavrilis. 2016. "The Ottoman Millet System: Non-Territorial Autonomy and its Contemporary Legacy." *Ethnopolitics* 15 (1): 24–42.

Barron, Patrick. 2014. "Introduction: At the Edge of the Pale." In *Terrains Vague*, edited by Manuela Mariani and Patrick Barron, 15–37. London: Routledge.

Bashkow, Ira. 2004. "A Neo-Boasian Conception of Cultural Boundaries." *American Anthropologist* 106 (3): 443–458.

Batty, David. 2012. "The Rise of the Gulf Art Scene." *The Guardian*, April 16.

Beaugé, G. 1986. "La kafala: Un système de gestion transitoire de la main-d'oeuvre et du capital dans les pays du Golfe." *Revue européenne des Migrations internationales* 2 (1): 109–122.

Beblawi, Hazem. 1987. "The Rentier State in the Arab World." *Arab Studies Quarterly* 9 (4): 383–398.

Benjamin, Walter. 1999. *The Arcades Project*. Cambridge, MA: The Belknap Press of Harvard University Press.

Berman, David. 1999. *Actual Air*. New York: Open City Books.

Bernard, Russell. 2011. *Research Methods in Anthropology*. 5th ed. Walnut Creek, CA: AltaMira Press.

Bishara, Fahad Ahmad. 2017. *A Sea of Debt: Law and Economic Life in the Western Indian Ocean, 1780–1950*. Cambridge: Cambridge University Press.

Bloom, Paul. 2016. *Against Empathy: The Case for Rational Compassion*. New York: Ecco Books.

Bourgois, Philippe, and Jeff Schonberg. 2009. *Righteous Dopefiend*. Berkeley: University of California Press.

Braudel, Fernand. 1972. *The Mediterranean and the Mediterranean World in the Age of Phillip II*. Translated by Siân Reynolds. New York: HarperCollins.

Brogden, Jim. 2019. *Photography and the Non-Place: The Cultural Erasure of the City*. Switzerland: Palgrave McMillan.

Broswimmer, Franz. 2002. *Ecocide: A Short History of the Mass Extinction of Species*. London: Pluto Press.

Bruslé, Tristan. 2009/2010. "Who's in a Labour Camp? A Socio-Economic Analysis of Nepalese Migrants in Qatar." *European Bulletin of Himalayan Research* 35–36: 154–170.

Buras, Nir Haim. 2019. *The Art of Classic Planning: Building Beautiful and Enduring Communities*. Cambridge, MA: The Belknap Press of Harvard University Press.

Burt, John A. 2014. "The Environmental Costs of the Coastal Urbanization in the Arabian Gulf." *City* 18 (6): 760–770.

Castles, Stephen. 1999. "International Migration and the Global Agenda: Reflections on the 1998 UN Technical Symposium." *International Migration* 37 (1): 5–19.

Chandra, Uday, and Irene Promodh. 2020. "A Divided City in a Time of Pandemic: Dispatches from Doha." *City & Society* 32 (2).

Choudhury, Masudul A. 1998. "Development Cooperation in the Islamic Perspective." In *Studies in Islamic Social Sciences*, 180–218. London: Palgrave Macmillan.

Constable, Nicole. 1997. *Maid to Order in Hong Kong: Stories of Filipina Workers*. Ithaca, NY: Cornell University Press.

cooke, miriam. 2014. *Tribal Modern: Branding New Nations in the Arab Gulf*. Berkeley: University of California Press.

Crapanzano, Vincent. 1980. *Tuhami: Portrait of a Moroccan*. Chicago: University of Chicago Press.

Crystal, Jill. 1990. *Oil and Politics in the Gulf: Rulers and Merchants in Kuwait and Qatar*. Cambridge: Cambridge University Press.

Crystal, Jill. 2005. "Public Order and Authority: Policing Kuwait." In *Monarchies and Nations: Globalisation and Identity in the Arab States of the Gulf*, edited by Paul Dresch and James Piscatori, 158–181. London: I.B. Tauris.

Dakkak, Nadeen. 2020. "'An Immense Cargo of Wanderers Seeking Their Own Destruction': Migration to the Arab Gulf States in Arabic fFiction." PhD diss., University of Warwick.

D'Andrade, Roy. 1995. "Moral Models in Anthropology." *Current Anthropology* 36 (3): 399–408.

Davis, Carlo. 2013. "World's Highest Density of Millionaires in Qatar, Study Finds." *Huffington Post*, June 11. https://www.huffpost.com/entry/highest-density-millionaires_n_3417275.

Davis, Mike. 1990. *City of Quartz: Excavating the Future in Los Angeles*. New York: Verso.

De Bel-Air, Françoise. 2017. "Demography, Migration, and the Labour Market in Qatar." *GLMM Explanatory Note #3*. https://gulfmigration.grc.net/media/pubs/exno/GLMM_EN_2017_03.pdf.

De Bel-Air, Françoise. 2018. "Asian Migration to the Gulf States in the Twenty-First Century." In *South Asian Migration in the Gulf*, edited by Mehdi Chowdhury and S. Irudaya Rajan, 7–34. Cham: Palgrave Macmillan.

Debord, Guy. 1983. *Society of the Spectacle*. Detroit: Black and Red.

Degen, Monica, Clare Melhuish, and Gillian Rose. 2017. "Producing Place Atmosphered Digitally: Architecture, Digital Visualization Practices and the Experience Economy." *Journal of Consumer Culture* 17 (1): 3–24.

Diop, Abdoulaye, Trevor Johnston, and Kien Trun Le. 2015. "Reform of the Kafala System: A Survey Experiment from Qatar." *Journal of Arabian Studies* 5 (2): 116–137.

Diop, Abdoulaye, Yaojun Li, Majed Mohammed H. A. Al-Ansari, and Kien T. Le. 2017. "Social Capital and Citizens' Attitudes toward Migrant Workers." *Social Inclusion* 5 (1): 66–79.

Douglas, Mary. 1966. *Purity and Danger: An Analysis of Concepts of Pollution and Taboo*. New York: Praeger.

Dresch, Paul. 2006. "The Place of Strangers in Gulf Society." In *Globalization and the Gulf*, edited by John Fox, Nada Mourtada-Sabbah, and Mohammed al-Mutawa, 200–222. London: Routledge.

DuBois, W. E. B. 2010. *The Philadelphia Negro*. Philadelphia: University of Pennsylvania Press.

Durkheim, Emile. 2014. *The Division of Labor in Society*. New York: Simon and Schuster.

Easterling, Keller. 2014. *Extrastatecraft: The Power of Infrastructure Space*. London: Verso.

ECSWA. 2007. *International Migration and Development in the Arab Region: Challenges and Opportunities*. U.N. Population and Development Report. Third Issue. New York: United Nations.

Eldem, Edhem. 2013. "Istanbul as a Cosmopolitan City: Myths and Realities." In *A Companion to Diaspora and Transnationalism*. Edited by Ato Quayson with Girish Daswani. Blackwell.

Elsheshtawy, Yasser, ed. 2008. *The Evolving Arab City: Tradition, Modernity & Urban Development*. London: Routledge.

Elsheshtawy, Yasser. 2010. *Dubai: Behind an Urban Spectacle*. London: Routledge.

Elsheshtawy, Yasser. 2017. "Urban Enclaves: Scenes from Abu Dhabi and Dubai." Paper presented at the *Migrants in Global Cities: Experiences from Asia, the Middle East and Europe* workshop, Singapore, October 31.

Elsheshtawy, Yasser. 2019a. "Real Estate Speculation and Transnational Development in Dubai." In *The New Arab Urban*, edited by Harvey Molotch and Davide Ponzini, 235–255. New York: New York University Press.

Elsheshtawy, Yasser. 2019b. *Temporary Cities: Resisting Transience in Arabia*. London: Routledge.

Elsheshtawy, Yasser. 2022. *Riyadh: Transforming a Desert City*. London: Routledge.

Engels, Frederick. 1993. *The Conditions of the Working-Class in England in 1844*. Oxford: Oxford University Press.

Exell, Karen, and Trinidad Rico. 2016. *Cultural Heritage in the Arabian Peninsula: Debates, Discourses and Practices*. London: Routledge.

Fisher, Mark. 2009. *Capitalist Realism: Is There No Alternative?* Winchester, UK: Zero Books.

Fisher, Mark. 2014. *Ghosts of My Life: Writings on Depression, Hauntology and Lost Futures*. Winchester, UK: Zero Books.

Fishman, Robert. 1987. *Bourgeois Utopias: The Rise and Fall of Suburbia*. New York: Basic Books.

Fletcher, Richard, and Robert A. Carter. 2017. "Mapping the Growth of an Arabian Gulf Town: The Case of Doha, Qatar." *Journal of the Economic and Social History of the Orient* 60 (4): 420–487.

Foucault, Michel. 1974. *The Archaeology of Knowledge*. London: Tavistock.

Frantz, Elizabeth. 2011. "Exporting Subservience: Sri Lankan Women's Migration for Domestic Work in Jordan." PhD diss., London School of Economics and Political Science.

Fuccaro, Nelida. 2009. *Histories of City and State in the Persian Gulf*. Cambridge: Cambridge University Press.

Furedi, Frank. 2003. *Therapy Culture*. London: Routledge

Furedi, Frank. 2020. *Why Borders Matter: Why Humanity Must Relearn the Art of Drawing Boundaries*. Taylor and Francis.

Gamburd, Michele R. 2000. *The Kitchen Spoon's Handle: Transnationalism and Sri Lanka's Migrant Housemaids*. Ithaca, NY: Cornell University Press.

Gardner, Andrew. 2005. "City of Strangers: The Transnational Indian Community in Manama, Bahrain." PhD diss., University of Arizona.

Gardner, Andrew. 2008a. "Consumer Culture in Al Khaleej." Paper presented at the annual meeting of the American Anthropological Association, San Francisco, California, November 21.

Gardner, Andrew. 2008b. "Strategic Transnationalism: The Indian Diasporic Elite in Contemporary Bahrain." *City and Society* 20 (1): 54–78.

Gardner, Andrew. 2009. "The Amalgamated City: The Alternatives of Wealth in the Neoliberal Landscape of Doha, Qatar." Paper presented at the annual meeting of the American Anthropological Association, Philadelphia, Pennsylvania, December 5.

Gardner, Andrew. 2010a. *City of Strangers: Gulf Migration and the Indian Community in Bahrain*. Ithaca, NY: Cornell University Press.

Gardner, Andrew. 2010b. "Engulfed: Indian Guest Workers, Bahraini Citizens and the Structural Violence of the Kafala System." In *The Deportation Regime: Sovereignty, Space, and Freedom of Movement*, edited by Nicholas De Genova and Nathalie Peutz, 305–349. Durham, NC: Duke University Press.

Gardner, Andrew. 2010c. "Labor Camps in the Gulf States." *Viewpoints: Migration and the Gulf*. The Middle East Institute.

Gardner, Andrew. 2011a. "Gulf Migration and the Family," *The Journal of Arabian Studies* 1 (1): 3–25.

Gardner, Andrew. 2011b. "Lazy Arabs: A Reconceptualization of the Qatari 'Rentier Economy.'" Paper presented at the annual meeting of the Society for Applied Anthropology, Seattle, Washington, March 31.

Gardner, Andrew. 2012a. "Rumour and Myth in the Labour Camps of Qatar." *Anthropology Today* 28 (6): 25–28.

Gardner, Andrew. 2012b. "Why Do They Keep Coming? Labor Migrants in the Gulf States." In *Migrant Labour in the Persian Gulf*, edited by Mehran Kamrava and Zahra Babar. New York: Columbia University Press.

Gardner, Andrew. 2014. "How the City Grows: Urban Growth and Challenges to Sustainable Development in Doha, Qatar." In *Sustainable Development: An Appraisal from the Gulf Region*, edited by Paul Sillitoe, 343–366. Oxford: Berghahn Books.

Gardner, Andrew. 2015a. "Migration, Labor and Business in the Worlding Cities of the Arabian Peninsula." IDE Discussion Paper #513, IDE-JETRO, Tokyo, Japan.

Gardner, Andrew. 2015b. "Gatekeepers, Imagineers, and the Development of Qatar's Knowledge-Based Economy." Paper presented at the Center for Gulf Studies biannual symposium at the American University of Kuwait, Kuwait City, March 14.

Gardner, Andrew. 2017. "The Journey to Arabia." *Anthropology Now* 9 (3): 73–90.

Gardner, Andrew. 2018. "Reflections on the Role of Law in the Gulf Migration System." *Journal of Legal Studies* 47 (January): 1–19.

Gardner, Andrew. 2019. "Imperial Diversity." *Areo Magazine*, October 9. https://areomagazine.com/2019/09/to10/imperial-diversity/.

Gardner, Andrew. 2021a. "A Window To Urban Arabia." *Anthropology Now* 12 (3): 64–73.

Gardner, Andrew. 2021b. "Migration, Activism, Justice, and an Academic Career in Anthropology." Paper presented to the Department of Sociology and Anthropology at the University of Puget Sound.

Gardner, Andrew. 2021c. "Beyond Exception." Review of *Beyond Exception*, by Ahmed Kanna, Neha Vora, and Amelie Le Renard. *Middle East Journal* 75 (2): 348–351.

Gardner, Andrew. 2023. "Cosmopolitanism and Urban Space in Doha, Qatar." *Journal of Arabian Studies* 11(2): 210–222.

Gardner, Andrew, Silvia Pessoa, Abdoulaye Diop, Kaltham Al-Ghanim, Kien Le Trung, and Laura Harkness. 2013. "A Portrait of Low-Income Migrants in Contemporary Qatar." *Journal of Arabian Studies* 3 (1): 1–17.

Gardner, Andrew, Silvia Pessoa, and Laura Harkness. 2014. "Labour Migrants and Access to Justice in Contemporary Qatar." London: Open Society Foundation and London School of Economics Middle East Centre.

Geertz, Clifford. 1973. *The Interpretation of Culture*. New York: Basic Books.

Gehl, Jan. 2011. *Life between Buildings: Using Public Space*. Washington, DC: Island Press.

Gengler, Justin. 2021. "Society and State in Post-Blockade Qatar: Lessons for the Arab Gulf Region." *Journal of Arabian Studies* 10 (2): 238–255.

Gilroy, Paul. 2000. *Against Race: Imagining Political Culture Beyond the Color Line*. Cambridge MA: The Belknap Press of Harvard University Press.

Gulf Times. 2019. "Qatar Freehold Zones 'to Spur Investments in Real Estate.'" August 1. https://www.gulf-times.com/story/638063/Qatar-freehold-zones-to-spur -investments-in-real-e.

Günel, Gökçe. 2019. *Spaceship in the Desert: Energy, Climate Change, and Urban Design in Abu Dhabi*. Durham, NC: Duke University Press.

Gupta, Akhil. 2008. "Globalisation and Difference: Cosmopolitanism Before the Nation-State." *Transforming Cultures eJournal* 3 (2).

Gupta, Akhil, and James Ferguson. 1997. *Culture, Power, Place: Explorations in Critical Anthropology*. Durham, NC: Duke University Press.

Habermas, Jurgen. 1991. *The Structural Transformation of the Public Sphere: An Inquiry into a Category of Bourgeois Society*. Boston: MIT Press.

Hall, Peter. 1980. *Great Planning Disasters*. London: George Weidenfeld and Nicolson Limited.

Hanieh, Adam. 2018. *Money, Markets, and Monarchies: The Gulf Cooperation Council and the Political Economy of the Contemporary Middle East*. Vol. 4. Cambridge: Cambridge University Press.

Hannerz, Ulf. 2005. "Two Faces of Cosmopolitanism: Culture and Politics." *Statsvetenskaplig Tidskrift* 107 (3): 199–213.

Harris, Marvin. 1979. *Cultural Materialism: The Struggle for a Science of Culture*. New York: Random House.

Harvey, David. 1989. *The Condition of Postmodernity*. Oxford: Basil Blackwell.

Harvey, David. 2008. "The Right to the City." *New Left Review* 53: 23–53.

Hay, Rupert. 1959. *The Persian Gulf States*. Washington, DC: Middle East Institute.

Hertog, Steffen. 2019. "A Quest for Significance: Gulf Oil Monarchies' International Strategies and Their Urban Dimensions." In *The New Arab Urban: Gulf Cities of Wealth, Ambition, and Distress*, edited by Harvey Molotch and Davide Ponzini, 276–299. New York: New York University Press.

Hewison, Robert. 1987. *The Heritage Industry: Britain in a Climate of Decline*. London: Methuen.

Ho, Elaine Lynn-Ee, and Laavanya Kathiravelu. 2020. "More Than Race: A Comparative Analysis of 'New' Indian and Chinese Migration in Singapore." *Ethnic and Racial Studies* 45 (4): 636–655.

Holmes, Seth. 2013. *Fresh Fruit, Broken Bodies: Migrant Farmworkers in the United States*. Berkeley: University of California Press.

Holston, James. 1989. *The Modernist City: An Anthropological Critique of Brasília*. Chicago: University of Chicago Press.

Hopper, Matthew. 2015. *Slaves of One Master: Globalization and Slavery in Arabia and the Age of Empire*. New Haven: Yale University Press.

Hosoda, Naomi. 2020. "Survival Strategies and Migrant Communities in the Arab Gulf states: A Case of Filipino Workers in the UAE." In *Asian Migrant Workers in the Arab Gulf States*, edited by Masako Ishii, Naomi Hosoda, Masaki Matsuo, and Koji Horinuki. Leiden: Brill.

Hubbard, Ben. 2016. "A Physician-Turned-Artist Offers a Diagnosis for Islam's Holiest City." *New York Times*. December 2.

Ishii, Masaki, Naomi Hosoda, Masaki Matsuo and Koji Horinuke. 2020. *Asian Migrant Workers in the Arab Gulf States: The Growing Foreign Population and Their Lives*. Leiden: Brill.

Iskander, Natasha. 2020. "Qatar, the Coronavirus, and Cordons Sanitaires: Migrant Workers and the Use of Public Health Measures to Define the Nation." *Medical Anthropology Quarterly* 34 (4): 561–577.

Iskander, Natasha. 2021. *Does Skill Make Us Human? Migrant Workers in 21st-Century Qatar and Beyond*. Princeton: Princeton University Press.

Jacobs, Jane. 1961. *The Death and Life of Great American Cities*. New York: Random House.

Jones, Calvert. 2019. "Adviser to the King: Experts, Rationalization, and Legitimacy." *World Politics* 71(1): 1–43.

Jureidini, Ray and Said Fares Hassan. 2020. "The Islamic Principle of Kafala as Applied to Migrant Workers: Traditional Continuity and Reform." In *Migration and Islamic Ethics: Issues of Residence, Naturalisation and Citizenship*, edited by Ray Jureidini and Said Fares Hassan. Leiden: Brill.

Kanna, Ahmed. 2011. *Dubai: The City as Corporation*. Minneapolis: University of Minnesota Press.

Kapiszewski, Andrzej. 2006. "Arab Versus Asian Migrant Workers in the GCC Countries." Paper prepared for the United Nations Expert Group Meeting on International Migration and Development in the Arab Region, Population Division, Department of Economic and Social Affairs, United Nations Secretariat, Beirut, May 15–17.

Kathiravelu, Laavanya. 2016. *Migrant Dubai: Low Wage Workers and the Construction of a Global City*. London: Palgrave Macmillan.

Khalaf, Sulayman. 2006. "The evolution of the Gulf city type, oil, and globalization." In *Globalization and the Gulf*, edited by John Fox, Nada Mourtada-Sabbah, and Mohammed al-Mutawa, 244–261. London: Routledge.

Khalaf, Sulayman. 2010. "Dubai Camel Market Transnational Workers: An Ethnographic Portrait. City & Society 22 (1): 97–118.

Kitto, H. D. F. 1951. *The Greeks*. London: Penguin Books.

Klinenberg, Eric. 2018. *Palaces for the People*. New York: Crown Publishers.

Kluckhohn, Clyde. 1951. "The study of culture." In *The Policy Sciences*, edited by D. Lerner & H. D. Lasswell, 86–101. Stanford, CA: Stanford University Press.

Kolson, Kenneth. 2001. *Big Plans: The Allure and Folly of Urban Design*. Baltimore: The Johns Hopkins University Press.

Koolhaas, Rem. 1995. "Singapore: Portrait of a Potemkin Metropolis. Songlines . . . or 30 Years of Tabula Rasa." In *S, M, L, XL*, edited by Rem Koolhaas & Bruce Mau. New York: Monacelli Press.

Koolhaas, Rem. 2002. "Junkspace." *October 100*, Obsolescence (Spring): 175–190.

Kotkin, Joel. 2005. *The City: A Global History*. New York: Modern Library.

Kovessy, Peter. 2015. "More shops and cinemas coming to renamed 'Asian Town' in Qatar." *Doha News.* May 4. https://www.dohanews.co/more-shops-and-cinemas-coming-to-renamed-asian-town-in-qatar/

Kroeber, Alfred L. and Clyde Kluckhohn. 1952. "Culture, a critical review of concepts and definitions." *Papers of the Peabody Museum of American Archaeology and Ethnology, Harvard University,* 47(1). Cambridge, MA.

Lasch, Christopher. 1979. *The Culture of Narcissism: American Life in An Age of Diminishing Expectations.* New York: W. W. Norton

Le Corbusier. 1967. *The radiant city: Elements of a doctrine of urbanism to be used as the basis of our machine-age civilization.* New York: Orion Press.

Lebkicher, Roy, George Rentz and Max Steineke. 1960. *Aramco Handbook.* New York: Arabian American Oil Company.

Leonard, Karen. 2002. "South Asian Women in the Gulf: Families and Futures Reconfigured." In *Trans-status Subjects: Gender in the Globalization of South and Southeast Asia,* edited by Sonita Sarker and Esha Niyogi De. Durham, NC: Duke University Press.

Lévi-Strauss, Claude. 1963. *Structural Anthropology.* Translated by Claire Jacobson and Brooke Grundfest Schoepf. Basic Books: New York.

Lewis, Oscar. 1959. *Five families.* New York: Basic Books.

Lindquist, Johan. 2015. "The Anthropology of Brokers and Brokerage." In *International Encyclopedia of Social and Behavioral Science.* 2nd ed, 870–874. Amsterdam: Elsevier.

Longva, Anh Nga. 1997. *Walls Built on Sand: Migration, Exclusion and Society in Kuwait.* Boulder, CO: Westview Press.

Longva, Anh Nga. 2006. "Nationalism in Pre-Modern Guise: The Discourse on Hadhar and Badu in Kuwait." *International Journal of Middle East Studies* 38 (2): 171–187.

Lori, Noora. 2012. "Temporary Workers or Permanent Migrants? The Kafala System and Contestations of Residency in the Arab Gulf States." Note de l'Ifri, Center for Migrations and Citizenship, November.

Lori, Noora. 2019. *Offshore Citizens: Permanent Temporary Status in the Gulf.* Cambridge: Cambridge University Press.

Lukianoff, Greg, and Jonathan Haidt. 2019. *The Coddling of the American Mind: How Good Intentions and Bad Ideas Are Setting Up a Generation for Failure.* New York: Penguin Books.

Mah, Harold. 2000. "Phantasies of the Public Sphere: Rethinking the Habermas of Historians." *Journal of Modern History* 7 2(1): 153–182.

Mahdavi, Pardis. 2016. *Crossing the Gulf: Love and Family in Migrant Lives.* Stanford: Stanford University Press.

Makower, Tim. 2012. *Drawing from Msheireb: Twelve Artists on a Changing Neighborhood. Doha, Qatar.* Doha: Bloomsbury Qatar Foundation Publishing.

Malinowski, Bronislaw. 1922. *Argonauts of the Western Pacific: An Account of Native Enterprise and Adventure in the Archipelagoes of Melanesian New Guinea.* London: Routledge and Kegan Paul.

Marcus, George, and Michael Fischer. 1986. *Anthropology as Cultural Critique.* Chicago: University of Chicago Press.

Marx, Karl. 1996. "The Eighteenth Brumaire of Louis Bonaparte." In *Marx: Later Political Writings,* edited by T. Carver, 31–127. Cambridge: Cambridge University Press.

Mater, Ahmed. 2016. *Desert of Pharan: Unofficial Histories behind the Mass Expansion of Mecca.* Zurich: Lars Müller.

Mazzarella, William. 2003. *Shoveling Smoke: Advertising the Globalization in Contemporary India.* Durham, North Carolina, NC: Duke University Press.

McDonough, Tom. 2009. *The Situationists and the City*. London: Verso.

Mehrotra, Rahul and Felipe Vera. 2015. *Kumbh Mela: Mapping the Ephemeral Megacity*. Cambridge, MA: Hate Cantz, Harvard University.

Mehta, R. M., F. Vera, D. L. Eck, D. Mehta, and D. Mehta. 2015. *Kumbh Mela: Mapping the Ephemeral Megacity*. Ostfildern: Hatje Cantz; Cambridge: Harvard University.

Melhuish, Clare, Monica Degen, and Gillian Rose. 2016. "'The Real Imaginary That Is Here': Understanding the Role of Digital Visualisations in the Production of a New Urban Imaginary at Msheireb Downtown, Doha." *City & Society* 28 (2): 222–245.

Menoret, Pascal. 2014. *Joyriding in Riyadh: Oil, Urbanism, and Road Revolt*. Cambridge: Cambridge University Press.

Migration Policy Institute. 2022. Global Remittances Guide. https://www.migrationpolicy .org/programs/data-hub/global-remittances-guide.

Mintz, Sidney. 1986. *Sweetness and Power: The Place of Sugar in Modern History*. New York: Penguin.

Mohammad, Robina, and James Sidaway. 2016. "Shards and Stages: Migrant Lives, Power, and Space Viewed from Doha, Qatar." *Annals of the American Association of Geographers* 106 (6): 1397–1417.

Molotch, Harvey, and Davide Ponzini. 2019. *The New Arab Urban: Gulf Cities of Wealth, Ambition, and Distress*. New York: New York University Press.

Moore, Henrietta. 1999. *Anthropological Theory Today*. Cambridge: Polity Press.

Moskowitz, Eva. 2001. *In Therapy We Trust: America's Obsession with Self-Fulfillment*. Baltimore, MD: Johns Hopkins University Press.

Msheireb Properties. 2021. "About Msheireb Downtown Doha." https://www.msheireb .com/msheireb-downtown-doha/about-msheireb-downtown-doha.

Mumford, Lewis. 1961. *The City in History*. New York: Harcourt, Brace & World.

Murrain, Paul. 1996. "Congress for the New Urbanism Charter: Developing an Agenda for Action." *Urban Design International* 1: 183–187.

Nagraj, Aarti. 2020. "New Mega Urban Development Project, Masar, launched in Saudi's Makkah." *Gulf Business*, June 30. https://gulfbusiness.com/new-mega-urban -development-project-masar-launched-in-saudis-makkah/.

Nagy, Sharon. 1997. "Social Diversity and Changes in the Form and Appearance of the Qatari House." *Visual Anthropology* 10 (2–4): 281–304.

Nagy, Sharon. 1998. "'This Time I Think I'll Try a Filipina': Global and Local Influences on Relations between Foreign Household Workers and Their Employers in Doha, Qatar." *City & Society* 10 (1): 83–103.

Nagy, Sharon. 2000. "Dressing Up Downtown: Urban Development and Government Public Image in Qatar." *City & Society* 12 (1): 125–147.

Nagy, Sharon. 2004. "Keeping Families Together: Housing Policy, Social Strategies and Family in Qatar." *MIT Electronic Journal of Middle East Studies* 4 (Spring): 42–58.

Nagy, Sharon. 2006. "Making Room for Migrants, Making Sense of Difference: Spatial and Ideological Expressions of Social Diversity in Urban Qatar." *Urban Studies* 43 (1): 119–137.

Nanda, Serena. 1989. *Neither Man nor Woman: The Hijras of India*. Belmont, CA: Wadsworth Publishing.

Natasi, Michele. 2019. "A Gulf of Images: Photography and the Circulation of Spectacular Architecture." In *The New Arab Urban*, edited by Harvey Molotch and Davide Ponzini, 99–129. New York: New York University Press.

Naufal, George. 2011. "Labor Migration and Remittances in the GCC." *Labor History* 52 (3): 307–322.

Niblock, Tim, and Monica Malik. 2007. *The Political Economy of Saudi Arabia*. London: Routledge.

Norbakk, Mari. 2020. "The Egyptians of Qatar: An Ethnographic Exploration of Middle-class Expatriation in the Arabian Gulf." PhD diss., University of Bergen.

Ong, Aihwa. 2006. *Neoliberalism as Exception: Mutations in Citizenship and Sovereignty.* Durham, NC: Duke University Press.

Onley, James. 2007. *The Arabian Frontier of the British Raj: Merchants, Rulers and the British in the Nineteenth-Century Gulf.* Oxford: Oxford University Press.

Onley, James, and Sulayman Khalaf. 2006. "Shaikhly Authority in the Pre-Oil Gulf: An Historical–Anthropological study." *History and Anthropology* 17 (3): 189–208.

Osella, Filippo, and Caroline Osella. 2000a. *Social Mobility in Kerala: Modernity and Identity in Conflict.* London: Pluto Press.

Osella, Filippo, and Caroline Osella. 2000b. "Migration, Money and Masculinity in Kerala." *Journal of the Royal Anthropological Institute* 6 (1): 117–133.

Othman, Nasser. 1984. *With Their Bare Hands: The Story of the Oil Industry in Qatar.* London: Longman.

Oxford Business Group. 2015. "New Economic Zones in Qatar Attract Investment and Develop Local Talent." https://oxfordbusinessgroup.com/analysis/new-economic -zones-qatar-attract-investment-and-develop-local-talent.

Palgrave, William G. 1866. *Narrative of a Year's Journey through Central and Eastern Arabia.* Volume 2. 3ed ed. London: Macmillan.

Patterson, Orlando. 2018. *Slavery and Social Death: A Comparative Study, with a New Preface.* Cambridge, MA: Harvard University Press.

Pessoa, Silvia, Laura Harkness, and Andrew Gardner. 2014. "Ethiopian Labor Migrants and the 'Free Visa' System in Qatar." *Human Organization* 73 (3): 205–213.

Pollalis, Spiro N., and Nader Ardalan. 2018. *Gulf Sustainable Urbanism—Past.* Volume I: *Toward a Sustainable Urbanism in the Gulf Analysis of the Past.* Cambridge, MA: Harvard College.

Pollan, Michael. 2006. *The Omnivore's Dilemma.* New York: Penguin.

Rahman, Md Mizanur. 2020. "Recruitment of Bangladeshi Migrants in the Arab Gulf States: A Typology of Work Visas." In *Asian Migrant Workers, in The Arab Gulf states: The Growing Foreign Population and Their Lives,* edited by Masaki Ishii, Naomi Hosed, Masaki Matsuo and Koji Horinuke, 236–242. Leiden: Brill.

Raymond, André. 2008. "The Spatial Organization of the City." In *The City in the Islamic World,* edited by Salma K. Jayyuse, volume 1, 47–70. Leiden, Netherlands: Brill.

Rizzo, Agatino. 2019. "Predatory Cities: Unravelling the Consequences of Resource-Predatory Projects in the Global South." *Urban Geography* 40 (1): 1–15.

Rizzo, Agatino, and Anindita Mandal. 2021. *Predatory Urbanism: The Metabolism of Megaprojects in Asia.* Cheltenham: Edward Elgar.

Roberts, Nicholas P. 2021. "A Sea of Wealth: Sayyid Saʿid bin Sultan, His Omani Empire, and the Making of an Oceanic Marketplace." PhD diss., University of Notre Dame.

Robbins, Richard. 2005. *Global Problems and the Culture of Capitalism.* 3rd ed. Boston: Pearson Education.

Rudofsky, Bernard. 1964. *Architecture without Architects: A Short Introduction to Non-Pedigreed Architecture.* New York: Museum of Modern Art.

Rustin, Michael. 2008. "Introduction: Social Science Perspectives on the 2012 London Olympic Games." *Twenty-First Century Society* 3 (3): 279–284.

Said, Edward. 1978. *Orientalism.* New York: Vintage Books.

Salama, Ashraf, and Florian Wiedmann. 2016. *Demystifying Doha: On Architecture and Urbanism in an Emerging City.* London: Routledge.

Samin, Nadav. 2015. *Of Sand or Soil: Genealogy and Tribal Belonging in Saudi Arabia.* Princeton: Princeton University Press.

Sardar, Ziauddin. 2014. "The Destruction of Mecca." *New York Times*, Opinion, October 1.

Saunders, Doug. 2010. *Arrival City: How the Largest Migration in History is Reshaping our World*. New York: Vintage Books.

Scheper-Hughes, Nancy. 1992. *Death Without Weeping: The Violence of Everyday Life in Brazil*. Berkeley: University of California Press

Scott, James. 1985. *Weapons of the Weak*. New Haven: Yale University Press.

Scott, James. 1999. *Seeing Like a State: How Certain Schemes to Improve the Human Condition Have Failed*. New Haven: Yale University Press.

Sennett, Richard. 1970. *The Uses of Disorder: Personal Identity & City Life*. New York: W. W. Norton.

Smith, Adam. 1937. *The Wealth of Nations*. New York: Modern Library.

Smith, Christian. 2014. *The Sacred Project of American Sociology*. Oxford: Oxford University Press.

Snoj, Jure. 2019. "Population of Qatar by Nationality—2019 Report." August 15. http://priyadsouza.com/population-of-qatar-by-nationality-in-2017/.

Soja, Edward W. 1996. *Thirdspace: Journeys to Los Angeles and Other Real-and-Imagined Places*. London: Wiley.

Spradley, James P. 1979. *The Ethnographic Interview*. Belmont, CA: Wadsworth Group.

Tylor, Edward. 1958. *Primitive Culture: The Origins of Culture*. Part 1. New York: Harper.

Venturi, Robert, Denise Scott Brown, and Steven Izenour. 1972. *Learning from Las Vegas*. Boston: MIT Press.

Vertovec, Steven. 2007. "Super-Diversity and Its Implications." *Ethnic and Racial Studies* 30 (6): 1024–1054.

Viramma, Josiana Racine, and Jean-Luc Racine. 1997. *Viramma: Life of an Untouchable*. London: Verso Books.

von Grunebaum, G. E. 1955. "Islam: Essays in the Nature and Growth of a Cultural Tradition." *American Anthropologist* 57 (2), Part 2, Memoir No. 81.

Vora, Neha. 2013. *Impossible Citizens: Dubai's Indian Diaspora*. Durham, NC: Duke University Press.

Walker, Lesley. 2015. "Qatar Ministry Publishes Maps with 'No Go' Housing Zones for Workers." Doha News, October 5. https://dohanews.co/qatar-ministry-publishes-maps-with-no-go-housing-zones-for-workers/.

Walters, William. 2002. "Deportation, Expulsion, and the International Police of Aliens." *Citizenship Studies* 6 (3): 265–292.

Watts, Michael. 2004. "Violent Environments: Petroleum Conflict and the Political Ecology of Rule in the Niger Delta, Nigeria." In *Liberation Ecologies: Environment, Development, Social Movements*, edited by Richard Peet and Michael Watts. 2nd ed., 250–272. New York: Routledge.

Wolf, Eric. 1956. "Aspects of Group Relations in a Complex Society." *American Anthropologist* 58 (6): 1065–1078.

Wolf, Eric. 1982. *Europe and the People without History*. Berkeley: University of California Press.

Wolfe, Charles R. 2016. *Seeing the Better City: How to Observe, and Improve Urban Space*. Washington, DC: Island Press.

Wright, Andrea. 2021. *Between Dreams and Ghosts: Indian Migration and Middle Eastern Oil*. Stanford: Stanford University Press.

Wu, Rufina, and Stefan Canham. 2008. *Portraits from above: Hong Kong's Informal Rooftop Communities*. Berlin: Peperoni Books.

Zeihan, Peter. 2022. *The End of the World Is Just the Beginning*. New York: HarperCollins.

Index

www.ingramcontent.com/pod-product-compliance
Lightning Source LLC
Chambersburg PA
CBHW030839270326
41928CB00007B/1125